EBS

Educational Ideas of
Dr. Annie Besant and J. Krishnamurti

Educational Ideas of Dr. Annie Besant and J. Krishnamurti

Dr. Jaya Mukerji
Lecturer
Department of Education
Allahabad Degree College
Allahabad

ADHYAYAN PUBLISHERS & DISTRIBUTORS
Delhi-110094

Published by
Adhyayan Publishers & Distributors
L-9 B, Street No. 42, Sadatpur Extension
Delhi-110094 (India)
Ph.: 011-22191282, Fax No.: 011-22199182
email-adhyayanpublishers@yahoo.com

Educational Ideas of Dr. Annie Besant and J. Krishnamurti

© Author
1st Edition 2006
ISBN 81-89161-57-1

Printed in India

Published by Harish Chandra Yadav for Adhyayan Publishers & Distributors, Delhi. Laser Typesetting at V. M. Graphics and Printed at Tarun Offset Printers, Delhi.

Dedicated to
my Grandfather

Late Shri Shiv Krishna Mukerji

Foreword

India is faced with challenges, which have to be urgently, and successfully met. Education may be regarded as the most effective instrument to meet the challenges ahead. Value-crisis in Indian society is one of the most important challenges, which should be met urgently. Education seeks to enrich life by developing values and a taste and sensitivity for perceived excellence and quality of life.

Jiddu Krishnamurti has advocated for absolute freedom to think and speak. He hopes for a permanently better world. Dr. Annie Besant has influenced not only currently Indian politics but also education. The efforts of both the educators have contributed a lot in the field of value education.

Dr. Jaya Mukerji has studied the educational ideas of Dr. Annie Besant and Krishnamurti in an excellent manner. Both these educational philosophers are a bit difficult to be understood. Dr. Jaya Mukerji has done a good job by writing a book to explain the ideas of both of these educators in a lucid style. Dr. Jaya Mukerji is a brilliant scholar of education who is teaching degree classes of a reputed constituent college of the University of Allahabad. Her book merits recognition by scholars of India as well as abroad.

I wish Jaya ji a glorious and prosperous educational career.

R.S. Pandey
Dean, Faculty of Arts (Retd.)
University of Allahabad

Preface

The tremendous discoveries of science, the incredible development of technology and speedy communications have rendered physical comforts only a push button away from human beings. This notwithstanding, mental peace, tranquility and true happiness, remain elusive for them. In the maze of man's material success his social and moral values, and indeed his entire philosophy seem to be lost. The retrieval of what man has lost by way of values is only possible through constructive philosophy and proper education. Learning to adopt an attitude in the present era which is one of comprehension and not of exclusiveness, one of understanding and not of mere tolerance, of appreciation and assimilation of whatever is valuable and not of hatred and fanaticism, can only be possible through the teachings of different seers, who from time to time have given their views on enriching the quality of life and society. They have made many suggestions in this regard and there are many centres which are attempting to give shape to the suggestions of such seers through activities like their own educational centres, societies and publications. Prominent among them may be mentioned the names of Dr. Annie Besant and J. Krishnamurti.

The lives of Dr. Annie Besant and J. Krishnamurti were intricately interwoven and overlapping, yet their philosophies blossomed differently. Indeed they were like two roses of different colours on the same plant. The study of their philosophies and educational ideas make a fascinating exercise. There are, no doubt, some expected similarities in their educational thoughts, but it is the understanding of the differences that calls for a thorough comprehension of their philosophies. Such a comprehension becomes all the more necessary so as to enable one to incorporate their educational thoughts in the present system of education, thereby bringing about in it a very desirable qualitative transformation. The unique and close relationship of Dr. Annie Besant and J. Krishnamurti and their comparatively divergent philosophies and educational ideas are a great fountain of knowledge of values. This, per se, interested the Researcher to carry out this study and assess its relevance in the context of the present situation.

This study has been done along the following lines: In the first chapter which is introductory, the researcher deals with the significance of the problem, purpose of the study and the research methods adopted. Lives and times of Dr. Annie Besant and J. Krishnamurti have been dealt with in chapter two, as events during this period influenced and shaped their thoughts. Philosophical perspectives on life in general are highlighted in the third chapter. To understand their educational ideas it is necessary to understand their general philosophy. A detailed account of the educational ideas of these two great thinkers has been given in the fourth chapter. This description includes the different aspects of education, such as, concept of education, aims of education, curriculum, methods of teaching, concept of school, role of teacher and student, concept of discipline and also the practical application of their educational ideas. In the fifth chapter, the researcher presents conclusions drawn from the comparative study and moves on to find out their contemporary relevance and offers suggestions.

For completion of this work I am deeply grateful to a number of persons without whose help and encouragement this work would not have been possible. First and foremost, I express my deep sense of gratitude and indebtness to my supervisor, Dr. Vidya Agarwal, Reader, Department of Education, University of Allahabad, for her painstaking help and constant guidance. To Prof. R. S. Pandey, Retired Head Department of Education, University of Allahabad, with whom

I have often had fruitful discussions regarding this work. I owe a special vote of thanks and gratitude. He not only helped me in giving shape to this work, but also provided valuable information from time to time. I cannot express my gratitude in full measure to Prof. Manas Mukul Das, Department of English, University of Allahabad, without whose help the understanding of Krishnamurti's philosophy would have remained an enigma to me, and because of whom I had access to rare manuscripts and information on Krishnamurti. I have to say the same regarding Smt. Gyan Kumari Ajeet, member of Besant Education Fellowship, member of National Committee Theosophical Order of Service India, and ex-secretary of its U.P. Federation, with whose help I had access to valuable sources of information regarding Dr. Annie Besant. My thanks are due to members of the staff of the Rajghat Education Centre as well as Kamachha, for their help and cooperation. To Prof. P.C. Saxena (Retd.), Department of Education, Univ. Allahabad, Prof. K.S. Misra, H.O.D. Education, Prof. P.K. Sahoo, and all members of the staff of Department of Education, University of Allahabad, I am grateful in no small measure for their help and encouragement. I shall be failing in my duty if I do not acknowledge the patience and forbearance of all my family members during the execution of this work.

Jaya Mukerji

Contents

	Preface	ix
1.	Introduction	1
2.	LIFE AND TIMES OF DR. ANNIE BESANT AND J. KRISHNAMURTI	8-60
	[A] Life and Times of Dr. Annie Besant	8
	[B] Life and Times of J. Krishnamurti	30
3.	PHILOSOPHICAL IDEAS OF DR. ANNIE BESANT AND J. KRISHNAMURTI	61-105
	[A] Philosophical Ideas of Dr. Annie Besant	61
	[B] Philosophical Ideas of J. Krishnamurti	77
4.	EDUCATIONAL IDEAS OF DR. ANNIE BESANT AND J. KRISHNAMURTI	106-209
	[A] Educational Ideas of Dr. Annie Besant	106
	[B] Educational Ideas of J. Krishnamurti	148
	[C] Educational Institutions of Dr. Annie Besant and J. Krishnamurti, visited by the Researcher	194
5.	Comparison, Conclusions, Suggestions	210
6.	Bibliography	243
	Index	253

1
Introduction

In the strife stricken world of today, it is time to take a second look at our educational system. The rapid strides in all fields of education are breath-taking. Man seeks to master the field of his choice and is indeed achieving excellence in his speciality. He has success to display and can bask in the glory of material satisfaction. The pace of education, imparting technical perfection, leaves little time for pondering over human values. Man in his pursuit of knowledge has become insensitive and harsh. This is the root cause of turmoil in society.

We must therefore 'Revisit' values and incorporate them in our system of education. A value-based education can go a long way in preventing a devastating cataclysm in society. Almost all seers and thinkers have realised this. Many have views on values, which are not exactly identical, and differ even more, on the manner of integration of these in the regular educational curriculum. To the educationist therefore falls the important task of pondering over this situation. As a first step a deep study of the philosophy and educational ideas of such thinkers both in absolute and comparative terms becomes necessary. This alone will provide a proper insight into the values, which are missing from today's blueprint of education and indicate methods of incorporating them.

Education aims at learning of skills, acquiring of information, inculcation of knowledge, refinement of natural instincts and building of character. Therefore it should be an instrument for value seeking and character building. Unfortunately in the contemporary era this is not so. The present are turbulent and troubled times, the society is restless, discontented and fragmented. There is much talk on education that is value based and the affirmation that this would bring about a transformation in society. The partakers in this discussion include the world population, which has constituted many bodies and committees to look into the matter. Mention of the United Nations Organisation (UNO), United Nations Educational, Scientific and Cultural Organisation (UNESCO), and others may be made in this regard. At the National level the government of India has from time to time formed different commissions for this purpose. Some of them which have emphasised the need for a value based education are the Mudaliar Commission (1952), Kothari Commission (1964-66) and also the National policy on Education (1986) with modifications undertaken in 1992.

A successful value based educational plan, nevertheless, still remains elusive and gives rise to the feeling that value integration in educational patterns have perhaps been only an intellectual exercise till today. There are a number of restraining factors which are perhaps responsible for the current situation. Prominent among these may be mentioned, a market oriented race for development, science and technology, materialism and individualism. The concept of values themselves has been the subject of debate and still remains controversial. They may be of various types and categories and may be derived from several sources such as religion, science, secularism and so on. These would tend to have different hues under different circumstances, but values which are purely human such as truth, love, peace are of more perpetual relevance. With all good intentions the educationists have been unable to incorporate the latter values effectively in our system of education which now is in urgent need of a total reconstruction. The focus of education should shift from materialistic gains to a qualitatively rich life.

Introduction

Looking into the history of India, the importance given to such values in the past becomes apparent. The ancient systems of education which were practised in India, such as in Gurukuls and Monasteries were all essentially value based and imparted in students, in a carefully thought of manner, a deep respect for some cherished human qualities such as truth, honesty, love, faith etc. As time advanced, the gateway to globalisation opened and the pace of man's pursuit of modernisation overtook the ancient system of imparting and imbibing human values. There was no denial that globalisation and modernisation were desirable and indeed the need of the hour. The problem was that modernisation bereft of values was creating a generation which lacked sensitivity, and a society which was intolerant and prone to unrest. *The question that confronts us now is how best to blend the intricacies of modern scientific knowledge and technology with pure human values.*

Seers have made many suggestions in this regard, and there are many centres which are attempting to give shape to the suggestions of such seers through activities like their own educational centres, societies and publications. Prominent among such seers may be mentioned the names of Dr. Annie Besant and J. Krishnamurti. Their lives had a close inter-relationship and their times were partially overlapping. Dr. Annie Besant propounded a rich philosophy based on Hindu religion and ancient Hindu scriptures and texts, and from it formulated an elaborate educational system which sought to impart education of modern science and technology along with cherished human values as propounded in ancient Hindu scriptures. She proceeded to draw up a detailed blueprint of education which not only aimed at building a strong character and inculcating a national spirit but also accepted all that was good in the western type of education.

J. Krishnamurti on the other hand, in spite of his early close association with Dr. Annie Besant had a philosophy which was entirely different. Proceeding from "setting man free", "You are the world" to "Truth is a pathless land", "looking at oneself in the mirror of relationship", "Freedom is at the beginning", J. Krishnamurti spawned a new lexicon which gave an entirely different meaning, depth and dimension to all these words and was, infact, the key to the understanding of his philosophy and educational ideas. His philosophy generated educational thoughts which emphasised learning by discovery from the text of life, without a guru or a teacher, in a joyful process of dialogue and sharing.

The researcher has, in this study, focused attention on the methods which Dr. Annie Besant and J. Krishnamurti have employed in imparting a value based education, together with a contemporary type which is the demand of the era of science, technology and commerce. Unquestionably the amalgamation of value based education and conventional type of education is not simple and it is fraught with difficulties such as time, dedication, expenditure and a proper understanding of the philosophy behind educational thoughts. *The significance of the problem lies in how best one can overcome these difficulties and arrive at a practical solution for incorporating basic human values in our present day educational curriculum.* Today we are in need of a suitable paradigm for a value based educational system. The study of educational thoughts of both Dr. Annie Besant and J. Krishnamurti offer interesting possibilities.

Purpose of the study

To make the study purposeful and informative, the researcher proposes to procure data, analyse and utilise it and to proceed with the work along the following lines:

1. To make an in-depth study of the educational ideas of Dr. Annie Besant and J. Krishnamurti, from available primary and secondary sources, for a comprehensive understanding and lucid interpretation of their thoughts. To make a similar study of the primary and secondary sources for a comprehension of their philosophies, to the extent that is necessary for understanding, appreciating and proper interpretation of their educational ideas. The life and times of a person have a deep impact on his philosophy, and for this purpose to make a

study of the life and times of both Dr. Annie Besant and J. Krishnamurti.

2. To define the aims of education, curriculum, methods of teaching, concept of school, discipline, role of student and teacher based on the educational ideas of Dr. Annie Besant and J. Krishnamurti.

3. To highlight some shortcomings in the present day system of education, and to note the similarities and differences in the educational ideas of Dr. Annie Besant and J. Krishnamurti; to identify and assess the emerging ideas that stand clearly apart from those that are in practice today, and to suggest their incorporation in the curriculum, with a view to bring about a qualitative improvement in the student's learning process.

The Method of Study

In order to study and compare the educational ideas of Dr. Annie Besant and J. Krishnamurti four main research methods have been adopted *viz.*, historical, analytical, descriptive and comparative.

Historical Method

To understand the philosophy and educational ideas of any great thinker or seer an understanding of the ground realities of his time is of paramount importance, as these undoubtedly influence the seer's thoughts and ideas. The way in which the study of such ground realities is done may be called the historical method, and there are two main sources of information on this subject, namely, primary sources and secondary sources.

Primary sources are first hand accounts of events recorded by the person himself or by an actual observer or participant in an event.

Secondary sources of information are summaries of information gathered from primary sources. Secondary sources are accounts of events that were not actually witnessed by the reporter. He or she may have talked with an actual observer or read an account recorded by an observer, but his testimony cannot be called that of an actual participant or observer.

The researcher has adopted the historical method to study the life and times of Dr. Annie Besant and J. Krishnamurti, and also to understand their philosophies and educational ideas in their proper context. The sources of information, both primary and secondary, have been mentioned and reviewed in appropriate sections of this thesis.

Analytical Method

According to Carter V. Good, et al (1953), "Analysis is a process which enters into research in one form or the other from the very beginning." It consists, in general of two steps, gathering of data and the analysis of these data. In the present study, the researcher has gathered all the data, from several available sources - both primary and secondary. This data has then been analysed under the following heads–

(a) The biographical sketch (b) The philosophy of life (c) The concept of education (d) The aims of education (e) the concept of curriculum (f) The methods of teaching (g) The concept of school (h) The role of teacher (i) The role of student (j) The concept of discipline.

Descriptive Method

Descriptive Method as defined by Best (1982), describes and interprets "what is". Although it is primarily concerned with the present, it nevertheless looks to past events and influences as they are connected to current conditions. Keeping this in mind, the researcher has used the descriptive method to explain the educational ideas of Dr. Annie Besant and J. Krishnamurti in present day context.

Comparative Method

In educational research, comparative method is used to compare the ideas of two or more persons or methodologies. It means to examine two or more entities, by putting them side by side and looking for similarities and dissimilarities between them. In the present study the comparison has been made between the educational ideas of Dr. Annie Besant and J. Krishnamurti.

The present study is a rare, interesting and objective comparison of educational ideas of two great seers-Dr. Annie Besant and J. Krishnamurti. Rare because, to the best of the researcher's knowledge, very few or perhaps no such comparison is readily available.

The comparison is interesting because it was Dr. Annie Besant who first chose and groomed J. Krishnamurti for being a "World Teacher". In J. Krishnamurti's tender years when he had lost his mother, Dr. Annie Besant showered on him, her love, care and affection to the extent that J. Krishnamurti addressed her as "Mother" in his letters. In later years, the Theosophical Society and Dr. Annie Besant provided him a world forum to become known as a world teacher. Yet J. Krishnamurti chose a path of his own, in response to an inner voice or experience, just as Dr. Annie Besant had done decades earlier. The comparison is objective because the researcher has not attempted to label either person's educational thoughts as the superior one, but has rather made a dispassionate comparison of the salient features. The researcher has further attempted to find out the contemporary relevance of the educational thoughts of both these thinkers.

2

[A] Life and Times of Dr. Annie Besant

Dr. Annie Besant lived from 1847-1933. C. Jinarajadasa wrote in his biography of Dr. Annie Besant, in September 1932:

> On October 1st next Dr. Annie Besant completes her 85th year. She is so well known throughout the world that any facts concerning her are eagerly read by everybody. She has lived such a dramatic life that in many ways she stands symbolic of some phases of the world's development. Her Autobiography, written in 1893, brings the story of her life to 1891, when Madame Blavatsky passed away. That book reveals such dramatic events that it is one of the most fascinating biographies to read. But since then so much more has happened in her life that there is no adequate biography today.[1]

Dr. Annie Besant's life was many faceted. She was a clergyman's wife but in her own right she was also an atheist campaigner, socialist propagandist, trade union agitator, birth control promoter, critic of capitalism and colonialism, and a fighter for women's rights. All these phases lasted till her mid-forties, after which began her Theosophical career and subsequent activities in India.

Dr. Annie Besant, a former President of the Theosophical Society, lived in India for forty years, and served her in every field of national life. Dr. Annie Besant's name was a household word in India and October 1st, which is her birthday, is celebrated by the various branches of the Theosophical Society, not only in India, but in practically every country of the world, as a day of remembrance and gratefulness. *The milestones in her career were greatly influenced by the social milieu of her times.*

The Early Years

Dr. Annie Besant was born in London on 1st October, 1847, in an aristocratic family. She lost her father at an early age and as a result experienced financial difficulties, being supported by the earnings of her mother, of whom she was extremely fond, and from whom she inherited her mystical and imaginative qualities.[2] The presence of these traits in Dr. Annie Besant possibly influenced her in joining the Theosophists later in life.

At this early age she experienced the differentiation between a male and a female child, prevalent in England in those days, as her mother took great pains to educate her son in deference to the wishes of her late husband, while her own education was considered of secondary importance.

The Educational Career

Little Annie's educational career started under the perfect guidance of Miss Marryat, who according to Dr. Annie Besant, "had a perfect genius for teaching".[3] Miss Marryat was a rich spinster and her earnest desire to teach young children drove her into this work. The children of her school were brought up in a new way, in a healthy, cheerful atmosphere with freedom of thought and expression, devoid of rote learning. Her way of teaching resembled the Montessori Method. Dr. Annie Besant's scholastic temperament and the quality of "personal self-denial for the good of others"[4] were to a great extent nurtured by Miss Marryat. Dr. Annie Besant wrote of Miss Marryat: "No words of mine can tell how much I owe her, not only of knowledge, but of that love of knowledge which has remained with me ever since as a constant spur to study"[5].

After her schooling under Miss Marryat's guidance, Dr. Annie Besant came back to her mother and read Catholic books of education, longed to spend her time in worshipping Jesus. As Dr. Annie Besant recalled: "...it nestled warm at my heart for ever, that idea of escaping from the humdrum of ordinary life by some complete sacrifice lured me onwards with its overmastering fascination."[6]

This tendency towards complete sacrifice was strongly buried within her ever since childhood, which she later proclaimed as having acquired from her past life and regarded it to be the strongest trait of her present life.

Stormy Married Life

At the age of twenty, Dr. Annie Besant married an English clergyman, Rev. Frank Besant. The stormy phase of her life started after her marriage. Being a devout Christian, she was attracted by a clergyman as she thought that by virtue of his very office, she would come nearer to God. However, she soon began to question several of the Christian dogmas, was not able to understand the Christian traditions and make logic out of it.

In order to hide her depression and boredom, she took to writing. Her first income had been a source of great delight as she felt a sense of independence. But even this sense of independence was snatched from her with the realisation that "all a married woman earned by law belonged to her owner, and that she could have nothing that belonged to her of right."[7] However, she continued to write.

Real happiness came into her married life when she gave birth to a son in 1869 and a daughter in 1870. The babies now occupied most of her time and she plunged into the pleasures of motherhood. Both her children fell ill in 1871 and the seriousness of their illness raised some fresh doubts in her mind. The problems were such as, "...The meaning of 'goodness' and 'love'; as applied to a God who had made this world, with all its sin and misery..."[8] Here it will not be out of place to mention that Mrs. Annie Besant had become a Freethinker[9]. She started reading books of Theistic writers like Grey, and Agnostics[10] like Mathew Arnold. Her skepticism grew deeper and deeper and she often thought how God being good, allowed the evil and misery to exist in the world. To get rid of her mental tension, she engaged herself in social work. She found immense satisfaction in nursing the sick, a fact which she herself had admitted in her autobiography:

> I think Mother Nature meant me for a nurse, for I take a keen delight in nursing anyone, provided only that there is peril in the sickness, so that there is the strange and solemn feeling of the struggle between the human skill we wield and the supreme enemy Death. There is a strange fascination in fighting Death step by step, and then is felt to the full where one fights for life as life, and not for a life one loves.[11]

She also started to involve herself in raising the lot of the agricultural labourers and helped the Agricultural Labourers' Union. During her militant years she came into contact with Mr. and Mrs. Scott. Mr. Thomas Scott had been engaged in issuing pamphlets on heretical thought, and Mrs. Annie Besant wrote her first freethought essay for him. Though she kept her name anonymous, she had acknowledged in the essay that it was written by the wife of a beneficed clergyman.

Such happenings show how Mrs. Annie Besant's views on religion were changing. She could not reconcile the religious doctrines with the behaviour that she found in actual practice in the outside world. She thought that whatever one preached, should also be observed truthfully in one's daily life.

In the spring of 1873, she entered the empty Sibsey Church and suddenly got the urge to deliver a speech on *Inspiration Of The Bible*, to rows of empty pews. This was her first lecture, and the force and expression with which she uttered the words convinced her that she had the great gift of speech which was hidden from her uptil now. Later on this very gift turned out to be the greatest delight of her life, and she became one of the best orators of the world.

She suffered a great deal in her married life. So terrible was her matrimonial tragedy that once, taking some poison in her hand, she thought of drinking it and so ending the horror of it all. As she was about to drink it she heard a clear voice of stern reproval, which said to her, "O Coward, coward who used to dream of martyrdom and cannot stand a few years of woe".[12] The voice seemed like a whip that hit her, who had read lives of martyred saints since the days of girlhood. She immediately threw the bottle out of the window and never forgot the voice.

The spirit of revolt in Mrs. Annie Besant broke her marriage, after which she returned to her mother with her little daughter, the son being with his father. She chose to face the brutal world all alone at the young age of twenty-six, because she felt that what she did not believe, she could not pretend to believe.

Beginnings of an Independent Life

Still in her twenties, endowed with beauty and charm to match her aristocratic features, which were by no means assets in a lonely woman in those days, she entered the field of public life in 1873, and with that began a new chapter in her life. By earning a living, doing needlework, working as a governess, writing pamphlets for Mr. Scott, she supported herself and her little daughter, as in the meantime she had lost her beloved mother. This, notwithstanding, she probed deeply into the grave questions of God, man's reason and conscience. Often she would go out to study at the British Museum, and would say that she would have her dinner in town, the said dinner being conspicuous by its absence. *It was perhaps the pangs of hunger that she faced; the struggle for existence that she experienced that moulded her into a socialist later on in life.*

Intellectual life and Revolutionary spirit

Mrs. Annie Besant came to know of the *National Secular Society*, an organisation for promotion of Freethought, through a journal, *National Reformer*, and made acquaintance with its editor, Mr. Charles Bradlaugh, which grew into a challenging companionship. Mrs. Annie Besant became an atheist and joined the *National Secular Society*, which had as its motto, "We Search For Truth." According to Mrs. Annie Besant, an atheist neither accepts nor rejects the unknown. He denies all that which contradicts with the knowledge which he already has, but he does not accept nor deny God, which is unknown to him, this being a wider definition as it encompasses the dictionary meanings, conveyed by the words, Agnostic and Atheist.

At this stage Mrs. Annie Besant did not believe in God as she had no proof of His existence. She believed in man's redeeming power, in man's elevation, growth through knowledge, love and work. She had an intense desire for improving the human condition, for bettering the world. She felt that Truth should be loved for its own pure sake. A man who believes in immortality, in reaping a reward, seeks only his own individual comfort, and for such a man Freethought has no place. To lead a noble life, to make men happy, to spread happiness around should be one's aims. When one leads such a life, "society will grow purer, freedom more settled, law more honoured, life more full and glad"[13] and that labour is one's own reward. *Heaven is attainable on earth not in some remote place, that is, in the clouds, unknown.* According to Dr. Annie Besant, while the theists hold that man is God-made and that evil exists by the will of God, atheists regard man as circumstance-made, and that the root cause of evil is ignorance. As she said, "educate the children, and give them fair wage for fair work in their maturity, and crime will gradually diminish and ultimately disappear"[14]. *Such was Dr. Annie Besant's philosophy by which she led her life from 1874 to 1886.* What she owed to Free thought was that it left the mind ever open to new truth and never rejected any new conviction that was based on solid grounds. However, there were many who opposed her views as they regarded Atheism to mean degraded morality. Dr. Annie Besant lost child custody on grounds of her atheism, but her subsequent agitations created much debate in liberal circles, eventually leading to changes in the repressive laws. In Dr. Annie Besant's words:

In the days when the law took my child from me, it virtually said to all women: "Choose which of those two positions, as wife and mother, you will occupy. If you are legally your husband's wife, you can have no legal claim to your children; if legally you are your husband's mistress, your rights as mother are secure". That stigma on marriage is now removed.[15]

Widespread Interests

From 1874 to 1889, Mrs. Annie Besant led a life of tremendous activity. She fought for justice for the industrial workers, became one of the pioneers of the labour movement in England. She delivered lectures in favour of Atheism and Radical Politics. In 1878, she wrote a book titled, *England, India And Afghanistan*. She strongly opposed powerful governments trying to suppress weaker nations.

In 1879, Dr. Annie Besant discovered that due to her atheism and so called immoral political activities, the doors of higher education were closed to her in England.

She actively embarked on Trade Union Activities and championed the cause of women workers.

Quest for Truth

Mrs. Annie Besant had always been probing deeply into certain problems of life. Kewal Motwani remarked: "During this period of intense activity and apprenticeship in the art and science of service of her fellowmen, her inner life remained equally vivid and dynamic. The search for Truth never subsided, the inadequacies and contradictions of life remained unsolved and she persisted in her search for Light and Life in the solitude of her heart."[16]

It is interesting to note here that whilst Dr. Annie Besant was busy promoting the freethought movement in England, Madame H.P. Blavatsky was busy setting up the Theosophical Society (1875) in the United States.

One incident deserves to be mentioned. As C. Jinarajadasa wrote in his biography of Dr. Annie Besant:

Whilst she was sitting in the Fleet Street office of the 'National Reformer', and brooding over her disappointments in the search of Truth, she suddenly heard a voice say to her: "Are you willing to give up everything for the sake of learning the Truth?" she replied instantly:

"Yes, Lord" she did not know who had spoken, but it was the same voice as on the earlier occasion.[17]

The voice that Mrs. Annie Besant heard was the same that had stopped her from taking poison when she was going through a stormy married life. From that time onwards she collected all her energies in search of Truth. It was her search for Truth that made her come across two volumes of Madam Blavatsky's *Secret Doctrine*, that "conceived of a great cosmic evolutionary plan in which divine potential is unfolded through an orderly progression, moving down from Spirit to Matter and back up again."[18] Instantly, she felt, as if her long tedious search was now over and that Truth stood in front of her, absolutely clear and pure. This was the turning point in her life, which led to the blossoming of her philosophy. She asked for an interview with the author and from that first sight of Madam Blavatsky, Dr. Annie Besant's total attitude towards life changed. She separated herself from her secularist friends and also to some extent from socialism.

For four years, she stayed on in England, giving teachings that affirmed the existence of Law or God, the one source of all life, the divine justice, the truth of karma and reincarnation, teachings that were totally different from what she had been preaching for the last fifteen years.

The Theosophical Society

A brief description of the Theosophical Society is sketched here before proceeding with Dr. Annie Besant's emergence in India.

The Theosophical Society had been founded in New York, America, on 17th November 1875 by Madame Helena Petrovna Blavatsky (a Russian lady) and Colonel Henry Steel Olcott (an American, a veteran of the Civil War, who was interested in spiritualism and mesmerism). Theosophy is a philosophy, which embraces the teachings of all religions, based on the concept of Universal Truth above all things else. The motto of the Theosophical Society is taken from Mahabharat which is as follows: 'Satyanasti Parodharmah' meaning 'There Is No Religion Higher Than Truth.' It is Divine Wisdom, whether called by its ancient Sanskrit name of 'Brahma Vidya', or its modern Greek name of 'Theosophia'. The term 'Theosophy' comes from the Greek words 'theos', god and 'sophia', wisdom. As practised in modern times, theosophy claims that all religions stem from the same roots of ancient wisdom, repeating myths and symbols, and that study of these secrets will lead to truth and spiritual oneness. The teaching of Theosophy partly lifts up the veil of the unseen world and tries to give a more accurate basis for conduct, a more rational appreciation of the causes and the effects that are seen in the terrestrial world. Theosophy borrows from many Vedic teachings along with the teachings of certain masters of a spiritual hierarchy channeled through particular individuals. The meaning of Theosophy is explained in the following lines:

> According to H.P. Blavatsky the term "Theosophy" dates back to the third century A.D. Ammonious Saccas and his disciples in Eclectic Theosophy saw that all religions shared three major ideas:
>
> 1) belief in one Supreme, Absolute deity as the Source of all; 2) humankind's immortal nature is a radiation from that deity; and 3) by making oneself as pure as the Source, one could receive the divine secrets. Such efforts are called "theurgy" or "divine work".[19]

It is also illustrated as:

> Theosophy is not a religion, it is religion *per se;* Theosophy is the Wisdom-Religion at the heart of all religions, found when all the encrustations, misinterpretations and superstitions are put away; ...Obviously the name "Theosophical Society" was neither vainly nor unintentionally chosen. It defines the connection between

the body of people who compose the Society and the transcendental knowledge which is the Wisdom-Religion and, the self-abnegating way of life which opens the soul to the Eternal, and prepares it to be a compassionate and wise server of the ailing world.[20]

The three declared objectives of the Theosophical Society are:

1) To form a nucleus of the universal brotherhood of humanity, without distinction of race, creed, sex, caste or colour.

2) To encourage the comparative study of religion, philosophy and science.

3) To investigate unexplained laws of nature and the powers latent in humanity.

"Theosophy is not a creed to be believed, but a life to be lived."[21] It lays stress on "clean life, open mind and pure heart".[22] The Theosophical Society is non sectarian, non political and non dogmatic. The bond of union of the members of the Theosophical Society is a common search and aspiration for truth. They hold that truth should be sought by study, by reflection, by service, and not imposed by authority as a dogma. One who joins the Theosophical Society is not asked to give up the teachings of his own faith, but to live up to its teachings of spiritual life, recognising the unity of all, to live in harmony with people of his own faith and people of other faiths. The Theosophical Society maintains the right of individual freedom of thought for every member. All in sympathy with the objects of the Society are welcomed as members.

Life in India

Founders of the Theosophical Society wanted to visit India, the land of the sages, to see what India had once been to the world, and what she might be again. They wanted to study the facts about Oriental religious philosophies, especially the pure esoteric teachings in the Vedas, and in the philosophies of the Buddha, Zoroaster and Confucius, so as to develop the 'inner psychic self' and also to bring about a 'Brotherhood of Humanity' by drawing together the East and the West, so that each may supply the qualities lacking in the other and develop more fraternal feelings among nations. *It was this intention of the Founders of the Theosophical Society, that finally paved the way for Mrs. Annie Besant's visit to India.*

Mrs. Annie Besant arrived in India on 16th of November, 1893. *She considered this date as her new birth and called India her 'sacred Motherland'*[23], as from this Indian soil she had received a wealth of knowledge. She expanded the old philosophies and poured forth that continuous stream of knowledge, which amazed the cultured Hindus of the land.

In 1895, after an extensive tour of India, she took up her residence in Benares, the sacred city of India, at her beloved home 'Shanti Kunj'. She devoted the first fifteen years to the promotion of education and advocacy of reform of the social structure of India that had become crystallised in dead customs and habits. During this period she saw and understood from close quarters the Hindu religion in all its vastness as also some of its shortcomings. She became well versed in Sanskrit and read many classics. Dr. Annie Besant was of the opinion that, the philosophy and religion of India's greater days, while holding the essence of her past, also reflected the glory of her future. Just like an individual needs spiritual, moral, intellectual and physical upliftment for all round development, similarly, a nation too needs to be developed spiritually, mentally, emotionally, physically, and to bring about such an upliftment, Dr. Annie Besant directed her attention towards the following areas – educational, political, social, religious.

Educational Activities

To build a great world empire and a strong united India, education was given the topmost priority in her thoughts.

For the untouchables she opened *Olcott Pancham School at Adyar. Many other schools were opened*, some of which are mentioned below.

The Annie Besant School at Allahabad was set up under her inspiration. Schools for girls and boys were started in

Varanasi. With the blessings of Dr. Annie Besant, a school started functioning at Adyar, where teaching was done according to Montessori Methods. The school continues to function till today.

She *started the famous Central Hindu College* at Varanasi in 1898. Dr. Annie Besant's work in the Central Hindu College from 1898 to 1913 is beautifully expressed in the speeches, which she delivered, on the anniversary gatherings of the College, contained in the seventh Volume of *The Besant* Spirit. As George Arundale wrote:

> The Central Hindu College became famous throughout India not only as a seat of Indian learning and culture, not only as an abode of fine physical prowess in all kinds of games, but even more as a home in which every member of the family learned how to become an Indian gentleman and a worshipper of his Motherland.[24]

It was Dr. Annie Besant's intention, to establish similar institutions, on the lines of this college, all over the country, this being the Mother of other Hindu Colleges.

The core teaching of Central Hindu College was religious, that is, giving stress on Hindu religion and morality; but so far as the acquisition of knowledge was concerned, it rested on Western secular foundation, on Western training. Dr. Annie Besant emphasised on teachers being only those persons who had the love of Hinduism in their hearts, and for whom the primary urge was in love of teaching and not pecuniary benefits. The students and teachers of the Central Hindu College came from different parts of India. Thus it was a national institution and not a local one. Dr. Annie Besant tried to enlist the support of prominent people from all parts of the country in her educational work. She also turned her attention to *women education*. Dr. Annie Besant formed the *Young Men's Indian Association* in 1914 in Madras. This association gave shelter to young people so that they could find a healthy place to live in, while continuing with their studies or earning a livelihood.

Dr. Annie Besant formed the *Sons and Daughters of India*, to train men and women into noble citizenship, and to instill into the coming generation a deep religious and patriotic spirit. The pledge of the Order had a twofold objective: 1. To promise to treat as Brothers, Indians of every religion and every province; 2. To make Service the dominant Ideal in life.

Dr. Annie Besant started the *Indian Scouting Movement* so as to develop a sense of service and world citizenship in the minds of the participants. To foster national system of education in India, she set up around forty schools, colleges and even a university. A scheme for promotion of national education was launched in Calcutta in December 1917. This new *Indian National University Scheme* was to be independent of government. Its Vice Chancellor was R.N. Tagore. The governing body was composed of the leading educationists of India. In July 1918, the first college was opened at Damodar Gardens, Adyar, leased to it by the Theosophical Society. Its curriculum consisted of literature, science, agriculture, commerce.[25]

Dr. Annie Besant wished to transform the Central Hindu College into a United India University including Hindus as well as Muslims. Owing to religious rivalry, a separate Muslim University was established at Aligarh. In response to this, Pandit Madan Mohan Malviya, planned to set up a separate Hindu University at Benares. The idea became very popular and Dr. Annie Besant agreed to the inclusion of the Central Hindu College as part of the proposed University and, *in 1911, Central Hindu College became the nucleus of the Banaras Hindu University*.

Dr. Annie Besant, who always stood for the ideal of selfless service, gave away the results of all her labour into the hands of Pt. Madan Mohan Malviya. On 14th of Dec, 1921, the Hindu University conferred upon Annie Besant its Honorary Degree of Doctor of Letters in "grateful recognition of her invaluable cooperation in establishing the University."[26] From then onwards she was referred to as Dr. Annie Besant.

Freed from the responsibility of guiding the Central Hindu College, Dr. Annie Besant formed the *Theosophical Educational Trust in 1913*. Its aim was to establish schools and colleges which would be open to students of every faith, and where religious teaching would be given the utmost importance. Soon a number of schools and colleges in different parts of India came under the control of that body.

A cultural centre called the 'Brahmavidyashrama' was opened at Adyar in 1922. It was to be "a meeting place for the East and the West in its spirit, its scheme of studies and its personnel."[27] This centre attracted a number of students and Dr. Annie Besant took active part in it.

Political Activities

Dr. Annie Besant emerged on the political scene of India at a time when the British were consolidating their hold on the country by stifling its cultural and political conscience, through its own motivated system of education, resulting in a feeling of despair and inferiority among the Indians, and completely negating their will to struggle for any national cause. In fact, such was the situation that educated Indians were happier to identify themselves with the Britishers and become alien for their own native brothers. This is not to say that there was no undercurrent of dissatisfaction. A movement of protest and struggle was afoot in a haphazard and scattered manner. The early Congress leaders were moderate in their demands. They believed in constitutional agitation within the law. They had a strong feeling that with British help and guidance, would India secure her national unity and national freedom. While the Congress was continuing its agitation along constitutional lines, a different wave of nationalism was sweeping over Bengal and Maharashtra. These were the extremists who believed in the force which alone would compel the British to hand over power to Indians. The moderates thought that Indians must be given enough training before they could be the master of their own destiny. Therefore, they believed in gradual attainment of self government, within the British Empire. Matters became worse after World War I, when India felt, that in spite of her cooperation she was not adequately compensated. On coming to India in 1893, Dr. Annie Besant devoted herself to the cause of social and educational upliftment of the Indians, but with the passage of time, she felt that no real improvement was possible without raising the political status of India.

As S.R. Bakshi remarked:

> Undoubtedly Besant emerged on the political scene of India at a time when the Raj was deeply involved in the global war and she was able to arouse the aspirations of the people towards a decision which promised them a new hope, with new political ideas and ways of life. During this time, the people of India became well aware of the fact that there was no one to push forward their constitutional demands hitherto put forward in the annual session of the Indian National Congress. Politics appeared to be inert and colourless and a stronger grip with a dynamic personality who could launch an agitation with the support of the people or could negotiate with the British bureaucracy was the need of the hour.[28]

Dr. Annie Besant was *neither a moderate nor an extremist. She was a radical*, a bridge between the two. She believed in a radical change of a constitutional nature, in quick result - oriented political activities. This *made her launch the Home Rule Movement.*

Dr. Annie Besant launched the All India Home Rule League in September 1915. *She successfully unified a politically fragmented India and brought the moderates, extremists, Muslim League together on a common platform of the All India Home Rule League.*

Dr. Annie Besant stressed that the question of Home Rule for India was no question of party politics, it was a question of principle, of the liberation of a people from autocratic rule. Her preference of the term 'Home Rule' over 'Swaraj' (self rule or self government) implied control over a 'National Household'. She wanted Home Rule but under the British Crown. She wanted liberty for India but within the British Federation - Dominion Status – independence within India, with an equal and friendly link with Britain through the Crown. Under her the press became powerful in spite of repression.

With the arrival of Gandhiji on the political scene, the Indian political picture showed an extremist hue and complete independence became the focus in the Congress programme. Gandhiji advocated the non-cooperation movement. He recommended the renunciation of government titles, boycotting of the legislatures, law-courts, government educational institutions and foreign goods; emphasis was laid on the promotion of Swadeshi goods by means of reviving hand-spinning in every home. Dr. Annie Besant regarded Gandhiji's non-cooperation movement as a 'muddle-headed diplomacy'.[29]

Though Dr. Annie Besant had a deep respect for Gandhiji as a person, she felt that Gandhiji's policy had come in the way of solid political, industrial and educative work and stirred up fanaticism and violence primarily due to the following reasons:

1. By drawing the youth of the land into such movements resulted in unnecessary anarchy and the movement in turn was prevented from being peaceful. She felt that the youth of the land should not be allowed to take the plunge all of a sudden, when their thinking power had not developed sufficiently to enable them to take wise decisions. Moreover, it created indiscipline in educational institutions and such students had their career ruined forever.
2. It was essential to have a functioning government to look to the day-to-day affairs. By paralysing the government of the day, it resulted in further confusion and anarchy.
3. Such policy was against the Hindu shastras, against Dharma as it injured the very foundation on which a society rested, that is, on cooperation.
4. It gave rise to racial hatredness.

Between 1923 and 1925, Dr. Annie Besant rallied the moderate group opposed to Gandhiji, and drafted a constitution that proposed Dominion Status for India within the British Empire, and limited the franchise to educated

Indians. With Gandhiji's philosophy of 'Satyagraha' beginning to win the hearts of the majority of Indians, Dr. Annie Besant's vision began to loose popularity. She moved away from active work and passed away at Adyar on 20th September 1933.

Social Activities

Dr. Annie Besant had involved herself in social work while she was in England. When she arrived in India, she again occupied herself in such works. She believed that a nation was an assembled human body, and just as a man in his present life suffers for the sins that he had committed in the past, similarly a nation too had to suffer for the wrong deeds done by the group of human beings that constituted it. India had sinned too. India had not accepted the Shudras as the younger brothers of the family and had ill-treated them. Also over the years caste was based on birth and not on quality. Dr. Annie Besant had quoted from the Mahabharat "A Brahman who shows the qualities of a Shudra is a Shudra and not a Brahman; that the Shudra who knows the quality of a Brahman is a Brahman and not a Shudra..."[30].

Dr. Annie Besant believed that India had to suffer for her wrong deeds. It was perhaps due to her wrong acts that India suffered from foreign invasions. Dr. Annie Besant stated that, "...she (India) has finally expiated the debt of being made the servant of another Nation, and thus has paid to the uttermost the debt that she owed to the karma that she had made..."[31]

According to Dr. Annie Besant no class can rise until she has her own self-respect. A man who is always treated with contempt from childhood cannot respect himself and, therefore, cannot rise. She hence asked the Theosophists to *treat the Shudras, the down-trodden as younger brothers* and show them due respect.

She opened schools for untouchables and 'Olcott Pancham School' at Adyar is one such example. She *laid stress on social equality, abolition of child marriages, purdah system that kept women in physical and mental seclusion,* abolition of the system of Devadasis and raised her voice against child labour. She improved the lot of widows "by making them the willing helpers of their sex, by training them as teachers and as nurses, and by thus making widowhood a consecration to the service of humanity"[32] She founded the *All India Women's Association* of which she was the first President. This association involved itself in social work and encouraged girls to receive education. This association also gave women the right to vote and believed that men and women should have equal status, for only then can a nation be strong.

Dr. Annie Besant took out campaigns against child marriages and since 1929, marriage before 14 for girls and 18 for boys has been forbidden by law. Now this has been increased to 18 and 21. She also drew attention to family planning.

She set up the *Theosophical Order of Service* in 1908. It is a social service organisation associated with the Theosophical Society. Its motto is "A union of all who love, in the service of all that suffers."[33] Dr. Annie Besant believed that the more one serves others, the more his life is enriched. As Radha Burnier states: "Theosophical Order of Service is a strong activity within the larger work of the Theosophical Society"[34]. Other institutions formed by Dr. Annie Besant for social work were, The Sons and Daughters of India, Scouting, Young Men's Indian Association. A brief account of their working has already been given under Dr. Annie Besant's educational activities.

Dr. Annie Besant believed that social awareness can be inculcated into the minds of the individuals when they are rightly educated. Therefore, she undertook her social work through the means of education. As pointed out in the journal Wake up India:

> Social reform in those days was especially divorced in its orientation from Hindu religion and philosophy. The social reform she (Dr. Annie Besant) advocated was aimed at removing outworn customs and accretions, which had encrusted the faith of the people.[35]

Exponent of the Essential Unity of All Religions

Dr. Annie Besant knew that India's greatness lay in her spiritualism, philosophy and religion which emphasised the unity of life, that there is an all pervading Life, of which all lives are a part. She found that in India there was more hope of spiritual revival than anywhere else. As she herself reiterated:

For spirituality is more easily awakened in India than elsewhere. The spiritual heart here is only sleeping, whereas in some other lands it has scarcely yet come to birth; for you must remember that in this land is the birthplace of every religion, and that from India outwards, religions have made their way.[36]

After the death of Colonel Olcott in 1907, Dr. Annie Besant became the President of the Theosophical Society. Theosophy finds a common basis of all religions and unites them all. Dr. Annie Besant had in 1922 written a prayer for daily repetition, which is still read at all the programmes of the Theosophical Society. The lines are as follows:

O Hidden Life! vibrant in every atom;

O Hidden Light! shining in every creature;

O Hidden Love! embracing all in Oneness;

May each who feels himself as one with Thee

Know He is also One with every other.[37]

The Theosophical Society with its stress on Universal Brotherhood, tried to convince the members to learn to trust the Divine in them and to lead a life of love and selfless service. Dr. Annie Besant applied the Theosophical idea of Brotherhood to all departments of life.

Skills of Written Expression

Dr. Annie Besant was a skilled writer. At the beginning of her career, she had written stories for children. After coming to India she wrote books on Indian culture and the various religions that existed in India. Through these books she made the people of India and of other lands become aware of the greatness of the various Indian religions. She translated *The Bhagavad Gita* into English. She wrote books on Theosophy, spiritualism, philosophy, and education. She edited magazines like *The Theosophist*[38], *Wake up India*, and newspapers like *Commonweal* and *New India*. *Wake up India* was the magazine started by her and is still being published from Adyar. The magazine promotes the movement for "right citizenship, right values, and right means". Some of her many interesting books to which the researcher had access are listed below:

The fundamental teachings of Theosophy are explained in simple and clear terms in her books, *The Ancient Wisdom, The Riddle of Life, The Inner Government of the World, A Study In Consciousness*. Books like *Karma, Rencarnation, Seven Principles of Man* have discussed these subjects in details. *The Universal Law Of Life, The Laws Of The Higher Life, The Doctrine Of The Heart, Meditations: On The Path And Its Qualifications*, reflect on the virtues that a man must possess in order to reach the stage of human perfection. The *Universal Law Of Life* contains two addresses by Dr. Annie Besant at the World Parliament Of Religions in September 1893 at Chicago on the themes The Supreme Duty and Theosophy and Ethics. Dr. Annie Besant's concept of Truth is based on the Hindu scriptures. This is beautifully expressed in her books *The Wisdom Of The Upanishads* and *Hints On The Study Of The Bhagavad Gita*. Her fundamental principles of nation building and educational ideas covering all departments of life – statecraft, industry, economics, culture, social life, are very beautifully expressed in the book *Builder Of New India*. This book is a compilation of *The Besant Spirit Series* containing seven volumes, of which the seventh volume entitled *Essentials Of An Indian Education*, and the second, *Ideals In Education* reflect the implications of the Upanishad and Bhagavad Gita on her educational ideas. Her *Autobiography* is the most comprehensive and authentic source of her life and times, extending from 1847 to 1891, that is, till she joined the Theosophical circle. The researcher was fortunate in having access to all these books and many more. Constraints of space preclude their further elaboration.

Dr. Annie Besant was also a great poet. The Universal Prayer of the Theosophical Society which begins with the words "O Hidden Life..." was composed by her in 1922. It is still repeated in all the programmes of the Theosophical Society. She has also composed beautiful poems like *God Save Our Motherland, God Save Our India* and *O Master I Have Promised* and also drew up the musical score for them.[39] She was a great musician and could play the piano very well.

In conclusion it may be said, that before coming to India, Dr. Annie Besant had been identified with practically every radical social movement in England. She brought with her to India this rich experience of social and political protest. She was also a member of the Theosophical Society and an ardent supporter of Theosophical ideas. In India she worked for her independence and national upliftment. In all that she did there was a religious and educational overtone. This had the strong support of her own religious and scholastic temperament.

References

1. A Short Biography Of Dr. Annie Besant, pp. 1-2.
2. Annie Besant-An Autobiography, pp. 14-15.
3. ibid., p. 23
4. ibid., p. 27
5. ibid., p. 24
6. ibid., p. 51
7. ibid., p. 58
8. ibid., p. 81
9. A person who forms his opinions about religion independently of tradition, authority or established belief.
10. A person who believes that the human mind cannot know whether there is a God, or an ultimate cause, or anything beyond material phenomena. Whilst the atheist rejects all religious belief and denies the existence of God, the agnostic questions the existence of God, heaven etc. in the absence of material proof, and in unwillingness to accept supernatural revelation.
11. Annie Besant - An Autobiography, p. 97.

12. A Short Biography Of Dr. Annie Besant, p. 6.
13. Annie Besant - An Autobiography, p. 138.
14. ibid., p. 146.
15. ibid., p. 194.
16. Three Great Sages-Sri Aurobindo, Dr. Annie Besant, J. Krishnamurti, pp. 29-30.
17. A Short Biography Of Dr. Annie Besant, p.15
18. Encyclopaedia Of Mystical and Paranormal Experience, p. 611
19. ibid., p. 612.
20. The Theosophist, November 2000, p. 43.
21. Anand Lodge: Theosophical Society, Allahabad (Pamphlet) 12th August, 1994, p. 3.
22. Introduction To Theosophical Society (pamphlet) 1997-1998, edited by Secretary, U.P. Federation Theosophical Society, Smt. Gyan Kumari Ajeet.
23. A Short Biography Of Dr. Annie Besant p. 23.
24. The Besant Spirit, Volume 7, p. vi
25. A Short History Of Theosophical Society, p. 427.
26. ibid., p. 446.
27. ibid., p. 453.
28. Annie Besant Founder Of Home Rule Movement, p. 14.
29. Builder Of New India, p. 92.
30. ibid., p. 322.
31. ibid., p. 319.
32. ibid., p. 331.
33. The Theosophist, March 2000, p. 231
34. Theosophical Order Of Service, pamphlet of U.P. Federation Theosophical Society (1999).
35. Wake Up India, April June 2000, p. 5.
36. Builder Of New India, p. 362
37. A Short History Of Theosophical Society, p. 460.
38. A journal started in October 1879 by Madame Blavatsky and Colonel Olcott in which Indian and Western Oriental scholars could write about the secret wisdom hidden under the myths of antiquity.
39. Prakash Punj: Annie Besant (pamphlet), p. 23.

2
[B] Life and Times of J. Krishnamurti

Jiddu Krishnamurti, who pointed his finger towards Truth, who wanted "to free humanity from all cages, from all fears", who was trained to play the role of the World Teacher - a title about which he always had reservations - was in no way different from an ordinary man who has to undergo the difficulties, toils, sufferings, and agonies during his life.

The various phases of Krishnamurti's life are interesting and show how he freed himself from the clutches of the materialistic, selfish, egoistic world in order to discover the extraordinary riches that lie beyond the scope of the mind, to discover what is reality, what is timeless, what is joy, what is love. *The narrative is biographical and the movement of Krishnamurti's life is traced chronologically from the time he was born till his death. To give coherence to his varied and diverse experiences, events in his life have been reviewed in brief under various sections.*

The Early Years

Krishnamurti was born on the 11th of May, 1895 at Madanapalli, in South India. He was brought up in a highly orthodox family with strictly conservative beliefs, and spent the early years of his life in a milieu of caste system, untouchability, strict observance of rituals.[1]

Krishnamurti was the eighth child of his parents, and was named after Sri Krishna who had himself been an eighth child. "The name 'Krishnamurti' means 'in the likeness of God'. Jiddu is his surname which is derived from the name of the village where his ancestors lived."[2] He belonged to a Telugu - speaking Brahmin family and his father, Jiddu Narianiah, was a rent collector employed by the British.

Krishnamurti had a very neglected childhood. His mother, Jiddu Sanjeevamma, died when he was only ten years old and was deprived of a mother's warmth, care and love early in life. He was deeply attached to his younger brother, Nityananda, with whom intense bonds remained till the latter's death at Ojai, California in 1925.

Krishnamurti began his educational career at the age of six at Kadiri. Having a frail constitution and being a "vague and dreamy" child, not at all eager to learn from books, but being so dreamy as to appear mentally retarded at times, he fell far behind other boys of his age and was often punished by his teacher in school. This "vague and dreamy" countenance perhaps mirrored the free and vacant mind which persisted throughout his life.

Discovery by Theosophists

After the death of Krishnamurti's mother, the fortunes of his father declined and he was relieved of his position in the Revenue Department. Having been a Theosophist for quite sometime, that is since 1881,[3] he was invited by Mrs. Annie Besant, the President of the Theosophical Society, to stay in Madras at Adyar, and work for the Society. He gratefully accepted the invitation and settled at the headquarters of the Society from 1909. He brought with him four of his sons, including Krishnamurti.

It was here that Krishnamurti was picked out one evening on the beach to be the vehicle for the World Teacher from a crowd of other Indian boys by Charles Webster Leadbeater, a leading figure in the Theosophical Society, who claimed to be clairvoyant. Most Theosophists at that time believed that the Lord Maitreya, the World Teacher, was soon to manifest in human form, as two thousand years ago he had manifested in the body of Jesus and before that in the body of Sri Krishna. Leadbeater, had remarked that the boy had "the most wonderful aura he had ever seen, without a particle of selfishness in it."[4] This remark of Leadbeater's is very significant as it points out to the clean and pure mind which Krishnamurti had, which never desired to have anything for himself-money, power, position, or publicity, and which prompted him to step down the hierarchical ladder, from the peak of glory being proclaimed the Messiah or Saviour, and reach out to the masses, to mingle with the vast multitude and become one with the universe. The belief of Annie Besant, based on Lord Krishna's promise in The Bhagavad Gita to return to earth for saving the good and destroying the evil, made her see in Krishnamurti this reincarnation and the makings of a World Teacher.

After having picked him up, both Mrs. Annie Besant and C.W. Leadbeater offered to take Krishnamurti in their care; and at this stage his father readily agreed. As there was a special bond of affection between the two brothers, Krishnamurti and Nityananda, Mrs. Annie Besant decided to adopt both the children. This is how Krishnamurti came into the Theosophical Circle. The two children found in Mrs. Annie Besant a source of inexhaustible affection and love which they were deprived of at a very tender stage, when their mother died. Krishnamurti started to address her as his "Mother" as is seen in his first letter dated 24th December, 1909 to Mrs. Annie Besant.

Dec. 24th, 1909.

My Dear Mother,

Will you let me call you mother when I write to you? I have no other mother now to love and I feel as if you were our mother as you have been so kind to us. We both thank you so much for taking us away from home and letting us sleep in your room; we are so happy there, but we would rather have you here, even if we had to sleep at home. They are so kind to us, they have given beautiful bicycles, and I have learnt to ride mine, and I go out on it each day. I have ridden 31½ miles, and I shall add some more this evening. I have seen you sometimes in the shrine-room, and

I often feel you at night and see your light. I send very much love.

Yours loving son
Krishna[5]

He had written this letter from Adyar to Mrs. Besant who had gone to Benares to attend the annual convention of the Theosophical Society.

Efforts of Leadbeater

Leadbeater began to teach the two boys himself with the help of some of his Theosophical friends. Leadbeater gave them nourishing diet, regular exercise, adequate rest and insisted on scrupulous cleanliness of their bodies. One of his chief concerns was to eliminate fear in them. English was the subject most emphasised so that they would be able to communicate with Mrs. Besant when she returned to Adyar. The early training that Krishnamurti received under Leadbeater's guidance was meant to prepare him for the role of the World Teacher that he was supposed to play in the near future. Under the instruction of the great masters he developed spiritually, led from one initiation to another. He is also said to have developed some power of clairvoyance.

The boys underwent spiritual training under Leadbeater's own occult master, Kuthumi, who, with other masters, was said to live in an ever young human body in a ravine in Tibet, and who could be visited nightly on the astral plane during sleep. Kuthumi accepted the boys as his pupils and Krishnamurti took his first occult Initiation on January 11th, 1910.[6]

The first initiation is a step forward to disciplining the ego and realising the importance of the powers of spirituality of the Great Masters.[7] The stiff qualifications necessary for the first initiation have been described in detail by Mary Lutyens.[8]

AT THE FEET OF THE MASTER

The true laws of life and conduct which the master taught Krishnamurti for his first initiation on the path of discipleship were written down by Krishnamurti and later published in the form of a small booklet titled *At The Feet of The Master* which has been translated into twenty - seven languages. This booklet is signed by Krishnamurti's 'star' name, 'Alcyone'. This 'star' name meant that when investigations into his past lives were undertaken by Leadbeater, Krishnamurti and the people with whom he was associated in those lives were given names of stars, to secure for them a certain amount of anonymity. The significance of this book is that it reflects some early formative stages of Krishnamurti's life which were to undergo tremendous changes in the years to come.

Order of the Star in the East

In 1911 an organisation was formed under the leadership of George Arundale, Principal of the Central Hindu College at Benares, named *The Order of the Rising Sun* to bring together those members of the Theosophical Society who believed in the imminent possibility of the re-incarnation of the Lord in the form of Krishnamurti, to help in preparing the world to receive him and thus to create a favourable spirit of welcome and reverence. A few months later, on the advice of Mrs. Annie Besant and Leadbeater, its name was subsequently changed to *The Order of the Star in the East* and was turned into an international organisation. Mrs. Annie Besant and Leadbeater were made Protectors of the new Order and Krishnamurti was made the Head. A quarterly magazine, printed at Adyar and called the *Herald of the star*, with Krishnamurti as its nominal editor was also started.

Krishnamurti's stay in Europe (1912-1921)

The members of the Theosophical Society took great care in training Krishnamurti as they were concerned with the development of events as preparation for the coming of a "World Teacher", and one comes to know about it from the letters written by Leadbeater to Mrs. Anne Besant from 1909 to 1913 concerning the progress and education of Krishnamurti and his brother Nityananda, published in *The Theosophist*, from June to October 1932, a magazine issued by the Theosophical Society. Both the boys were taken to Europe by Mrs. Annie Besant in 1912 for being properly educated. They were educated privately by a group of learned Theosophists such as C. Jinarajadasa,[9]. George Arundale[10], A.E. Wodehouse, elder brother of P.G. Wodehouse, who had been Professor of English at Elphinstone College, Bombay, and moved to Benares after getting interested in Theosophy. The accent was on the proper use of language. It was hoped that both boys would pass into Oxford or Cambridge or, failing that, into London University.

As the various stages of Krishnamurti's life unfold one finds him going through the pangs, agonies, cravings of an ordinary human being, but Krishnamurti's true self was all the time unfolding, slowly, secretly, hidden even from himself. The influence that other people have had on him from time to time has been entirely superficial. Though he was strictly kept under Theosophical influence, nothing touched him. He hated publicity and longed for a normal life. In one of his letters to Lady Emily Lutyens, a Theosophist and wife of architect Edwin Lutyens, he had written, "why did they ever pick on me?"[11]. As Krishnamurti said in one of his dialogues on the influence of Theosophy on himself, at Vasanta Vihar in December 1980:

> I was not conditioned by the teaching. I mean by this, it came in and it came out. Sir, I would say that they tried to condition me; they tried to say that this is the life, you are going to take. They tried to induce me to accept their church, cannons, and all that... I can assure you that none of that mattered. All that thing never touched that boy.[12]

Krishnamurti failed in his matriculation three times and Mrs. Annie Besant, losing all hopes of Krishnamurti ever passing the examination, sent him to Paris to learn French in 1920. Krishnamurti had by now entered the stage of youth. In 1921, Krishnamurti went to Holland on being invited by Baron Philip Van Pallandt Van Eerde who had offered to make over to the Order of the Star his beautiful eighteenth century ancestral home, Castle Eerde at Ommen. It was here that Krishnamurti fell in love with an American girl named Helen Knothe, a niece of Miss Cornelia Dijkgraaf, National Representative of the Star in Holland and daughter of Frank Knothe who had a successful clothing business in New Jersey. But this love which he had experienced for the first time in his life had to be sacrificed as he was asked by Mrs. Annie Besant to leave Europe at the end of 1921 and to come to India to begin his life's work as a lecturer for Theosophy and the Order of the Star in the East. Mrs. Annie Besant had once written to Krishnamurti: "A man called to highest service loses 'the lower life', and if he is brave enough to let it go, he finds a splendid and changeless happiness"[13]. These lines were noted down by Krishnamurti in his diary, and unknowingly he led his life along them. In one of his letters to Dr. Annie Besant, he wrote, "...I honestly mean to do this and I will do this at all costs. I will take my life very seriously, help and make others happy...I will do my best, my holy mother and no man can do more."[14] That he fully believed that his work would lie in India is shown by his writing to Lady Emily in 1920:

> Mother dear it has got to be sometime in this life. Mrs. Besant has not yet sent for me. If she does we shall have to put our feelings in our respective pockets and I shall certainly go to India.[15]

Also to Mrs. Annie Besant he wrote, "...I want to gain everything that the West can give and then turn my face to India where I am sure I shall work..."[16].

The Spiritual Experiences

Due to Nityananda's poor health, the brothers were advised by the doctor to go to California in 1922. It was hoped that the climate of that country would bring about a lasting improvement, which it did for sometime to begin with. There they were left to themselves entirely doing all the work by their own hands. They lived in a small house in the Ojai Valley which was named 'Arya Vihara'. It was a beautiful valley full of orange groves.

There at Ojai, Krishnamurti passed through intense spiritual experiences that completely transformed his life. These experiences were recorded by his brother Nityananda and were also witnessed by one Miss Rosalind who attended upon Krishnamurti during those days of spiritual awakening preceded by pain and physical torture.[17]

After the Ojai experience Krishnamurti's life changed. As he wrote to Lady Emily on the 2nd of September, 1922:

> So mother you see I have changed and with that change in me, I am going to change the lives of my friends. ...I am going to help the whole world to climb a few feet higher...You don't know how I have changed, my whole inner nature is alive with energy and thought and I am sure my ego has come down decidedly...[18]

From that time onwards Krishnamurti started to refer to himself only in the third person as "K", or as the impersonal "we", to suggest an absence of the "I", the ego's sense of "individuality. Most of his friends and followers started calling him "Krishnaji"– the suffix "ji" being a term of respect. Krishnamurti took on a new stature and had no more doubts as to what his mission in life was to be. He began to write poetry and continued to do so for several years. He started to write an article, a sort of prose poem which appeared in the *Herald* under the title *The Path* in 1923.

In the years that followed Krishnamurti's spiritual experiences continued and often he felt an intense pain and would put his head down and become unconscious.[19]

Discord with Theosophical Society

The years 1925 turned out to be of immense significance not only for the Theosophical Society and the Order of the Star in the East, but also in the personal life of Krishnamurti.

While Krishnamurti was at Ojai, California, looking after his sick brother, important events were witnessed by all those who attended the second star camp held at Ommen, Holland in 1925. In the absence of Krishnamurti, Head of the Star organisation, Mrs. Annie Besant suddenly announced the names of seven Apostles, to assist the vehicle prepared for the Great One. This announcement, in fact, raised a great storm everywhere and even Dr. Annie Besant had to clarify herself in America and elsewhere later on. Krishnamurti was shocked. "He felt that something infinitely precious, sacred and private had been made publicly ugly and ridiculous, cheap and vulgar."[20] Later on when he stepped out of the Theosophical Society in 1930, *he saw the cause of most Theosophical difficulties in the system of occult communications and thought that the occult had usurped the place of the spiritual*, that Theosophy was no longer the experience of the Truth by each person but only experienced by a few, who as a result, become mediators revealing the divine wisdom.

The Great Bereavement

The moment of 'The Great Bereavement', the shocking news of his brother Nitya's death, which Krishnamurti received in November 1925, when he was on board ship bound for Colombo, is a very crucial period of his life which eventually led to the flowering of his teaching. Krishnamurti was quite sure that Nitya would not be allowed to die as the Masters had assured him and so he accepted the invitation of going to Adyar, Madras to attend the Jubile Convention of the Theosophical Society. In the words of Shiva Rao[21], Krishnamurti was, "heart broken, disillusioned".[22]

After that tragic incident his entire philosophy of life - the implicit faith in the future as outlined by Mrs. Besant, Leadbeater and Nitya's vital part in it appeared to be shattered to pieces and afterwards he never mentioned the Masters. He learned to stand totally alone. Krishnamurti had gone through an inner revolution, transformation which had given him a new strength, a new enthusiasm to face the world, and Leadbeater who had gone to the port to receive him, greeted Krishnamurti with the words, "Well, at least *you* are an Arhat"[23], meaning that Krishnamurti at any rate had passed the Fourth Initiation. Krishnamurti now totally moved away from the idea of gurus or masters and refused to accept any comforting lies. He had now freed himself totally from all his friends, his books, his associations. By that time Krishnamurti's mission in life was clearly marked out and he set out to "free humanity from all cages, from all fears,"[24] to instill in them an intensive desire to seek Truth which could not be found in any outward form or "shelters of comfort"[25] but only in oneself.

Dissolution of the Order of the Star

Krishnamurti dissolved the Order of the Star in August 1929 at the Ommen Gathering in the presence of Mrs. Annie Besant and 3000 star members, since he did not want the Order "to be a vessel which holds the Truth and the only Truth".[26] He did not want to have followers. He said: "...I maintain that Truth is a pathless land, and you cannot approach it by any path whatsoever, by any religion, by any sect..."[27]

He wanted to free humanity from all types of bondage, from all types of spiritual organisation, theory, belief that captivate man and cripple him and make him weak, which prevent him from opening, unfolding, flowering. He wanted to free man from all fears - from the fear of religion, salvation, spirituality, love, death, from the fear of life itself. Here an article of Radha Burnier in which she has beautifully sketched the reason of Krishnamurti's stepping out of the Theosophical Society deserves mention:

> The connection between Krishnamurti (Krishnaji as he was affectionately known) and the Theosophical Society was broken not because he left as many members believe, but because people were not ready to listen to a profound message given in terms they were not accustomed to hearing. It is not the first time that this happened. The Jews would not listen to Jesus when he came to teach. The majority of Hindus did not respond for long to what the Buddha had to say. Most people like to revert to their accustomed thoughts, their habits, their convenient theories and ideas even when they are shaken up, or radical change is both difficult and "inconvenient". But everything which is profound is radical. Truth cannot temporize and compromise, and we like to compromise and have the best of both worlds. In the Mahatma Letters, it is made very clear that one who is earnest about the Path must abandon all his accustomed modes of thinking and ways of action. So members of the Theosophical Society, should have been prepared to hear a new message. But when Krishnaji began to speak in a radical way, there were many who could not listen.

The very fact that he denied to himself all authority was radical. Those who expected the "World Teacher" to manifest through Krishnamurti had, as he himself declared in 1927, a picture in their minds of what would be said and what the function of Krishnamurti would be. A picture is a static, material form projected by the mind, and Krishnaji pointed out that as long as the picture was static, people were happy and satisfied. When the picture came alive they were disturbed. Obviously, it is so much more convenient to deal with something which does not speak or act, except as the person wants. An image can be made to play a role which satisfies. It was expected of the "World Teacher" that he would tell people what to believe, define the "truth" and the role his followers were to play. Many may have liked an important role for themselves as followers and interpreters. But when the teaching came and Krishnaji denied his authority, repudiated all following, refused any interpretation, it deflated the ego-sense of some would be followers and dismayed others.[28]

The Aftermath

In 1930, Krishnamurti stepped out of the limited circle of the Theosophical Society into the wide world and was accepted by the world. Now he belonged to the vast ocean of humanity, to the whole world and not just to the small circle of Theosophical Society. Krishnamurti who had earlier longed for total renunciation of becoming a sanyasi in India, now abandoned this idea completely. He now realised that his work had to be in the world, that he must go out and talk to the masses instead of waiting for the few to approach him. The full flowering of his teachings had begun. The Camps at Ommen and Ojai were now open to the public, and Krishnamurti, wanting to be free of all responsibilities, resigned from the various Trusts of which he had been a member. He continued to pursue his mission now with great enthusiasm, traveling, giving talks in Europe, India, America, Australia, and holding gatherings at Ommen and Ojai. Wherever he went he had packed audiences to listen to him. Many of his old friends moved away from him as they were not ready to give up their belief or their positions of prestige which they had held so far. New people took the place of those who abandoned him and donations towards his work continued to pour in. Krishnamurti's own personal source of income was the £ 500 a year settled on him by Miss Dodge,[29] all other income came from donations and the sale of his books. After Nitya's death, Rajagopala[30] looked into his financial matters. He continued to live at Arya Vihara when he was at Ojai. Throughout his life he had been held, protected in his childhood days by the affection and concern of his father and later by the Theosophical Society, their expectations, their belief, their hopes of the role he was to play as the World Teacher. After his stepping out of the Theosophical Society he was inwardly and outwardly free. No one was there to charter his activities or question him.

In the Service of Humanity

For the next sixty years Krishnamurti probed deeper and deeper into the real meaning of life. He traveled all over the world holding seminars, giving talks. He was trying hard to find words in which to convey an understanding of what to him was Truth. He moved away from his poetic mysticism to the hard and rational language of science. He met people from all strata of society like scientists, psychologists, educationists, scholars, politicians or sanyasis, students, and the poor. Krishnamurti was fond of children and would always come closer to the younger generation as he felt that it was the young who had "the power to fall in love, to give oneself completely"[31], that he found so lacking in the older people.

Between the years 1933 to 1939 Krishnamurti visited India several times, giving talks to large audiences. With the death of Mrs. Besant in 1933 and the election of George Arundale as President of the Theosophical Society in 1934 Krishnamurti lost touch with the Theosophical Society completely Krishnamurti however, visited the Theosophical Society Headquarters at Madras on November 3, 1980 for the first time after 46 years at the request of Radha Burnier who now had become the President of Theosophical Society and continues to be so[32]. Krishnamurti had spoken of the Theosophical Society as an organised belief, and disliked the idea of a Guru who would lead his followers and show them how far advanced they were on their spiritual path.

A significant development took place in Krishnamurti's life during the phase of the Second World War. Krishnamurti was in Ojai in 1939 when the Second World War broke out in Europe. Krishnamurti spent nearly eight years in Ojai as the war put a restriction on his travels. However, the quiet time that he spent in Ojai was something "very creative and joyous".[33] While he was enraptured by the beauty of the quiet place, the rest of the world shook and trembled from the brutalities, exploitations, horrors of the war. The solitude and proximity to nature along with hours of meditation helped him to make amazing discoveries within himself. The public talks he gave at the Oak Grove in 1944, 1945, 1946 were concerned chiefly with the knowledge of the self. Those quiet years were of great importance to Krishnamurti as it resulted in the flowering of his teaching and the writing, which, encouraged by Aldous Huxley, was later published as *Commentaries on Living*. When asked about his years in Ojai, Krishnamurti said: "I think it was a period of no challenge, no demand, no outgoing. I think it was a kind of everything kept in, everything held in; and when I left Ojai it all burst."[34]

On the 15th of August, 1947, India became independent and Jawaharlal Nehru, her first Prime Minister. The birth pangs of Independent India were indeed painful. The partition of the country was violent and bloody, and post partition chaos prevailed. The new rulers of India, most of whom had spent half their lives in prison, were suddenly called upon to restore order and to deal with a refugee problem the magnitude of which was never encountered before. They were however sensitive enough not to believe like the masses that with the end of British rule in India a new age based on secularism, socialism, equalitarianism had emerged. The ideals that had carried them through the years of political struggle had crumbled under them, and they were left helpless, bitter, confused, sorrowful, fearful.

It was at this juncture that Krishnamurti visited India. He could sense the seething unrest and could foresee the chaos and violence that lay ahead. "The house is burning,"[35] he passionately told those who listened, but the intensity and urgency were missing in those who heard him.

Most people in India had witnessed the freedom struggle and the power of a mass movement, and they felt that to build a new India vast numbers of people should launch a new struggle for values. Krishnamurti told them, "to create a new structure I must be the architect, the builder as well as the workman.' When asked what one man could do, he said, 'You think in terms of large movement, large actions, large responsibilities, but you do not take responsibility. Why don't you begin to clean your front doorstep, the part of your street which is yourself ?"[36]

Between 1948 and the early 1960s, Krishnamurti was busy with his talks and personal meetings. The years 1964 to 1969 were also a time when Krishnamurti's attention was greatly diverted to the West. New people had gathered around Krishnamurti and taken charge of his financial and other interests. They arranged for his tour schedules, talks, publication of his works. This was the time when the foundations came into existence in India, England, America.

Dialogues

The last fifteen years of Krishnamurti's life marked the rise of dialogues as a profound means of exploring the nature of reality, truth. There were innumerable dialogues, question and answer meetings, seminars, unscheduled informal small-group discussions and conversations. He traveled to Europe, India, America at the ripe old age of eighty. He held summer gatherings at Saanen in Switzerland and autumn gatherings at Brockwood Park, Hampshire, England. He used to spend a month or more each year during the decade 1976 to 1986 at Vasant Vihar in Madras, India, and also visited the schools set up by him. Altogether he had a very heavy schedule and met many people, gave interviews, or met them at lunch, where the conversation would go on long after the meal. He wrote a number of books and in his last years was deeply concerned with how his work was to be carried on after his death. He wanted no interpreters of his teaching since he did not want to create another authority, another belief, another organisation to dispense Truth. According to him Truth has no limitations. It is not encompassed by any belief, or religion, or dogma. He wanted people to read his books and hold discussions as discussion is not interpretation. Krishnamurti was interested in building study centres where people concerned with his teaching could go and study it. He wanted his schools and the Foundations to work in a cooperative spirit and continue to flourish. Engaged till the last in all these activities, Krishnamurti passed away in Ojai, California at the age of ninety on 17th February 1986. The institutions founded by him and the message he gave to the world are sustained by the vigour that they imbibed from him and people all over the world continue to perpetuate it.

Relationships

So far as Krishnamurti's relationships with people are concerned, some deserve mention as they had profoundly influenced Krishnamurti's work. As in this thesis a comparison has been made between Dr. Annie Besant and J. Krishnamurti at various stages, an attempt has been made to give a summarised account of their relationship in the life and times of Krishnamurti too.

Throughout their lives, Dr. Annie Besant and Krishnamurti were to spend little time together. Despite this fact there was a very close bond between the two. From the moment Dr. Annie Besant saw Krishnamurti at Madras in 1909, she started to love him immensely and continued to do so till her death in 1933. Dr. Annie Besant's earliest letters to Krishnamurti reflect the intensity of love that flows out, to embrace the child and protect him. As a boy Krishnamurti wrote to her every week describing his dreams, his studies, his little problems, experiences. He even refered to her as "my mother". As he had been deprived of a mother's love at a very young age, he looked to Annie Besant for the affection and love of a mother. During his childhood Annie Besant played the role of a mother, always protecting, caring; later on she played the role of a teacher, concerned about Krishnamurti's education and as the years passed she desired to play the role of a disciple and sit at his feet to listen to his words. When Krishnamurti dissolved the Order in 1930, Krishnamurti's views had such a profound influence on Annie Besant that she, all of a sudden closed down the Esoteric Section of the Theosophical Society, but on the protestations of the leaders of the movement, she opened it again. She also told Krishnamurti that she wanted to resign as President of the Theosophical Society and desired only to sit at his feet and listen to the teaching, but he refused to let her do so. On hearing Krishnamurti's resignation from the Theosophical Society she wondered how Krishnamurti would survive the cruel world as she was aware of his total lack of wordly values. As Pupul Jayakar has mentioned in her biography of Krishnamurti that Dr. Annie Besant convinced B. Sanjeeva Rao and his wife, Padmabai, eminent educators and her close friends, to resign from the Theosophical Society and help Krishnamurti in his work.[37] Many members of the Theosophical Society resigned following Krishnamurti, and those who held fast, took a hostile attitude. But Annie Besant became vague and vacillated between acceptance and avoidance. During the last phase of her life, she had completely lost her memory, but she recognised her dearly beloved son, and Krishnamurti's deep love and respect for her persisted throughout his life. She was the only person he never forgot throughout his life. He refered to her always as Dr. Annie Besant although she had only an honorary degree conferred on her by the Hindu University at Benares in 1921. As Pupul Jayakar has mentioned in her biography of Krishnamurti :

> She was an influence not in moulding or giving direction to his mind and teaching, but in providing the ground of a total security of love. He had seen the fire in her blaze and sink to embers, but the warmth and unselfish love of Mrs. Annie Besant was perhaps the one constant factor in his early life.[38]

Some other persons who may be mentioned in this connection are Alain Naude, a South African and lecturer at the University of Pretoria, also a professional pianist. He arranged Krishnamurti's talks with distinguished persons. Also arranged talks with students of Harward.

Vanda Scaravelli, daughter of an Italian aristocratic landowner, arranged for periodic talks by Krishnamurti at Saanen.

In India, Nandini Mehta, daughter-in-law of Sir Chunilal Mehta and her sister Pupul Jayakar, Rao Sahib Patwardhan, Achyut Patwardhan and their father were of help.

David Bohm, Professor of Theoretical Physics at Birkbeck College, London University, attended Krishnamurti's talks in Europe and California since 1961. During the year 1980, eight dialogues took place between Krishnamurti and David Bohm, and these dialogues together with another five which took place at Brockwood Park, were published under the title, *The Ending of Time*.

Some Facets of Krishnamurti

A question often arises in one's mind as to what kind of a person was Krishnamurti? What were his habits, likes and dislikes? Was he an ordinary human being? Therefore, an attempt has been made in this thesis to give a brief account of a few facets of Krishnamurti's personality, before proceeding to consider his educational activities.

The key to the understanding of Krishnamurti is the critical and minute appreciation of the value of the silent, vacant mind. In his educational thoughts, in his talks and writings, he has always emphasised the necessity of an open mind, of a vacant mind that is unclustered by thoughts, by memories of the past, a mind that is intensely aware of what is around. It is only such a mind that can unravel the mysteries that lie deep within oneself. Commenting on his vacant mind, Mary Lutyens in her book *The Open Door* has quoted Krishnamurti from his journal. "He has never been hurt, though many things happened to him, flattery and insult, threat and security. It was not that he was insensitive, unaware: he had no image of himself, no conclusion, no ideology."[39]

It was perhaps due to this vacant mind that his early life seemed to move in a different sphere, in a closed and protected orbit, in the midst of an international Theosophical network. None of the goals, methods of the Theosophical Society touched him and he had no fear of going against Leadbeater, against Theosophy, against authority at a later stage. He finally stepped out of the Theosophical Circle saying that he wanted "to set man free". This was perhaps the result of his experiences during meditations which also prompted him to negate the "I" within him and address himself in the third person. Krishnamurti had never dwelt in the past, never carried the burden over from one day to another, nor was he concerned with the future. As Mary Lutyens has mentioned in her book, *The Years Of Fulfilment* that Krishnamurti remembered nothing of his childhood and youth except what had been told to him. This was not due to carelessness, but on the contrary, it was due to his extraordinary alertness. His mind was sharply focused on the present.[40]

Another characteristic that he retained all along was an intense observation of nature. Mary Lutyens in her book *The Open Door* has quoted Krishnamurti from his journal:

> As a young boy he used to sit by himself under a large tree near a pond in which lotuses grew. They were pink and had a strong smell. From the shade of that spacious tree he would watch the green snakes and the chameleons, the frogs and the water snakes[41].

Again Sunanda Patwardhan wrote:

> He used to talk to the trees and plants. He was so gentle. For a couple of years, some young trees were not growing well in Vasant Vihar. He would talk to them: "Come on, old lady, grow." He seemed to have an extraordinary oneness with nature, trees, plants and animals[42].

While observing nature closely he ultimately found himself united with nature, his consciousness having blended into every form of creation and he could sense the presence of "the Beloved" who resided in every blade of grass, in the flowing waters of the river, in the open skies, in mountain tops– such experiences were a source of tremendous joy to him.

Another facet that cannot be overlooked is his sense of belonging everywhere and nowhere in particular. Wherever he went he mingled with the crowd. When he came to India he wore his pyjamakurta and the traditional-style dhoti and while staying in the West he wore his western outfit. He considered himself raceless and without nationality.

Educational Activities of Krishnamurti

A brief account of Krishnamurti Schools, Study Centres, Foundations in India and Abroad is being given on the basis of information gathered from articles, journals, souvenirs, personal interviews.

Krishnamurti's guidelines to the schools were on two fronts - one was creating the right atmosphere to bring about a different kind of mind, and the other was with regard to the nature of the organisation that would manage the place. What would make the place alive and different was to be the spirit of self-awareness on the part of individuals and this had to be attempted by a group of teachers working together.

Description of Krishnamurti Schools Abroad

Oak Grove School, Ojai

R.E. Mark Lee has written in his article, A Guest On This Earth: "In 1975, Krishnamurti and the foundation started the Oak Grove School with three children and two teachers. The school was started with the intention to create a unique learning environment that would meet the needs of children facing a world in conflict, outwardly and inwardly."[43]

The school has boarding facilities for high school students and educates approximately 200 students, aged 5 to 18, each year. The 150 acre campus, surrounded by towering mountains, includes the grove of ancient oaks, where Krishnamurti most frequently spoke in the United States over the course of sixty years.

Brockwood Park Educational Centre

The centre was started by Krishnamurti in January 1969 with the sole object of discovering whether it was possible for students and staff from many nationalities and cultures, to live together as a family, to understand through daily contacts in the school, ways in which they as representative of mankind, have been conditioned and to free themselves from these limiting factors. As one older student wrote in 1972, "This Brockwood is a place where one can learn what it means to meet life." [44]

The centre is international, co-educational, and residential, and is not run for financial gains. Meals are vegetarian. Age of students range from 14 to 25 years and they come from over 20 different countries. It is essential that the school remains small in size, bearing in mind the fundamental question of what is being attempted, which is primarily, to bring into being an entirely new approach to living and to relationship, through self knowledge and at the same time to provide through academic education, a heuristic type of learning, where no matter what the subject, one was invariably studying oneself. There is a closely associated group of staff and students, living, working and playing together, to learn the art of living in their daily contacts with one another, and to cooperate without the imposition of psychological authority.

Description of Krishnamurti Schools in India

Krishnamurti Foundation India manages the following schools– Rishi Valley in Andhra Pradesh, Rajghat at Varanasi, Bal Anand at Bombay, The School in Madras, The Valley School at Bangalore, The Bhagirathi Valley School in Uttar Kashi, and the Sahyadri School near Pune.

The Rishi Valley Education Centre

The Rishi Valley Education Centre in India begun with the initiative of Krishnamurti in 1931, is a co-educational English medium school, which yearly educates approximately 350 students aged 8 to 17, some of whom board at the school. Located not far from Krishnamurti's birthplace, Rishi

Valley was selected by Krishnamurti as an appropriate site for a school. This had a beautiful but barren landscape which was later rendered sylvian by the students of Rishi Valley by tree plantation campaigns.

Today, the Rishi Valley Education Centre also oversees a rural education programme, operating some 18 satellite schools in impoverished hamlets around the valley. Rishi Valley School has a well qualified faculty who are not only concerned with the academic progress of their students, but also with their ability to work for a better future. Rishi Valley's educational philosophy is based on the notion that education must cater to the changing needs of students, for instance – how to preserve the environment? How to motivate first generation learners so that they do not drop out?[45]

Rajghat Education Centre

Rajghat School in Varanasi is the second Krishnamurti School founded in India. Details of this school are given in the chapter, *The Educational Ideas of J. Krishnamurti.*

Bal Anand School

Bal Anand School in the heart of Bombay is an after-school centre where opportunities for creative work are given to children from under privileged families in an atmosphere of affection and freedom. The children learn arts and crafts, music and yoga, and are taken to the countryside, to cultural events and to meet people from all walks of life to give them a broader outlook on the world. The centre, which was started in 1975, also operates a regular pre-primary day care facility, and provides nourishing snacks to all children in attendance.[46]

The School-KFI

The School-KFI stands in the middle of a shady grove in a quiet and peaceful place, in the heart of Madras and not far from the headquarters of the Krishnamurti Foundation India. It is a co-educational, English medium day school. The school offers an excellent programme of preschool education where child care is the essence. The following account of G. Gautam aptly describes the place:

> Students, from Kindergarten to Class-XII come happily to school. The school is a context for being with friends for students and teachers alike. A wide variety of experiences are introduced to children...students go out of the campus for field visits and study tours. Nature study on the rich campus forms an important part of Environment Studies. The teaching staff body meets twice every month for half a day to share experiences, draw insights and keep the intention in focus.[47]

The Bangalore Education Centre–The Valley School

The Valley School is situated at Haridvanam, ten miles from Bangalore. It was started in July 1978. The 104 acre campus 'Haridvanam' is picturesque, surrounded by hills, farms and forests. Its name 'Haridvanam' was given by Krishnamurti. The word 'Harid Vanam' is a Sanskrit word meaning 'green forest'. It is a co-educational, English medium day school; educating children aged 5 to 16.[48]

Uttar Kashi Education Centre

Uttar Kashi Education Centre is situated on the banks of the Bhagirathi, in the middle of the Garhwal Himalayas. On the left bank of the Bhagirathi is the Bhagirathi Valley School and on the right bank is the Uttar Kashi Retreat. Together they form the Uttar Kashi Education Centre.

> The Bhagirathi Valley School, still in its infancy, hopes to be a residential home for children from poor and illiterate homes in the hill region. The challenge of the teachers is to see if they can retain the innocence and sensitivity of the children while providing first rate academic training. This demands enormous strength and pliability, a capacity to learn all the time.[49]

At present the director of the Bhagirathi Valley School is Rajesh Dalal and he has taken 36 students in the school and they are all being brought up in a different way.

Sahyadri Krishnamurti School

Krishnamurti talked of having a school in western India, especially Maharashtra. As per his wishes, Sahyadri Krishnamurti School was inaugurated on 10th of September 1995, at a distance of sixty-five kilometers from Pune by Sunanda Patwardhan.[50] The school has gained a very good reputation in a short time and is growing rapidly and gaining in strength and stability. Both Bhagirathi Valley and Sahyadri Schools were set up after Krishnamurti's death by the Krishnamurti Foundation India.

Study Centres

The Study Centre is intended to be a place for self reflection, meditation, study and silence. In the latter part of his life, Krishnamurti became concerned that mature individuals seriously interested in his work had no place to spend time with it, to study and reflect, because of the pressures of job and family. To meet their needs, he asked the Foundations to establish retreats and study centres near the schools that he had founded. In these study centres learning and enquiry go side by side. Teachers, parents and students are encouraged to deeply enquire into the fundamental questions of life and also learn about the intentions of Krishnamurti in establishing these schools. There are also independent study centres. They have facilities for using audio and video tapes of Krishnamurti, and also a library of his books, as well as a general library with books of a philosophical nature. Monthly meetings take place and facilities for people to stay exist. An account of Krishnamurti's vision of a study centre follows:

> ...It is a place for the flowering of goodness, where there is communication and co-operation not based on work, an ideal, or personal authority. Co-operation implies not around some object or principle, belief, and so on, but a sharing of insights. As one comes to the place, each one in his work, working in the garden or doing something (else), may discover something as he is working. He communicates and has a dialogue with the other inhabitants, to be questioned and doubted in order to

see the weight of the truth of his discovery... It is not a place for one's own illumination or one's own goal of fulfilment, artistically, religiously, or in any other way, but rather a place for sustaining and nourishing one another to flower in goodness..."[51]

Foundations

There are Krishnamurti Foundations in U.S.A., Latin America, Britain and India. Krishnamurti did not regard the foundations as religious organisations, but rather as functional bodies established essentially for the dissemination of the teachings. These Foundations consist of a group of dedicated workers who during Krishnamurti's lifetime arranged for his talks, published his writings, produced audio and video cassettes of his talks and dialogues. Today the Foundations maintain the schools, study centres, archives, and facilitate dialogues and gatherings. The primary responsibility of the members of the Foundations was to live the teaching in daily life. Krishnamurti wanted the members to work together in search of truth. As Krishnamurti said, "You have come together sharing in common something profound, as seekers after truth. You should keep your hearts open."[52]

Works of Krishnamurti

Krishnamurti's first book *Education And The Significance Of Life* was published in 1953 by Harper and Row in America and Gollancz in England. This is a thought provoking book on education, discussing important features about educating the child. Details have been discussed in the chapter on the educational ideas of Krishnamurti.

In 1954 Krishnamurti's second book *The First And Last Freedom* was published by Gollancz. The first part of the book consists of twenty-one chapters on such themes as- What are we seeking?, Individual and Society, Self-Knowledge, Fear, Desire; Can thinking solve our problems?, Self-deception. The second half is made up of Questions and Answers taken from various talks.

At Ojai in June 1961, Krishnamurti started writing about his inner states of consciousness which were later published in 1976 as *Krishnamurti's Notebook*.

An authentic report of Krishnamurti's talks in India and Europe between 1963-1964 was compiled into a book with sixteen chapters titled *Freedom From The Known*. This book was published in 1969 and it deals with Krishnamurti's ideas under such headings as Awareness, Conditioning, Consciousness, Death, Fear, Freedom, God, Love, Meditation etc.

The Urgency Of Change was published in 1971. It consists of deeply probing questions put to him by Alain Naude. This book also throws light on one of Krishnamurti's frequently recurring themes which deals with the ending of thought.

The first important Krishnamurti book from India titled *Tradition And Revolution* was published in 1972 in Delhi by Orient Longman. It was edited by Pupul Jayakar and Sundanda Patwardhan. It comprised thirty dialogues held during 1970-71 in New Delhi, Madras, Rishi Valley and Bombay with a small group of people from a variety of cultural backgrounds and areas – intellectuals, artists, politicians, sanyasis – whom Krishnamurti had been meeting since he went to India in 1947.

Beyond Violence was published in 1973. It deals with Krishnamurti's talks and discussions held in Santa Monica, San Diego, London, Brockwood Park, Rome. This volume is highly concerned with the radical transformation of the individuals, so as to go beyond the violence so widespread everywhere. To be free from violence implies freedom from everything that man has put to another man, belief, dogma, rituals; my country, your country, your god, my god, my opinion, your opinion.

The Awakening Of Intelligence was published in 1973. It is the longest and most comprehensive of all Krishnamurti's works. The volume is made up of seven parts, including 'Two Conversations between Krishnamurti and Prof. Jacob Needleman' at Malibou in 1971, 'Two conversations between Krishnamurti and Alain Naude' at Malibou in 1971,

'Two Conversations between Krishnamurti and Swami Venkatesananda' at Saanen in 1969 and 'A Conversation between Krishnamurti and Prof. David Bohm' at Brockwood in October 1972. In his first conversation with Prof. Needleman, Krishnamurti emphasised the importance of getting rid of all religious conditioning. The root of Krishnamurti's teaching is that everything can be discovered in oneself and that in understanding oneself one comes to understand others, for fundamentally we are no different from others. In the conversation with Alain Naude, Krishnamurti states that the function of the religious man is to make the human being realise that when there is order in the human being then there is order in the world for "the world is me, I am the world". Krishnamurti's attitude to gurus is clearly reflected in his conversation with Swami Venkatesananda. Krishnamurti's conversation with Prof. Bohm was on 'Intelligence'. It is as a result of his talks with David Bohm that Krishnamurti has come to speak more often on the ending of thought. He has been excited and encouraged by his discussions with Bohm in which he feels that a bridge has been opened between the scientific and the religious mind.

In 1973, Krishnamurti started writing another manuscript as he had done in 1961. The daily writings were published in 1982 under the title *Krishnamurti's Journal*. They reveal more about him personally than any of his other works.

Krishnamurti's views on education are beautifully illustrated in two of his books titled *Beginnings Of Learning* and *Krishnamurti On Education* published in 1974. *Beginnings Of Learning* consists of informal discussions between Krishnamurti and students and staff at Brockwood school. *Krishnamurti On Education* is comprised of discussions with students and teachers at Rishi Valley and Rajghat Schools.

During the Brockwood Gathering in 1978, Krishnamurti began to write fortnightly letters to his schools which he continued to do till March 1980. It was a means of keeping in close personal touch with the schools. A copy of each letter was given to every teacher and pupil.

The thoughts and talks of Krishnamurti have been published and translated into almost 50 languages and are widely read. To demonstrate the organic evolution of Krishnamurti's philosophic convictions *The Collected Works Of J. Krishnamurti* has been published. Contained in 17 volumes are the transcripts of over 800 talks and more than 2700 answers to questions asked in twenty countries. Here is the essence of Krishnamurti recorded through 34 years (1933-1967). The talks are excellently edited; many by Krishnamurti himself, and the index of both topics and questions are exemplary.

Unpublished Manuscripts

Gists of two important unpublished manuscripts of Krishnamurti, (minimally edited by Krishna Nath) to which the researcher had access are being given below.

1. On Life

This material is from an unpublished manuscript reproduced from the original in the Henry E. Huntington Library and Art Gallery, California, U.S.A. Topics are alphabetically arranged as follows: Action, Awareness, Character, Comfort, Completeness, Conflict, Conformity, Contemplation, Craving, Discipline, Ego, Experience, Exploration, Fear, Ignorance, Knowledge, Life, Loneliness, Love, Memory, Mind, Progress, Sorrow. Themes pertaining to daily life have been given in a condensed manner. In page 2 of the manuscript, an extract from New's Letter Ommen, Holland, No. 3, July 1934 is given which explains that Krishnamurti was preparing a new book; probably to be entitled, *Thoughts On Life*, which would be written by Krishnamurti himself and not be a compilation of talks given by him, or a collection of his thoughts taken from them. Krishnamurti delayed its publication as he felt that it needed further revision.

2. On Study Centres

This is another unpublished manuscript consisting of verbatim transcripts of the Report of the International Trustees' Meetings in Ojai, 1977. From these one gathers that the Study Centres and the Foundations are there to actually live the teachings. The Study Centres are a place of integrity, deep honesty and the awakening of intelligence in the midst of confusion, conflict and destruction that is taking place in the world. This in no way depends on any person or group of people, but on the awareness, attention and affection of the people who are there. It is not a place for one's own illumination but rather for sustaining each other and nourishing each other to flower in goodness. Perhaps the real centres are not out there in physical space and in the facilities created there. They are necessary, but not sufficient. The real centres are in the mind and heart of the persons living there.

In conclusion it may be said that, during the lifetime of Krishnamurti, he saw racial prejudice between the English and the Indians, class divisions amongst people of the same country, British imperialism as shown by the annexation of Egypt, Upper Burma by Britain, Boer War, increasing nationalism, outbreak of the First World War, Russian Revolution (of 1917), the formation of the League of Nations, the beginning of world depression in trade, rising to power of dictatorial rulers like Hitler, Mussolini, German invasion of Poland and outbreak of Second World War, the dropping of atom bombs, signing of treaties and forming of organisations like United Nations Organisation (1948), North Altantic Treaty (1949) in Washington, beginning of Cold War, formation of self governing states like India and Pakistan, Indo-Pak rift, Indo-China War, Korean War, Vietnam War, Cuban Missile Crisis, Arab-Israeli War, politics and party rivalries as nothing but the result of inner conflict in each human psyche. Though technology and science over the years had progressed tremendously as was depicted from the various experiments, inventions done in science, literature, art, philosophy, psychology, but the inward psychological states of man had not made much headway. He saw each individual as responsible for all the chaos and violence in the world. No ideologies, no religions, no authorities, no social reforms could ever end conflict and sorrow. The greed for power, wealth, and position was rooted in the heart of almost every individual, and Krishnamurti stressed on the clearing of the source. Every year, like the inexhaustible sun, he went round the world, without the paraphernalia of authority and status, awakening the light of intelligence among those who cared to listen to him.

Concluding Remarks

The lives of Dr. Annie Besant and J. Krishnamurti together spanned over an eventful century. Dr. Annie Besant experienced hardship and struggle in her early life, but was endowed with a spirit of resistance and defiance, a scholastic temperament questioning doctrines and dogmas. She came to India when the country was in turmoil. She embarked on a mission for the upliftment of India as a nation, and did so by arousing a religious fervour. Her picking of Krishnamurti into the fold of the Theosophical Society effectively set in motion a chain of events, where the lives of two great thinkers ran parallel for a while, and then separated to blossom into philosophies of their own. Krishnamurti had a mind, which was unable to accept the doctrines of the Theosophical Society for long. He had experiences during meditations, which made him see life differently. Krishnamurti's lifetime was marked with many events like wars and scientific discoveries. A nationalist movement or freedom struggle was not his priority, as by being achieved, they waned in significance.

References

1. The Years Of Awakening, pp. 1-2.
2. A Bibliography Of The Life And Teachings Of Jiddu Krishnamurti, p. xi.
3. The Years Of Awakening, p. 7.
4. ibid., p. 22.
5. ibid., p. 32.
6. ibid., pp. 36-37.
7. A Short History Of The Theosophical Society, p. 387.
8. The Years Of Awakening, p. 29.
9. Jinarjadasa was a student of C.W. Leadbeater. After taking a degree at Cambridge in Sanskrit and Philosophy, Raja,

as he was usually called, had become a valuable lecturer for Theosophy.
10. Principal Of Central Hindu College, Banaras.
11. The Years Of Awakening, p. 90.
12. A Vision Of The Sacred, p. 75.
13. The Years Of Awakening, p. 91.
14. ibid., p. 99.
15. ibid., p. 129.
16. idem.
17. See Krishnamurti: The Years Of Awakening by Mary Lutyens pp. 162-169 for Nitya's full account. Also for Krishnamurti's full account of this experience see pp. 169-172.
18. The Years Of Awakening, p. 175.
19. See Krishnamurti: The Years Of Awakening by Mary Lutyens, p 187 for the second spiritual experience that happened in 1923 at Ehrwald; p. 196 for the third that happened in Ojai, in 1923; p. 210 for the fourth that happened in Pergine in 1924. Another experience is given in Pupul Jayakar's book, 'J. Krishnamurti – A Biography', pp. 130-134.
20. The Years Of Awakening, p. 236.
21. A Sanskrit scholar, taught Krishnamurti and helped Annie Besant in the compilation of 'New India'
22. The Years Of Awakening, p. 238.
23. ibid., p. 239
24. ibid., p. 294
25. ibid., p. 279
26. ibid., p. 280
27. ibid, p. 293
28. Northern India Patrika, 11th May, 2001, p. 6.
29. A rich American Theosophist who lived in England.
30. A South Indian Brahmin, had been a protégé of Leadbeater's and had been sent to England in 1920 to go to Cambridge. He met Krishnamurti that year and started to work for him. After Nitya's death Krishnamurti appointed him Organising Secretary of the Order of the Star in the East and made him International Treasurer of the Order.

31. The Open Door, p. 9. Mary Lutyens recalls the talk that Krishnamurti gave at the age of 29 at Pergine.
32. The Open Door, p. 33.
33. The Years Of Fulfilment, p. 58 (Letter written to Lady Emily in August, 1943).
34. J. Krishnamurti - A Biography, p. 98.
35. ibid., p. 115.
36. ibid., p. 146.
37. ibid., p 82.
38. ibid., p. 84.
39. The Open Door, p. 4.
40. The Years Of Fulfilment, p. 34.
41. The Open Door, pp. 3-4.
42. A Vision Of The Sacred, p.100.
43. Krishnmurti Birth Centenary Souvenir 1995, p. 99.
44. ibid., p. 101.
45. An Introduction To The Life And Work Of J. Krishnamurti (1895-1986) – Unconditionally Free, Krishnamurti Foundation, America, 1995, p. 18.
46. ibid., p. 22.
47. Krishnamurti Birth Centenary Souvenir, 1995, p. 85.
48. An Introduction To The Life And Work Of J. Krishnamurti (1895-1986) – Unconditionally Free, Krishnamurti Foundation, America, 1995, p. 20.
49. Krishnamurti Birth Centenary Souvenir, 1995, p. 91.
50. Sunanda Patwardhan was born in 1927 and graduated from Madras University in 1947. The same year, she met Krishnamurti for the first time. It was the beginning of a lifelong commitment to Krishnamurti, his teaching and his work in India. With her husband, Pama Patwardhan, she was in charge of Vasant Vihar, the headquarters of Krishnamurti Foundation India, from 1976 to 1986.
51. A Vision Of The Sacred, pp. 110-111.
52. ibid., p. 82.

3
[A] Philosophical Ideas of Dr. Annie Besant

Philosophy is the backbone of all educational thoughts. Dr. Annie Besant's philosophical beliefs were based on Hinduism and Theosophy. To know the educational ideas of a thinker one has to first know his philosophy. This is conventionally studied under the following heads- Metaphysics (theory of reality), Epistemology (theory of knowledge), Axiology (theory of values), and the researcher proposes to do the same, for studying the philosophical ideas of Dr. Annie Besant.

Metaphysics

Under this, one studies about Truth, God, Soul, Universe.

Truth or Brahma

Dr. Annie Besant believed in an all-pervading Truth which she called 'Brahma'. Her concept of Truth is based on Hinduism. She observed:

> There is nothing else but Brahma. He is all and the universe is in Him. Its manifestation is only a manifestation of Himself. There is nothing there which was not there before, nothing in addition to Himself. Beings think there is something different, "Myself and

Him", but there is only He, unchangeable. It is not He and a Universe, but He as a Universe.[1]

And again

... Stage after stage the marvels of his manifestation; stage by stage the might of his unfolding; his quality of *sat*, of pure existence, comes forth in the unmoving creation, in the mineral kingdom, where existence only can be said to be shown. *Chit* and *ananda* are there concealed, and only *sat* is manifest. Then in the vegetable world the unfolding life shows us the beginning of pleasure and pain, the germ which develops into *ananda* in the later stages of evolution; and in the animal world there is shown forth also the germ of *chit*, which is to have its later and fuller evolution; and in man the germs are all partially manifested of *sat*, *chit* and *ananda* until at the end of the evolution *sat*, *chit* and *ananda* are perfectly developed in him. Then he is Brahma, he has become one.[2]

The Eternal is one unchangeable. It knows no present, no past, no future. Everything is there in one simultaneous, unchangeable reality of ever-present living. While His abode is said to be in the uppermost supernatural planes, His existence is manifest in all things. Theosophy believes in the 'Universal One Existence', the source of all beings, eternal and changeless, supporting all existences, all embracing. "He is self-existent, Infinite and Eternal, the One Life on which all lives depend, the One Existence from which all existences are drawn".[3]

God or Ishvara

This 'Universal Spirit', 'Universal One Existence' unfolds His powers in the universe and becomes manifest and known as Ishvara. He is the 'Brahma' performing the task of creation. This role involves a triplicity of functions and there is, therefore, a Trinity of the manifested God. According to the Hindu beliefs with which Dr. Annie Besant has fully agreed, the triple functions involve the role of God as Creator, Preserver, Destroyer cum Regenerator – Brahma, Vishnu, Shiva. Similar mention of triple manifestation in the form of Holy spirit, Son and Father is found in Christianity. Theosophists describe them as Third Logos, Second Logos and First Logos. Sparks from this Ishvara (manifest Brahma), result in creation of lesser Ishvaras and Jivatmas.

From the ether of space the Brahma or Third Logos creates with His breath seven different types of atoms which are mixed in different proportions resulting in the formation of seven different types of matter, where the essential composition is of the seven atoms created, differing only in the concentration patterns of the different atoms. The seven different types of matter comprise seven different planes, worlds or globes of the solar system. The lowest of these is the densest and the uppermost, the rarest. Each of these seven planes or globes is correlated with a distinct state of consciousness.

The two highest planes are the super spiritual planes—those of the Logoi. The lower of these two is the habitat of the Monad, the God in man. The next two are the spiritual planes reaching which man realises himself as divine. The next or the fifth plane is comparatively denser and is the intellectual plane, the sixth, the emotional and passional and that of desires and is called the astral, the lowest or the seventh is the physical plane. These may be depicted as follows:

1. ⎤
2. ⎦ Super spiritual (Rarest)

3. ⎤
4. ⎦ Spiritual

5. Intellectual
6. Astral
7. Physical (Densest)

In short, when unmanifest 'Brahma' manifests in the process of creation of the universe, He does this as Ishvara.

Spirit or Atma

Dr. Annie Besant's view on spirit is based on 'Brahma Vidya' meaning Divine Wisdom or Theosophy.

According to her concepts man is composed of seven principles. The Spirit or true Self of man belongs to the highest region of the universe, and this is universal, same for all, it is a part of God, "a spark from the divine fire"[4]. In his innermost nature, man is one with the Supreme Father. The Spirit or the true Self is clothed in perishable garments that feel the pain, anxiety which man unmistakably regards as himself. The identity in nature of the Universal and the Particular Self is best illustrated in Dr. Annie Besant's words: "This is to become an individual, reflecting the divine perfection, a son that grows into the likeness of his father"[5].

Atma or Spirit puts on successive garments, each garment belonging to a definite region of the universe and enables the Self to come into contact with that region or plane and acquire knowledge of it and work in it. This is how the Spirit gains experience and all its latent potentialities are gradually drawn out into active powers.

The seven principles of man are further classified into two groups - 'The Triad' is the deathless, immortal part of man's nature and pertains to the three higher planes - that is, Atma, Buddhi, Higher Manas. The 'Quaternary' pertains to the body, the mortal part and consists of the four lower planes. The immortal elements are named as spirit (atma) and soul (jivatma) and the mortal part is called body. This division of body, atma (spirit), jivatma (soul) has been accepted by many Christian thinkers such as St. Paul. In the Vedanta philosophy too, one finds this description of Jiva, Jivatma and Atma.

Atma is the "inseparable ray of the Universal and the One Self"[6]. It is that one Eternal Existence, wherefrom are all things and in which all things inhere. To get a clearer vision of what Dr. Annie Besant calls 'Atma' one has to first study the seven principles that constitute man.

The *'dense physical body'* of man is the first of the seven principles. It is made up of material molecules - with its five organs of sensation, its organs of locomotion, its brain and nervous system The *'etheric double'* is the second principle of man. It interpenetrates the 'dense body' and is composed of more subtle and rarer matter than that which is perceptible to the five senses. The 'etheric double' acts as the medium through which the life currents can be adapted by the denser particles. *'Prana'* or the life breath of every creature is the third principle of man's constitution and through the etheric double, 'Prana' exercises this controlling and coordinating force. The fourth principle of man is the desire-body or *'Kama Rupa'*. It consists of appetites, passions, emotions, desires, that is, it is confined to the passional and emotional nature.

The above four principles form the 'quaternary', the mortal part of man and is called by the Theosophists as the 'personality'. To make the personality 'human', it requires to be illumined by the mind for such a personality has passions, but no reason; it has emotions but no intellect; it has desires but no rationalised will.

The Thinker or *'Manas'* is the fifth principle of man. The 'Manas' is the immortal individual, the real 'I'. It gathers up within it the results of all past experiences and these act as causes moulding future lives. The general characteristics of the present body depend on the past lives of the Thinker on earth. The eternal divine Mind has two attributes – the Lower Manas and the Higher Manas. During earth - life, 'Kama' and the Lower Manas join together to form 'Kama-Manas'. Thus 'Kama-Manas' is the interweaving of the fourth principle of man with the lower part of the fifth. If the Kamic nature be strong and indisciplined the brain and body will prove itself inadequate to send forth to the outer world the light of the real inner man and the pure manasic light will be polluted. As the Lower Manas frees itself from Kama, it becomes the ruler of the lower part of man and shows more and more its true and essential nature. Attached to the spiritual part of man's nature is the conscience of man and "conscience is that instantaneous perception between right and wrong which can only be exercised by the spirit, which, being a portion of the divine wisdom and purity, is absolutely pure and wise"[7] This is *'Buddhi'* and it is the vehicle of *'Atma'*, the sixth and seventh planes respectively. This Buddhi works independently of reason, reason being a faculty of the physical brain which deduces inferences from premises and thus dependent on the evidence of other senses, cannot be a quality pertaining directly to the divine spirit. This 'Atma-Buddhi' unites with the mind principle or 'Manas' to form the human trinity.

The Monad or 'Atma-Buddhi' does not belong to anybody in particular but is 'the spiritual essence' energising in all. There is but one 'Atma-Buddhi' in the universe, the universal soul, present everywhere, immanent in all. Schematic representation of seven principles of man:

7. Atma
6. Buddhi
5. Manas
4. Kama
3. Prana
2. Etheric double
1. Dense physical body

Universe

Universe came into existence with unmanifest Brahma, manifesting as Ishvara. It consists of several solar systems, each consisting of a sun with its component of planets. The sun, being the source of life giving energy to the planets, may be regarded as the Ishvara of that system. This has been described as the Logoi of the system by the Theosophists and the solar system as a manifestation of such a Logoi.

Theosophy begins with the idea that the Universe and Man are primarily spiritual existences; that Spirit and Matter are not really two substances or are in antagonism, but are different stages of evolution of one substance. Planes are divisions in nature, distinguishable by the characteristics of its Spirit – Matter. Spirit-Matter differs within certain limits and works under certain laws.

Life and consciousness are at the core of the Universe. Consciousness shows itself working on each plane of the Universe, through the Spirit – Matter of the plane. Each stage involves an expansion of consciousness. The Universe is manifested in seven different forms of matter, subtle at the beginning, denser at the end, arranged in seven different stages of manifestation. Each plane of the Universe has life manifestations suitable to the plane on which they are manifested. The organisms of one plane are conscious of the organisms of the other depending on the power of sensation possessed by these organisms. Man by his physical sense comes into contact with the physical plane of the Universe.

Since man has in himself these seven different stages of existence he is able to investigate the whole Universe around him, becoming conscious of each plane in the Universe by virtue of the corresponding principle in himself. The Universe exists so that the purpose of the Self may be served, and His manifestations made possible.

> The universe exists for the sake of the Self, so that the germs of divinity, the embryonic Selves emanated from the supreme Self may unfold into the likeness of the parent God, whose nature they share, being truly partakers of the divine Nature.[8]

This holds true not only for our earth but according to Theosophists in six other planets also. These are Vulcan, Venus, Jupiter, Saturn, Uranus and Neptune, in addition to Earth[9] All of them contain six interlinked worlds each with the main planet as the turning point. Thus a chain of seven globes are formed, the globes being situated in pairs in the mental and astral planes through which the evolutionary life travels completing a so called evolutionary round. In case of earth, from mental through astral, back to mental. Several such evolutionary rounds in the different planets and their globes are necessary in the complete process of evolution.

Epistemology

This aspect of philosophy deals with questions regarding the possibility of acquiring knowledge about the nature of Truth, God, Soul and Universe, about the instruments or means of acquiring knowledge, the relationship of the knower and the known, the degree of directness or indirectness in the knowing process.

According to Dr. Annie Besant, the aim of human life is to realise the all pervading Truth, the one Universal Life. One can experience this through 'Brahma-Vidya' or God-Knowledge. This knowledge of God cannot be communicated by a teacher to the pupil, nor can be experienced through leading a life of seclusion in the mountains:

> This supremest initiation into the knowledge of the Self must be taken by each Self for itself when it is ready to open out into the fullness of its own Divinity. None else may give it; none else may impart it; only Brahma within can know Brahma without. So that the last, the final, the most lofty initiation is Self taken. None else may give it, nor may any withhold it.[10]

This implies that one can know the Universal Spirit, only by sharing His nature in oneself. One can know that which one shares. Dr. Annie Besant said:

> It is called in the Upanishad "the knowledge of Him by whom all things are known". It is a difficulty rather of our language that we speak in that sense of "knowledge", because knowledge implies a duality, or indeed a triplicity – the Knower, the Known and the Relation between them – whereas when the Spirit of man, who comes forth from Ishvara, realises his own nature, it is no longer a case of thinking or of knowing. It is a case of realising that identity. You know it is written again in the Upanishad: "He who says 'I know', he knows not", because the very word knowledge is an error in this realisation. In that, we do not say, "I know"; we say, "I am". This gives the primary meaning of the world "Theosophy".[11]

The Theosophist holds that man is essentially a spiritual being, emanating from the Universal Self or Universal Spirit and this Universal Self transcends all the beings in which it is manifested, and is alike in all.

Dr. Annie Besant regarded *Reincarnation and Karma* as fundamental facts in nature, on which the perfection of the individual depended. Reincarnation or the law of rebirth is "the unfolding of the human spirit through recurring lives on earth, experience being gathered during the earth life and worked up into intellectual faculty and conscience during the heaven life, so that a child is born with his past experiences transmuted into mental and moral tendencies and powers"[12] Every man enters into earth life without knowledge, conscience or discrimination.

He accumulates materials from the experiences that he undergoes, whether pleasant or painful, and builds into mental and moral faculties. These faculties make up his character. Thus the character which he brings to earth is self made and shows the stage he has reached in his long evolution.

It is also essential for one to understand the importance of Karma, or the law of causation while considering reincarnation. The law of causation states that "every action has a past which leads up to it; every action has a future which proceeds from it"[13]. As a man thinks or does, so he becomes. Thought, will, action create one's destiny as they build up character, opportunity and environment. The favourable or unfavourable nature of the circumstances into which one is born depends on the effect of one's actions in past lives in spreading happiness or unhappiness. Therefore, Dr. Annie Besant reiterated that man is the maker of his own destiny.

By repeated reincarnations under unbreakable law which makes each man reap exactly as he has sown, man attains his temporary goal–human perfection. Dr. Annie Besant has compared evolution to a spiral road winding round a hill in an ascending order, along which humanity slowly advances. However, there is 'a shortcut' to the goal of human perfection and men may reach that in advance of the bulk of their fellow men by strenuous exertions, noble and unselfish living, thus attracting the attention of the spiritual guardians of mankind, the Masters who will teach him how to quicken his evolution. Such men are the pupils or disciples of the Masters, who undergo five initiations or stages of widening consciousness. Dr. Annie Besant believed that there is a larger or Higher Consciousness than the waking brain consciousness of man and this exists in each one. Man can realise his true nature as the Higher Consciousness by tranquillising the senses and restraining the mind. The first step is to learn to control the body, by giving it adequate sleep, exercise and diet, thus keeping the body healthy. Health is not to be sacrificed in order to achieve delicacy and sensitiveness.

After having controlled and purified the body, one can make it sensitive to the higher vibrations by 'Vairagya' or dispassion. One must lose interest in the lower life and become indifferent to the temptations of the outer life. So long as one gets attracted towards the lower things of the world, the Higher Consciousness cannot use this man as its vehicle. The 'five initiations' that a disciple has to undergo in order to reach the stage of 'Perfect Man' are designed to this end. (The Riddle of Life, pp. 54-56).

The First Initiation

The First Initiation seeks to develop qualities of discrimination, desirelessness or dispassion, control of the mind and of speech and actions, inculcation of tolerance, confidence and the ability to see the Self in everything. A firm belief in Karma and Reincarnation is necessary. In Hindu religion such an Initiate is called the Wanderer or "Parivrajaka" and among the Buddhists "he who has entered the stream" or "Srotapanna".

The Second Initiation

In this stage the Initiate develops the powers of subtle bodies, that he may be useful for service. An initiate who has undergone the second initiation is called "Kutichaka" or Builder in Hindu religion and in Buddhism, "he who returns but once" or "Sakadagamin".

The Third Initiation

At this stage the Initiate acquires identity in nature of Particular and Universal Self and becomes the United or "Hamsa", "I am He" as mentioned in the Hindu religion. Such an individual is called "Anagamin" in Buddhist tradition which means "he who does not return".

The Fourth Initiation

At this stage the Initiate becomes the Super individual or "Paramahamsa", "beyond the I" as mentioned in the Hindu tradition and "the Venerable" or "Arhat" as given in Buddhism. He sees Self in everything and all things in the Self.

The Fifth Initiation

Here the Initiate has to throw away five "filmy fetters" that separate him from the Masters. These are:

  (i) Traces of desire for life in form
  (ii) Traces of desire for life in formless worlds
  (iii) Pride in the greatness of the task achieved
  (iv) Possibility of being disturbed by aught that may happen
  (v) Illusion that distorts Reality

After this, he becomes the "triumphant Son of Man" who has finished his human course. He becomes the "Perfect Man". Such a man has reached complete union with the Divine.

Axiology

The logical discussion of Truth and the interpretation of the means of knowledge is incomplete unless it is given a moral basis. Axiology is the theory of values. Its main problems are: What is good? What is evil? What is beauty? What is art? Under this branch of philosophy one attempts to interpret the values, ideals and aims of man's life. The views of Dr. Annie Besant pertaining to morality and aesthetics are studied under Axiology.

Any religion, philosophy or science is related to morality. Since one of the objectives of Theosophy pertains to a comparative study of religion, science and philosophy, Theosophy itself becomes the embodiment of the highest morality. Dr. Annie Besant observed that, "It (Theosophy) denotes a body of truths, or facts concerning God, man and the universe, and these may conveniently be classified under the three heads of religion, philosophy and science. On these truths is based its system of ethics, rational, inspiring and compelling"[14]. Theosophy believes in the One Life that manifests itself in everything and a harm done to one is a harm done to everyone. It seeks to evolve the inner law without imposing an outer by ever presenting to the members the highest ideals and infusing into them the loftiest aspiration. It presents to its members the highest moral teachings, the essentials of all religions.

Theosophists believe that man is the maker of his own destiny. As a man thinks so he becomes. As a man thinks, thoughts from him spread out to shape the thoughts and lives of other men. Thoughts of love and gentleness go out into the world to create the whole storehouse of love. Like the idealistic thinkers, Dr. Annie Besant believed in the power of thought.

Dr. Annie Besant believed that for a disciple to reach the stage of "Perfect Man", certain qualities were imperative. The disciple has to undergo five initiations and the fifth opens the gateway to the "Masters", the highest products of evolution. She quoted from the Bible, "Strait is the gate and narrow is the way that leadeth unto life, and few there be that find it"[15.]

1. Desire for union or love

The disciple must learn to identify himself with all, breaking down everything that separates man from man. That is why brotherhood is the most important objective of the Theosophical Society. The recognition of brotherhood is the first stage towards the realisation of non-separateness, which is necessary if the disciple is to progress. The disciple must be sensitive to the sufferings of all, so that he may be ready to help humanity. He must not brood over his own griefs or troubles, if he is to be identified with the sorrow of mankind.

2. Service

From the feeling of oneness springs forth the sense of service. Dr. Annie Besant observed, "Service is that which is done for love's sake for another. It is not true service which is paid with wages."[16] The world is not ruled by chance. Duties are obligations that one owes to those around. One lives by the constant sacrifice of other lives, so he must pay it back. One should obey those who are superior, should be gentle, affectionate and helpful. To be compassionate to everyone is the recognition of one Self in all.

3. Sacrifice

One must perform every act as a sacrifice, not for what it will bring to the doer but for what it will bring to others. People prepare themselves for some big sacrifice but forget the little things of everyday life. Man must train himself to begin every day with an act of sacrifice, the offering of himself to that One Life. Every word and each action in daily life should be a way of serving that one Universal Life. All that comes, the joys, troubles, anxieties, successes, failures must be regarded as an expression of His will.

4. Discrimination

Discrimination helps one to distinguish between the right and the wrong. One must see the right no matter by what path of sorrow or failure the right is to be found. One must strive to do the right thing in one's daily life, no matter what anguish or pain it may bring. Dr. Annie Besant observed: "There is a great difference between one who knows the spiritual life to be a reality and the man who only babbles about it but perceives it not, who clutches at and grasps for it, but inhales not its fragrant breath nor feels its exquisite touch."[17] Since 'Brahma is Truth' and He is in everything, everywhere and so is within each individual, one must practise truth in thought, speech and action. This wakes up the spiritual insight which pierces through every veil of illusion.

5. Dispassion

One must not seek the fruits of action as reward. A good deed should be done for the sake of its usefulness to others and not for the sake of praise or reward that the act might accrue. Dr. Annie Besant said, "Practice' does not mean only meditation, though this is the sense in which the word is generally used; it means the deliberate, unbroken carrying out of dispassion in the very midst of the objects that attract."[18]

6. Control of Thought

Every man sets the vibration rate of his mind and the vibrations that do not harmonise with that rate are flung aside. For instance, a lie will not take root in the mind of a man who thinks truth, and hate will not disturb a man who thinks love. A man must not let his mind to lie fallow, for then any type of thought can take root in his mind. He must so train his thoughts that only good ones come into his mind. When a concentrated mind is steadily directed to any object, with the view of piercing the veil and reaching the life, and drawing that life into union with the life to which the mind belongs, meditation is performed.

7. Control of Speech and Action

One must be true and gentle in his speech and make his actions as wise as he can, by using one's best thought and effort to judge what is right before he does it. He must train himself to perform action as a duty without consistently looking for any sort of personal gain.

8. Tolerance

One can find a place in the hearts of men by sympathy, tolerance, by speaking from their standpoint instead of asserting one's own. To be tolerant is to see a thing from others' point of view, and to speak from that standpoint in order help. The Self in each man knows his own path much better than the Self in anyone else can judge it for him. The Self in each one marks his own path according to the unfoldment that he desires and requires. Therefore one must not try to control or mould others according to one's own beliefs and ideas.

9. Endurance

There has to be a patient bearing of all that comes in one's life. What a man sows in his past life, he reaps in his present life, and the stings that give pain in life are only the payment of a debt. The truth of reincarnation when once understood gives one tremendous endurance.

10. Faith

The strong conviction or faith that nothing can shake the Self that lies within each, that one's essential nature is divine and the effort to realise it helps its growth, cheers the pilgrim in his path of evolution Dr. Annie Besant said: "For there is no reality to be found save in the profoundest depths of consciousness; there alone is the Real, there alone is the Eternal, and only for him who knows the Eternal and abides therein, only for him is there Peace."[19]

11. Balance

One must try to keep a calm balance of mind, try to look from the standpoint of others and avoid all extremes. One should not act impulsively but try to dispassionately see both sides as both may be required for the evolution of mankind. Dr. Annie Besant remarked:

> Yoga is literally union, and it means harmony with the divine Law, the becoming one with the divine Life, by the subdual of all outward-going energies. To reach this, balance must be gained, equilibrium so that the self...shall not be affected by pleasure or pain, desire or aversion.[20]

12. Liberation

When the disciple reaches a stage, where all his weaknesses have fallen away, when the fallacies of human nature have gradually been overcome, when his capacities of wisdom and love overcome his lower nature, comes liberation. Then just the will of God is one's directing force. It does not mean that one does not return to the mortal world, but that one is not obliged to return. It means that one has become immortal and that whenever the world wants his guidance he is ready to help. All interests of the lower world shut him out forever, save that of service, to work for the redemption of humanity.

References

1. The Wisdom Of The Upanishads, p.5.
2. Seven Great Religions, pp.12-13.
3. The Universal Textbook Of Religion And Morals, part I, p. 13.
4. The Seven Principles Of Man, p. 2.
5. idem.
6. ibid., p. 72.
7. ibid., p. 67.
8. An Introduction To Yoga, p. 2.
9. The Riddle Of Life, p. 7.
10. The Wisdom Of The Upanishads, p. 2.
11. The Inner Government Of The World, p. 2.
12. The Riddle Of Life, p. 23.
13. ibid., p.43.
14. Theosophy And The Theosophical Society, p. 3.
15. The Riddle Of Life, p. 53.
16. Meditations : On The Path And Its Qualifications, p. 12.
17. The Doctrine Of The Heart, p. 81.
18. Meditations : On The Path And Its Qualifications, p. 47.
19. ibid., p. 107.
20. ibid., pp.115-116.

3
[B] Philosophical Ideas of J. Krishnamurti

J. Krishnamurti's thought is centered on the individual. For any durable change to take place in society or in the world, first the individual has to change radically, completely. The thrust of whatever he said was directed unwaveringly to this end.

Krishnamurti's approach to life was holistic. Understanding his philosophy is like perceiving a beautiful fabric with interwoven threads indistinguishable from one another. His emphasis on holism is evident from the titles of some of his books : *The Wholeness Of Life, You Are The World.*

The educational ideas of Krishnamurti flow from his general philosophy. It is neither possible nor desirable to attempt to separate the two very rigidly. Similarly the conventional components of philosophy – metaphysics (theory of reality), epistemology (theory of knowledge), axiology (theory of values) – are difficult to discern as clear strands in his holistic approach. Krishnamurti's philosophy is, therefore, best comprehended as an unfragmented whole. Only later, out of deference to conventional methodology, could one, if need be, set out to unravel metaphysics, epistemology and axiology as separate entities.

This study has attempted to understand Krishnamurti's philosophy from the primary sources in the form of books and cassettes which are a record of Krishnamurti's lectures, journal writings, dialogues and interviews.

Krishnamurti conceived of life as the web of relationships through which one is connected to things, to people and to ideas, to everything. To understand life and the significance of existence is to understand oneself as related to and involved in all, that is to society and the world:

> To know ourselves means to know our relationship with the world – not only with the world of ideas and people, but also with nature, with the things we possess. That is, our life- life being relationship to the whole. Does the understanding of that relationship demand specialisation ? Obviously not. What it demands is awareness to meet life as a whole.[1]

For Krishnamurti *no transformation which did not radically change man would change the world*. A total psychological transformation of the individual was far more important than any political or economic restructuring. The individual was inseparably and organically linked to the world. There is in fact no dichotomy between the individual and society:

> The individual is essentially the collective and the society is the creation of the individual. The individual and society are inter-related are they not? They are not separate. The individual builds the structure of society and the society or the environment shapes the individual.[2]

The *individual is responsible for creating the world in which he lives, as what he is within is projected outward to constitute society.* Man is confused within. This inward psychological state is projected outward to constitute the world torn by rifts, hatreds, divisions. World events are the result of human behaviour and behaviour is the outcome of inner psychological state. The problem of existence is therefore rooted in the structure of human consciousness, which is fragmentary, incomplete and inadequate:

To observe holistically is to observe- or to listen to –the whole content of something. Normally, we look at things partially, according to our pleasure, or according to our conditioning or according to some idealistic point of view, we always look at things fragmentarily. The politician is mostly concerned with politics; the economist, the scientist, the businessman, each has his own concern, generally throughout life.³

The problem of existence is the concern of every individual and not merely of a few religious, philosophical, political, cultural or social leaders. *Each individual is a contribution to the prevailing confusion.* Therefore, to bring about a psychological revolution- a change in the constitution of consciousness, the intelligent co-operation of one and all, is necessary. It is essential that "one has to understand not as a theory, not as a speculative, entertaining concept, but rather as an actual fact-that we are the world and the world is us".⁴

The *problems of existence cannot be solved at the level of the fragmented consciousness from which they arise.* Any fragmentary approach, whether political, economic, social, religious or purely intellectual, can only multiply the problems further. Krishnamurti said:

> Order implies harmony in daily life. Harmony is not an idea. We are caught in the prison of ideas and there is no harmony in that. Harmony and clarity imply seeing things holistically, observing life as a total unitary movement – not, I am a businessman at the office and a different person at home; not, I am an artist and can do the most absurd and eccentric things; not this breaking up, or fragmenting, of life into various categories, the elite and the non-elite, the worker and the non-worker, the intellectual and the romantic, which is the way we normally live. See how important it is to treat life as a total movement in which everything is included, in which there is no breaking down, as the good and the bad and heaven and hell. See holistically so that when you observe your friend, or your wife, or your husband, you see holistically in that relationship.⁵

The *problem of human existence requires to be approached as a whole. One's response to environment, which is relationship, has to be spontaneous, immediate, free from thought of the result,* an action that is total, complete, *not based on preformed ideas.* Krishnamurti has said that "all that happens is coming in and flowing out –there is no retaining but always a flowing out. That state of mind has its own sense of beauty and 'continuity' which is not of time."[6] To be aware of the whole problem at once, one has to look at life as one inter-connected whole. Krishnamurti *regarded education, learning, meditation, religion, interacting with people, the daily round of activities, looking at a flower, going for a walk, as one inseparable interpenetrating continuity. Every moment of living is important.* The most important moment is *now* on which the whole of life focuses, the past converging on it and the future emerging from it. The concept of the present, the past and the future has been likened to the "trikal damaru of Shiva" by Prof. Manas Mukul Das. (Journal of the Inter University Centre for Humanities and Social Sciences, p. 45). If one visualises the movements of the 'trikal (tri : three, kal : time) damaru of Shiva', one may perceive the two cones meeting at the waist as the past and the future, and the point of the waist where past and future converge and intersect as the eternally flowing moment of the present. Shiva holds the damaru by the waist and plays with time striking the past and the future. Time, here, is *not chronological time, but subjective time,* time as one experiences it. *In subjective time the past is memory and the future, a projection of the memory as hope and fear.*

Krishnamurti considered living to be the only purpose of life, and living is always in the present and not in time, not in terms of past and future as hopes and fears. "What one does in daily life, how one acts, not at moments of crisis but actually everyday is of the highest importance."[7]

Krishnamurti insisted that truth must be realised in one's daily life. He considered truth as a full understanding of life and this itself amounts to happiness and perfection. Such a truth must be sought and found at the earliest *within the life span of the individual, one cannot search for happiness in another world.* One must find this in one's everyday life; in one's everyday action, thought and feelings one must be able to experience the vastness of life. *One must be aware that it is one's daily deeds that may create struggle and strife leading to the corruptibility of life.* It is only in one's everyday life that one can mirror one's purity or impurity and transform one's corruptibility into something totally new, fresh, creative. Without fully understanding the corruptible, the fleeting, the unessential, it is not possible to go beyond it.

Once Krishnamurti was asked by Pupul Jayakar what the teaching was. To this Krishnamurti replied that, the teachings, in a nutshell could be said to be merely this: "*Where the self is, the Other is not*"[8]. This forms the hub of his philosophy, from which several spokes radiate: Inner Revolution, Relationship, Freedom, Meditation, Intelligence. The hub and spokes comprise the full wheel of his thought. Therefore, before looking at all the ramifications of Krishnamurti's philosophy, one might first try to grasp the core that holds it all together and out of which the rest emerge. The crux, the central point of his philosophy is self naughting, the extinction, the perishing of the "me".

(A) Self-Naughting

Man who has evolved from the lower animals through a process of evolution retains in him many basic emotions inherited from them; for instance, the possessive instincts for food, sex, territory. Though man today stands perhaps at the highest rung of evolution, yet he has been unable to discard this urge to possess. Rivalry and jealousy between persons and groups – sects, religions and nations stem from this instinct. Krishnamurti proceeds to explore how there can be a total change in man away from the "me" and the "mine".

In his dialogues whether with a single listener or with a large audience, Krishnamurti always proceeded from the known. For instance, he never used the word "self" in the Upanishadic sense of "Atma" but in the way everyone used and understood the word in ordinary conversation.

By the word "self", Krishnamurti generally meant the "content of consciousness". The self is the accumulation through time, the gathering up of one's experiences as memory and the projection of the experiences into the future as hopes and fears. It is the conditioning of the mind arising from various aspects of one's background such as education, family environment, the sum total of the gross as well as subtle identifications one makes with nation, religion, ideals, beliefs, language, culture, race etc. All these add up to constitute the inner bondages, the conditioning, the mind, the "centre", the "self". Thus the content of consciousness is the conditioning, the centre and the self:

> Do we know what we mean by the self? By that, I mean the idea, the memory, the conclusion, the experience, the various forms of namable and unnamable intentions, the conscious endeavour to be or not to be, the accumulated memory of the unconscious, the racial, the group, the individual, the clan and the whole of it all, whether it is projected outwardly in action or projected spiritually as virtue, the striving after all this is the self...the self is dividing; the self is enclosing; its activities, however noble, are separative and isolating. We know all this. We also know those extraordinary moments when the self is not there, in which there is no sense of endeavour ...when there is love[9].

Since the "content of consciousness" is psychological memory acquired from the past and the hopes and fears projected into the future, Krishnamurti identified the self with time and thought. Later he explained that, by time and thought he meant psychological time and psychological thought:

> You know, there are two kinds of time: Time by the watch, the next minute, tonight, the day after tomorrow; and there is another kind of time which is created by the psyche inside one, by thought – "I shall be a great man", "I shall have a job", "I shall go to Europe" – that is the psychological future, in time and space. Now to understand chronological time by the watch and to

understand time as thought and to go beyond both, is really to be free of fear.[10]

Time is a movement which man has divided into the past, present and future. So long as he divides it he remains in conflict – the conflict of becoming, the conflict of not wanting to be what one is or wanting to become what one is not. Since conflict is not order or peace, therefore, living in divisions of time does not bring order or peace. One cannot want to be free of the self because then one is caught up in the paradoxical situation. The moment one says- I wish to extinguish the self, one is caught up in a desire of the self – the desire to experience a state when the self is absent, to become something that one is not, to arrive at a result.

The self as has been said earlier is psychological thought accumulated over time and projected in time. One's psychological thought is one's conditioning, one's way of looking, feeling, interpreting the world. It is one's attitudes and perspectives formed by one's conditioning, by one's identifying with one's nation/religion. One feels hostile towards another nation or religion, though all human beings are the same, being repositories of similar thoughts and emotions. So, it is the mind perceiving the world through its conditioning that makes enemies and friends.

It is thought that creates divisions in oneself-the "me" and the "not me", the higher and the lower, the Atma and the lower self. Thought divides one into many parts – his mental energy, his physical energy, his psychological energy. Thought divides one man from another – energy of a doctor, energy of a teacher, energy of a labourer and in this way thought divides the world into communist block, socialist block, democratic block, Hindu, Muslim, Christian, Buddhist and so on. It creates division and whenever there is division there is conflict. Thought creates effort and effort is resistance – I am this and I want to become that. Thought is mechanical since it is repetitive, conforming, comparing. It operates in knowledge and knowledge is in the field of the known. It is always operating within the limitations of the field of the known as it wants to remain in security, safety, certainty.

So the question is, can the human mind change, can the mind stop projecting itself? Krishnamurti, speaking to Allan Anderson said:

> So if that is clear, that the human mind has divided the world in order to find its own security, which brings about its own insecurity, then one must inwardly as well as outwardly deny this division, as we and they, I and you, the Indian and the European and the Capitalist and the Communist. You cut at the very root of this division. Therefore from that arises the question: Can the human mind which has been so conditioned for millennia, which has acquired so much knowledge in so many directions – can that human mind change, bring about a regeneration in itself and be free to reincarnate now?[11]

It is therefore interesting to see how Krishnamurti proceeds in this direction. *What is the relation between these two states of mind, the conditioned and the free?* This prompts one to examine what Krishnamurti meant by "the Other".

During the course of his dialogues, Krishnamurti used many descriptions to denote "the Other" in its different aspects: the immeasurable, the infinite, the timeless; the sacred, the beautiful, the sublime, god, truth, reality, benediction; the vast emptiness, silence; love, compassion, creativity. He also saw it as a state in which there was no duality, where the observer and the observed, the knower and the known became one, as a state of meditation where no meditator remained, as a state where the self ceased to be, where the mind only existed in the eternal present, in the continuously moving *now*, gathering no time in its flow. In the perception of "the Other" there is only the experience of the boundless in which everything *is* and in which there is no place for any other entity including that of an observer or a knower. It is also seen as a *state of emptying of the self* which is a necessary condition for receiving the Infinite Otherness. It is also perceived as a state inundated with the emotion of love, compassion and joy. Therefore, the use of different epithets for denoting the different aspects of "the Other".

Philosophical Ideas of J. Krishnamurti

The Infinite cannot be held in a receptacle, that is, the Infinite cannot be held by a mind confined by the boundaries of the self. It cannot be held by language which can but express the already known. Therefore, to try to know or to express "the Other" is to be caught in an impossible situation.

"The Other" can only come when the mind is free of itself- of its thoughts, beliefs, ideas, conclusions – that is, when the mind is absolutely empty, when there is consciousness which has no content, no time, no psychological thought. But this state cannot be desired. One cannot make any effort to reach it because all desire, all effort is centered around the self. Even the desire to become a great saint or to reduce oneself to a cipher are but desires of the self, and therefore, strengthens the self. Therefore, no activity which is geared to a desire for becoming can rid the mind of the self. Such activity would only strengthen the self that must perish for "the Other" to manifest itself. When thought that works in the field of the known tries to seek "the Other" then that "Other' is only a perception of thought, for that "Other" is projected out of the known past into the known future. What is required, therefore, is a state of passivity. The way could perhaps be the way of *passive action*, naturally, freely, spontaneously. This means the emptying of the consciousness of all will to become. Krishnamurti called it "*choiceless awareness*".

(B) Inner Revolution

Only a total inner psychological revolution can change the basic nature of man and therefore of society. Any superficial change in society would be overcome by man who remains confused within. Krishnamurti would often ask whether one could be free of all conditioning, whether one could say deeply, truly and honestly that one belonged to no country, no religion, no language, no culture, no tradition, whether one could see the world without a centre brought into being through one's identifications and mental conditionings. Can the centre dissolve? Can there be a mind without a self? Such a mind could be a harbinger of harmony. Such a mind would undergo a tremendous revolution, and would be completely whole, not projecting from the past, through the present, into the future. That means to live completely *now*, to die psychologically from moment to moment to everything that one has known. Eternity has no time. "That which is timeless, is now, not in some distant future."[12]

The titles of some of his books emphasise the need for a fundamental psychological revolution – *The Only Revolution, Tradition And Revolution, Urgency of Change*. The fundamental, radical revolution in the psychological realm cannot be brought about through psycho-analysis, through environmental awareness, or through effort. The action of psycho-analysis is partial in so far as it is a post-mortem operation which if accurately and laboriously pursued can only bring about an understanding of a certain event in the past. Besides, the action of psycho-analysis creates the division between the analyser and the analysed. Environmental pressure brings about conformity, and effort involves resistance and conflict. All these processes imply action based on memory and ideas. Such action is effective for bringing about a modified continuity of the past, but not for a total revolution, which implies freedom from the known: all the conditionings of the past gathered up as accumulated knowledge which constitutes the content of consciousness that intervenes in all action – thought and feeling as the actor's subtle self.

The urgency of an inner psychological revolution is implicit in this statement of Krishnamurti's:

> The crisis is not in the outer world, but in consciousness itself. And until we understand this crisis, not superficially, not according to some philosopher, but actually deeply understand it for ourselves by looking into it and examining it, we shall not be able to bring about a change.[13]

One of Krishnamurti's books is titled: *The Urgency of Change*. The passion, the interest, the seriousness, has to be there in oneself and this passion comes about only when one sees that he is responsible for the present state of chaos. This urgency is there when one understands himself truly and understanding implies direct perception, without implying time and effort, without the interference of thought.

This inner psychological revolution is not the result of an act of will, or the outcome of compulsion, pressure, influence. This can only be brought about through "choiceless awareness", spontaneously. What is required, therefore is a state of passive observation, and to understand such a state, one needs to understand his self and this is achieved by watching oneself in relationship.

(C) Relationship

Living is relationship. If there is no relationship, there is no living at all and then there comes about the whole chain of endless conflicts, separations, loneliness, fears, anxieties. As Krishnamurti observed:

> Life is a movement in relationship. If we do not understand what is implied in relationship, we inevitably not only isolate ourselves, but create a society in which human beings are divided, not only nationally, religiously, but also in themselves and thereby they project what they are into the outer world.[14]

Man exists only in relationship to everything around him. "And in that relationship, through observing one's reactions, thoughts and motives, one can see, non-verbally, what we are".[15]

To understand the workings of one's mind, to understand oneself, Krishnamurti has often advised one to watch one's mind "in the mirror of relationship". In *The Wholeness Of Life* he said : "One does not seem to be able to understand how extraordinarily important it is to see what one is actually, as though one is looking at oneself in a mirror, psychologically; thereby bringing about, a transformation in the very structure of oneself."[16]

Similar thoughts are expressed in other books: like *Beginnings Of Learning* (p. 80), *The First And Last Freedom* (p. 104), *You Are The World* (p. 49). To be, is to be related; life is relationship to things, people and ideas; and, therefore, Krishnamurti rightly perceived the problem of existence to be essentially a problem of relationship. Krishnamurti asked his listeners whether their relationship is through an image created by them, if so it is no relationship at all. Then it becomes a process of isolation and a society based on such relationships is isolating, and does not contribute to peace. Krishnamurti further observed:

> To be related means not to be dependent on each other, not to escape from your loneliness through another, not to try to find comfort, companionship, through another. When you seek comfort through another, are dependent and all the rest of it, can there be any kind of relationship? Or are you using each other?[17]

The image building might continue into making larger identifications, however great and vast the object of identification may be, its function is to condition the mind, to create the self, and therefore, divisions. Belief in God could be another form of identification with an idea. It could be the reaction of fear, which is the search for security, for continuity. That does not however mean that Krishnamurti did not accept the Sacred. But for him, the Sacred could not be a word or a belief.

The believer and the non-believer both are conditioned by their own belief, which is a product of their background, their social and political environment, their culture and tradition. Truth is not a matter of belief. Truth has to be discovered as a fact, Krishnamurti said: "Religion is not a matter of dogmas and beliefs, of rituals and superstitions, nor is it the cultivation of personal salvation, which is self-centred, it is the understanding of Truth which is not a projection of the mind."[18]

The only reality is "what is". In every type of relationship one begins to build an image around this reality and this is the beginning of a conflict which is never resolved. In order to understand "what is" one must have within one the quality which will enable one to do so, and this quality is being free within. When one observes objects like trees, flowers, clouds, the things outside one, then there is not only the space between the observer and the observed, the "physical space" or distance between the thing and the person observing, but also the space of memory, the distance created by seeing the object through one's previous knowledge of it. This psychological distance is the result of the image that the observer builds about the thing he observes. The image between the observer and the thing observed separates the observer and the observed and there is no direct contact between them. When one sees a tree, recognises it as a mango tree and thinks he knows all about it, he may not have noticed the shape of its branches, the texture of its bark, the tenderness of its leaves, the coolness of its shadow. When there is direct contact, there is no observer, just the observed. One is aware without any motive, image, conclusion, judgement, past knowledge and therefore, he has tremendous energy to relate with that which he is observing. One perceives the truth, the "what is" and it is the truth, the fact, that acts. To learn how to observe without the observer, without the past, without the image, one has to find out how to have a mind that is totally innocent. To have such a mind is to have freedom from within.

(D) Freedom

The very titles of the two books, *The First And Last Freedom, Freedom From The Known*, eloquently express Krishnamurti's emphasis on freedom.

Man in pursuit of more and more objects of desire and gratification, cultivating possessive relationships with family, group, nation etc. or taking refuge in ideology or religious dogma, is essentially seeking nothing but security and happiness. Happiness is the ultimate goal of human endeavour. Why is it that man is not successful in his endeavour? Why is it that despite his ceaseless search he is not able to find happiness? Krishnamurti's answer is because "happiness does not come when you are striving for it"[19]. Happiness cannot be found through acquisition. Happiness comes into being when there is love, goodness, when the mind is very quiet, silent, "listening timelessly to everything that is happening".[20] This implies a free mind.

Freedom does not mean that one is free to do what one likes. Nor does it mean freedom from something. Freedom implies observing holistically without barriers. "Freedom implies not the negation of the known but the understanding of the known and that understanding brings about an intelligence which is the very essence of freedom"[21] The subtle difference between negating and understanding the known is of paramount importance in the philosophy of Krishnamurti:

> To us the word, the concept is extraordinarily important, not the acts of seeing and doing. But having the concept, which is belief, an idea-having this – conceptual living, prevents us from actually seeing, doing; and therefore we say we have problems of action, of what to do or not to do, and the conflict that arises between the act and the concept.[22]

(i) Knowledge and Experience

Why is it that one has given so much importance to image, concept, knowledge, experience? It is because "the mind is isolating itself all the time in all its activities, building a wall round itself in order not to be hurt, not to have any discomfort, unhappiness, or trouble, it is isolating itself all the time in its self centred activity"[23]. This creates the centre in each one. It is this centre that influences one's process of enquiry.

Once Krishnamurti asked Swami Venkatesananda[24] (1969, in India) about what he meant by "Vedanta". To this the Swamiji had said that he meant "the ending of knowledge". Krishnamurti then asked why should one acquire knowledge, "why should not I, from the very beginning, see what knowledge is and discard it?"[25] In Krishnamurti's words "Vedanta", means the end of accumulating knowledge.

In the classical way of learning one accumulates knowledge, proceeds from the known to known and is vaguely promised freedom in the end, whereas Krishnamurti regards freedom of the mind from the very beginning as a continuous process which never ends. This entails freedom of listening, freedom of observation, freedom of learning, which never stops. Knowledge is, therefore, a hindrance to freedom, "to the open, to the unknown"[26]. It is a process of continuous storing up and from that storing up one reacts. It becomes the past. The known is the past and this past modifies the present, the unknown. This is clearly stated in Krishnamurti's talk at Rajghat, January 1956: "'Knowledge' he said, 'conditions your experience. If you want to experience reality directly you must strip your mind of all the knowledge. You cannot learn about reality or Truth. You can only have direct perception, direct experience of Truth now – immediately.'"[27]

(ii) Systems, Beliefs, Gurus and Organised Religions

When the mind works along a pre-constructed infrastructure it follows a pattern or a system. The mind seeks to act through a system primarily because it wants to be secure, to be sure of success, and secondly, because through a system one can act mechanically, thoughtlessly, without undergoing the trouble of thinking afresh everytime.

Two books: *A Wholly Different Way Of Living* and *The Awakening Of Intelligence* give one a direction regarding the views of Krishnamurti on reincarnation and the permanent soul. There can be no better way of expressing these views than quoting Krishnamurti himself from the book, *The Awakening Of Intelligence* :

> To find out what reincarnation means, which is to be born in a future existence, you must find out what you are now. If you believe in reincarnation what you are now? – a lot of words, a lot of experience, of knowledge... The remembrance of the failures, the hopes, the despairs, all that you are now, and that is going to be born in the next life...Or you think there is a permanent soul, a permanent entity...The moment you say there is a permanent soul, a permanent entity, that entity is the result of your thinking, or the result of your hopes, because there is so much insecurity, everything is transient, in a flux...So if you believe in a future birth, then you must know that the future is conditioned by the way you live now... So what you are now, what you do now, matters tremendously[28].

The mind often needs a teacher or a guru for guidance.

Such a state may also be described as ignorance, being unable to understand oneself. In the acceptance of authority there is conformity, there is following; and that breeds contradiction in oneself-the "what is" and "what should be", and therefore disorder, conflict. All communication is in the field of the known, and the unknown cannot be approached through the known:

> The moment the guru says he knows, then you may be sure he doesn't know. Because what he knows is something past, obviously. Knowledge is the past. And when he says he knows, he is thinking of some experience which he has had, which he has been able to recognise as something great, and that recognition is born out of his previous knowledge, otherwise he couldn't recognise it, and therefore his experience has roots in the past. Therefore it is not real.[29]

The guru cannot awaken one, he can only point out "what is". It is for the individual to discover for himself what is true.

(iii) Habit

Habits are formed by the mind in order to be secure, safe, certain, undisturbed. One falls into habits deliberately, or by being influenced or pressurised by others, or by fear. It implies a repetitive action which generally leads to a mechanistic way of living.

(iv) Fear

To discover Truth one needs to have direct perception. This direct perception is warped by fear. To quote Krishnamurti:

> Freedom concerns the whole habit forming machinery, and to understand this whole problem of habit forming one must be free to look at its mechanism. Perhaps we are afraid of that freedom too; and therefore we put freedom far away from us, in some heaven.[30]

Fear leads to belief, fear brings in comparison, that is,

a mind that measures all the time. Then the self wastes its energy by striving to do better everyday, instead of living with the "what is" and utilising its energy in understanding the "what is". Fear brings in choice, resistance, will, motive, compulsion, authority, pursuit of a system, method, guru, nurturing of habits, ideals, beliefs, tradition, knowledge. Fear is not something abstract. It exists in relationship – fear of loss, fear of death, fear from others, from self and so on. One is afraid of death because he is afraid of losing the known, the self which is nothing but a bundle of memories and thus pertains to the past. One cannot live in the present if one clings to the past. "Fear cannot be got rid of but it can be understood only when the things that produce the fear, like death, are understood".[31] To find out what is death, there must be freedom and there is no freedom if there is attachment, fear, desire for comfort. What is the truth before death? If that is not clear then what the truth is after death will never be clear. To understand death is to understand something which is closely related to life. Living is before death. Living is one's education, culture, beliefs, dogmas, rituals and on. One can only find the truth of it when there is order in this life. When there is a total complete holistic ending, something totally new is born. To find out the truth of death there must be the ending of the content of one's consciousness – a total freedom from the known. This means dying to everything that one knows from moment to moment –one's memories, tradition, and what one "should be". Truth is the life that one leads everyday, and without understanding it, one will never understand what love is, what beauty is, what death is, what freedom is.

Freedom is a state of being which is not the outcome of a desire to be free. The desire to be free causes its own bondage. When the mind understands this and sees the falseness of authority, then only does it perceive the truth, the "what is".

Order, virtue, goodness, humility, love, beauty are contained in the moment of the *now*. Hence they are free of the past, of the known. One's relationship is only in the *now*, not in the past. If one's relationship is ingrained in the past, which means, he is not related to the *now*, then he has no compassion, no order "so freedom is compassion, and that comes when there is the real deep realization that I am the world, the world is me. Freedom, compassion, order, virtue, goodness are one; and that is absolute".[32] Goodness implies the total absence of the "me", to move completely away from the mind's self-centered activity implies complete order, freedom, goodness.

(E) Meditation

It is the open mind and not an occupied mind that can discover what is true, that can see "what is" from moment to moment. *An occupied mind is a petty mind, enclosed within the self-defensive walls of the ego. The unoccupied mind is the silent mind, is the indivisible whole. So, the question that arises is how does the mind become quiet without effort, without control?* The moment one asks "how", one introduces a system. Therefore, there is no "how". This brings to light Krishnamurti's views on meditation and in this context it will not be out of place to mention that one of Krishnamurti's books is captioned *MEDITATIONS*.

In the words of Krishnamurti:

> You can't make the mind quiet, because *you* are the mischief-maker, you are yourself disturbed, anxious, confused-how can you make the mind quiet? But when you understand what quietness is, when you understand what confusion is, what sorrow is and whether sorrow can ever end, and when you understand pleasure, then out of that comes an extraordinary quiet mind; you don't have to seek it. You must begin at the beginning and the first step is the last step, and this is meditation.[33]

Meditation must begin with the total understanding of oneself. With the complete understanding of oneself there is an end to knowledge and therefore freedom from the known. *Meditation implies the ending of all strife, conflict inwardly and therefore outwardly.* As Krishnamurti put it:

> In uncovering what one actually is, one asks: Is the observer, oneself, different from that which one observes – psychologically that is I am angry, I am greedy, I am

violent; is that I different from the thing observed which is anger, greed, violence? Is one different? Obviously not. When I am angry there is no I that is angry, there is only anger. So anger is me; the observer is the observed. The division is eliminated altogether. The observer is the observed and therefore conflict ends.[34]

A major problem in one's life is conflict and from conflict all sorts of misery, disorder, chaos occur. To end this conflict one must find out how to act so that no conflict results. "A mind that is in meditation must find out what action is"[35] One has to see what one is actually doing, how one is actually living a life of conflict, acting fragmentarily, acting in contradiction. For this one has to be aware.

Meditation begins when one learns to listen to oneself, to enquire, to observe, to watch. It involves constant awareness, or what Krishnamurti referred to as "choiceless awareness". Awareness is not possible when one chooses. To choose a particular action that seems most satisfactory, rewarding, brings about conflict. If one is completely aware, aware of the flow of thoughts, aware of whatever is happening to oneself inwardly or outwardly, without attempting to give it any direction or purpose, then there is an action which is free from conflict and therefore holistic, complete. Mary Lutyens in *Years of Fulfilment*, explained "choiceless awareness" as:

> 'Choiceless awareness' were words that J. Krishnamurti was to use... over and over again and still uses. Choice implied direction, the action of the will. What Krishnamurti was talking about was awareness from moment to moment of all that was taking place inside oneself without any effort to direct or change it – a matter of pure observation, perception which would result in change without effort.[36]

According to J. Krishnamurti meditation can take place anywhere. It is not separate from one's daily life. Meditation can take place in a bus, or walking in the park or even looking at the faces of one's loved ones. It has no technique and cannot be learnt from anyone else. No one else can teach one how to quieten the mind or control one's wandering thoughts. If one forces the mind to be quiet and still, that is not meditation. All that is needed is total attention to whatever it is that one is saying, doing or thinking. This total attention is meditation. As Krishnamurti pointed out: "Meditation is complete attention without an object in which thought is absorbed"[37]

Thus the process of attention where there is no object, no concentration, no "me" operating, is meditation. Krishnamurti gives the example of toys to explain what is meant by total attention. He said just as toys absorb the interest of the child and the child becomes restless when they are taken away, similarly, with grown-ups the toys are their beliefs, ambitions, worshipping of gods ad so on, and they too become restless, confused, when their toys are taken away. Therefore, he pointed out that the toys become all-important for the adults and not the mind which is taken over by the toy, and to understand what attention is, one must be concerned with the mind and not with the toys of the mind.

One's life is based on thought which is measurable. Thought, the self, measures God. It measures its relationships with another through image. It tries to improve itself according to what it thinks it should be. This is the reason why one lives in a world of measurement and through that world of measurement one wants to enter into a world which is immeasurable, limitless. "Meditation is the seeing of 'what is' and going beyond it"[38] seeing the measure and going beyond the measure. In meditation there is nothing of the past, no repetition, no imitation, no following of systems, habits, methods, "there is death of everything known and the flowering of the unknown".[39]

An unoccupied mind is a mind that negates everything, not through effort but spontaneously. The discovery of the true, lies in the understanding of the false as false, and the false is understood for what it is, when the false values of life are discovered to be misfounded, then the false drops away of its own accord; no other action, no other discipline is necessary to free the mind from the illusion of the apparent.

According to Krishnamurti, "The awareness of inattention is attention"[40].

When one sees what is not meditation, then one understands what meditation is. For instance, concentration is not meditation as it involves attention directed to one single object, excluding all others. Prayer is also not meditation, for it involves repetition of mantras, involves an action based on idea, implying a self-centre. In meditation the mind is empty of both past and future and is therefore timeless. Solitude is not required, nor is it necessary, what is required is one's consciousness to be forever centered in the present.

There are no means, no method, no technique by which one can bring about that state of being in which creative action is possible. "Creativeness comes into being when there is constant awareness of the ways of the mind and of the hindrances it has built for itself,"[41] and there is an extraordinary tranquility, which is not put together or made up.

Meditation is a state of "not knowing"[42]. In this state one does not wait for an answer, one is totally alive, alert, active, sensitive, in this state of uncertainty one is already free from the thought "I know" and therefore it implies an unfragmented mind. One knows what is disorder and therefore rejects it completely. Having denied the disorder one is free-free to meet the ever fresh challenges of life with a new undivided total attention. Order can only come about when there is the cessation of total disorder in oneself. When the mind has come up to this state of absolute order, *it* itself becomes the sacred because it is absolutely orderly. Then there is no seeking, "for that which *is*, is sacred."[43] When there is love without hatred, jealousy, anger, prejudices, then that love itself is sacred and this love "is tremendously passionate. And therefore it acts immediately. It has no time interval between the seeing and the doing".[44]

(F) Intelligence

Krishnamurti in his book titled, *The Awakening Of Intelligence* talks of intelligence, as the action of understanding, which takes place in the "choiceles awareness" of the ways of the self. The direct perception of "what is", takes place in a silent mind, in the mind that is free from the occupation of becoming, of identification. Intelligence is the harmony of reason, emotion and action. It is different from intellect. Krishnamurti said, "Intellect is thought functioning independently of emotion, whereas, intelligence is the capacity to feel as well as to reason..."[45].

This whole technological world is based on thought with its measurement. Thought creates its own limitations. Thought creates fragmentation, divisions. It cannot bring about true relationship between man and man. Every culture has certain beliefs, ideals which regulate the lives of human beings, constantly creating images of oneself. All these create a conflict between "what is" and "what should be". Apart from the cultural patterns, conflict is created by the will. Will is independent of the fact, of "what is". It depends on the self, on desire and that desire or want is based on circumstances, on environment, on culture and is separated from the fact. Therefore, there is a resistance within one's mind.

Krishnamurti has talked of the freeing of the mind from the barriers imposed on it by knowledge. He has defined knowledge as a to and fro movement of human thought from one point of time to another necessarily based on past experiences or memories, and therefore incapable of going beyond the dimension of time. However, he says, the importance of this knowledge defined as movement along time be fully appreciated and understood. The benefits that have accrued to man through this knowledge are never to be under-rated. The question, however, persists, can man understand the importance of knowledge and yet see its limitations and go beyond it? Can man be free of time and yet still function in this world? Can man "enter into the immeasurable which has its own space and live in that world, free of time and yet function with time, with knowledge and all the technological achievements which thought has brought about?" [46]

Krishnamurti saw how it is possible for human thought to transgress this barrier of time. The mind is a bundle of memories, experiences, knowledge, which is the past. It operates in the field of the known. Can that mind which is the past, the old, be absolutely quiet, still, so that a new movement begins? If it forces itself to be quiet through effort, will, desire, then it is still operating in the past. This creates further division, conflict. *But when the mind understands the truth that as long as it functions in response to memories, accumulated knowledge, tradition, it can never discover anything new, then it becomes absolutely still, quiet. This understanding is intelligence.* Intelligence is the understanding that the "old brain"[47] can only function within the field of the known. The new dimension of love, freedom can only operate through intelligence. As Krishnamurti pointed out: "When the old brain sees that it can never understand what freedom is; when it sees that it is incapable of discovering something new, that very perception is the seed of intelligence, isn't it"?[48]

"Intelligence means to respond to a challenge rightly, adequately"[49] It operates when the mind, heart, body are in complete harmony, that is, when the mind has no fear, demands no pleasures, when the heart does not hurt others nor is itself hurt, when the body is very, very sensitive, which implies, to observe everything very closely, to be aware of what actually is without choice. That intelligence operates in this world morally; it brings about order and the beauty of order. Morality is order, is virtue, not the virtue or morality of society which is totally immoral. Intelligence is the perception of right values. It comes into being with the absence of the "me". It understands life as a whole. After all, it is the incomplete action, the conditioned response that brings about and strengthens the self, the "me". As long as action is incomplete, there is bound to be accumulation of experience which is responsible for the distortion of perception, which is the lack of intelligence. The incessant demand for fulfilment is due to incomplete action, and intelligence is total action which wipes out the sense of incompleteness entirely. Intelligence is the action of love arising out of the understanding of life as an undivided whole.

Having studied the holistic approach of Krishnamurti one is now in a position to comment on the conventional compartmentalisation defined earlier. Certain pertinent components emerge from the aforesaid discussions.

Under philosophical method one studies metaphysics, epistemology, axiology.

Metaphysics

Under metaphysics an attempt has been made to give Krishnamurti's views on truth, God, soul, reincarnation, immortality.

There is a total relatedness in Krishnamurti's philosophy. Anything which is not totally related does not conform to it. Unless psychologically the "I" is destroyed, there cannot be any experience of the infinite as has been discussed earlier under self-naughting.

Truth according to Krishnamurti cannot be conceived, it can only be discovered through the action of understanding arising with the "choiceless awareness" of "what is", and any description of truth or the transcendental reality either given by Krishnamurti or anyone else does not constitute Truth. Truth is not static, it is always changing. Truth is life and life has no permanency. Life has to be discovered from moment to moment. It cannot be taken for granted. If one takes it for granted that one knows life, then one is not living.

God or soul are projections of the mind. To Krishnamurti God is a living eternal reality which cannot be described but which each one must realise for himself.

Immortality is the infinite present. It would be useful to recall what has been said earlier that the most important moment is *now* on which the whole of life focuses, the past converging on it and the future emerging from it.

Krishnamurti is neither skeptic nor affirmative in absolute terms regarding reincarnation. He cautions against beguiling onself about visions of life reincarnated based on a person's possessions and beliefs in his present life. According to Krishnamurti such beliefs may lead to dreams of a rosy future existence while his living at the present moment continues to be foul. Permanent soul is the projection of the mind seeking shelter from insecurity, creating an image of so called permanent security for himself.

Epistemology

Under Epistemology, theory of knowledge, it may be pointed out that when the mind functions according to accumulated knowledge, it can never discover anything new as it only acts according to what it has stored up as past images and memories. The mind then moves from one fixed point of time to another necessarily based on past experiences and, therefore, incapable of going beyond the dimension of time. This creates fragmentation of consciousness and no true relationship is established. The direct perception of "what is" takes place in a silent mind, in the mind that is free from the occupation of becoming, of identification, of any image. Krishnamurti has, therefore, talked of keeping an open mind from moment to moment without previous image formation. He has discarded the images of the past or projection of human mind into the future and has emphasised living fully at the present moment, that is, *now*.

In Krishnamurti's case there is a different process of knowing the truth, knowing while working upon one's mind uninfluenced by past images. There is understanding of Truth from moment to moment without preconceived images, ideas or comparisons, opening the floodgates of one's mind as Truth flows in, grasping it in all its native significance and letting it flow by without exercising any hold on it, much like a flowing river as the torrent comes and flows by.

Understanding the Truth is not a relationship where observer and observed are separate. It assumes a complete and meaningful form where the distance between the observer and the observed wanes and the observer fades into the observed.

Axiology

Axiology, theory of values, is a pervasive element all through the holistic approach of Krishnamurti ranging from the self and the Other, viewing oneself in the mirror of relationship, without getting entrapped in the time cycle, and therefore comparison such as what one is and what one desires to be, thereby freeing one's mind of fear. Certain values such as good and evil, discipline and indiscipline have not been considered as absolute opposites of one another but rather of qualitative difference, depicted by the mind of a person which may cultivate good qualities superficially while retaining evils deep inside. A true understanding of "what is" will start the process of removal of deep seated evils within a person silently and without his knowing. What Krishnamurti has to say on celibacy would be a good example in this context.

> Not being able to find out how to live a chaste life one takes vows of celibacy and goes through tortures. That is not celibacy. Celibacy is something entirely different. It is to have a mind that is free from all images, from all knowledge, which means understanding the whole process of pleasure and fear.[50]

Proceeding further one may recall what Krishnamurti has to say on intelligence. Intelligence is the perception of right values. It comes into being with the absence of the "me". It understands life as a whole.

Throughout the aforesaid discussion the holistic vision of Krishnamurti decries division in any form in his philosophy. The comparison made initially with a beautiful woven fabric and its indiscernible threads is worthwhile recalling at this stage. The philosophy of Krishnamurti is indeed so vast and pervasive that no container can confine it within limits. Krishnamurti has often used different words on different occasions conveying the same meaning. For instance he has used the following phrases for denoting "the Other"– "the immeasurable", "the infinite", "the timeless"; "the sacred", "the beautiful", "the sublime", "god", "truth", "reality", "benediction"; "the vast emptiness", "silence"; "love", "compassion", "creativity". Similarly he has named self as "content of consciousness", "psychological thought", "psychological time", "the observer".

Philosophical Ideas of J. Krishnamurti

What needs to be emphasised is that Krishnamurti never claimed to be a teacher, in fact, he had once spontaneously said to Pupul Jayakar that "there is no teaching"[51]. Krishnamurti has on many occasions said that his philosophy has nothing new to offer. In this context again one recalls his conversation with Pupul Jaykar's nephew, Asit Chandmal in 1958 at Ranikhet when he said, "The straight line being the 'I' and the horizontal bar, the negation of the 'I'"[52]. The core message behind this was self-naughting - a message of truth which was discovered by Krishnamurti himself. The person is his own teacher.

With this background it would seem somewhat arbitrary and perhaps even redundant to separate educational ideas of Krishnamurti from his general philosophy. Nevertheless, an attempt has been made to focus on this aspect after a detailed study of the holistic approach. One may proceed to dwell on his educational ideas with the full conviction that these are not separate entities and consist of Krishnamurti's holistic approach to life.

Concluding Remarks

After a study of the philosophies of Dr. Annie Besant and J. Krishnamurti, a thought that engages the mind is, the extent to which their philosophical thoughts are in continuity of the Vedantic philosophy. Dr. Annie Besant's firm belief in "Brahma", the Supreme Truth and "Brahma Vidya", the Supreme Knowledge, by which man has knowledge of the God within him, and which comes in the final stages of his evolution, a knowledge with cannot be imparted by any guru, makes this continuity manifest. Perhaps, in the case of Krishnamurti such a continuity is more subtle. Whilst the word "Truth" remains the same, the contents shift focus and have different meanings. Dr. Annie Besant defines Truth in conventional and absolute terms and calls it "Brahma". Krishnamurti on the other hand, refers to it as an understanding of "what is" and "a pathless land" – an understanding of oneself in relationship (self knowledge) which comes in one's everyday life, without the help of any guru. Self knowledge is the naughting of the "I" and in

Vedantic interpretation could mean a step towards knowing the "Jivatma". This is against the backdrop of Krishnamurti saying that "the Sacred", could not be a word or a belief. Dependence on any religious literature has always been denied by Krishnamurti. Beliefs like reincarnation and permanent soul are considered as projections of the mind. According to Krishnamurti if one believes in a future birth then one must know that it is conditioned by the way one lives *now*. So what one is *now* is of tremendous importance. To this extent the similarity with Dr. Annie Besant's Vedantic philosophy of Karma influencing Reincarnation thus seems apparent, just as it reinforces Krishnamurti's views on the most important moment being *now*, the past converging on it and the future emerging from it.

References

1. The Penguin J. Krishnamurti Reader, p. 67.
2. Commentaries On Living, II series, p. 81.
3. The Wholeness Of Life, p. 207.
4. The Awakening Of Intelligence, p. 75.
5. The Wholeness Of Life, p. 208.
6. ibid., p. 209.
7. You Are The World, p. 48.
8. J. Krishnamurti – A Biography, p. 313.
9. The First And Last Freedom, p. 76.
10. Krishnamurti On Education, p. 35.
11. A Wholly Different Way Of Living, p. 14.
12. The Awakening Of Intelligence, p. 83.
13. You Are the World, p. 138.
14. The Awakening Of Intelligence, p. 75.
15. You Are The World, p. 110.
16. The Wholeness Of Life, p. 141.
17. The Awakening Of Intelligence, P. 78.
18. Commentaries On Living, III series, p. 92.
19. This Matter Of Cuture, p. 23.
20. idem
21. A Wholly Different Way Of Living, p. 25.

22. The Awakening Of Intelligence, p.188.
23. ibid., p. 475.
24. Swami Venkatesananda, Scholar and Teacher, asks to be identified only by his name.
25. ibid., p. 177.
26. On Learning And Knowledge, p. 13.
27. On An Eternal Voyage, pp. 12-13.
28. The Awakening Of Intelligence, p. 82.
29. ibid., p. 24.
30. ibid., p. 199.
31. ibid., pp. 204-205.
32. ibid., p. 131.
33. ibid., p. 98.
34. The Wholeness Of Life, p. 142.
35. idem.
36. The Years Of Fulfilment, p. 42.
37. Commentaries On Living, III Series, p. 336.
38. Meditations, p. 22.
39. ibid., p. 77.
40. ibid., p. 45.
41. Education And The Significance Of Life, p. 124.
42. The Awakening Of Intelligence, p. 313.
43. ibid., p. 217.
44. ibid., p. 216.
45. Education And The Significance Of Life, p. 63.
46. The Awakening Of Intelligence, p. 345.
47. ibid., pp. 403-404.
48. ibid., p. 411.
49. Education And Life's Challenges (Audio Cassette), January 1970.
50. The Awakening Of Intelligence, p. 82.
51. J. Krishnamurti –A Biography, p. 313.

4

[A] Educational Ideas of Dr. Annie Besant

Born of a strong urge to uplift the Indian nation from the trampled state under British rule, and realising that this was possible through proper education, Dr. Annie Besant who had herself deeply studied ancient Hindu Philosophy and also words of sages through holy books, formulated a pattern of education for India, which was eminently suitable to the ground realities of her times, and which allowed itself to be moulded through the years to conform with the contemporary situation. Such a dispensation must of necessity be intricate, involved and vast. For cohesive comprehension the researcher has discussed this under following captions:

    I   Preamble
    II   Goals of Education
    III   Organisation of Education
    IV   Methods of Teaching
    V   Concept of Schools in India
    VI   Educator/Teacher
    VII   Student
    VIII   Discipline

IX   Women Education
X   Mass Education

Preamble

The forms of education that Dr. Annie Besant advocated were subservient to situational changes, but the principles that she laid stress on were true for all times. She felt that in the scientific age there was need for the moral conscience to develop before knowledge advanced further. The most important industry was the industry of educating the people in the right way and creating the right individuals for the future.

In May 1909, Dr. Annie Besant delivered lectures in London which were compiled into a book titled, *The Changing World*, in which she described deadlocks in every sphere of human thought and activity-in art, science, economic and social conditions and in international relations. She believed that this state of affairs was a prelude to the beginning of a new civilisation in the building up of which India was to play an important role. She gave a call to recreate ideals, discover new methods which would appeal to the great masses of mankind. She expected a free India to impart her spiritual wealth to the new civilisation. With political freedom, India would be able to give the proper place to education and culture. She pointed out that the future citizen is moulded by the way the present day education makes him. Therefore, education must be one's foremost concern at every moment of existence. She believed education to be "the corner-stone of the new world order."[1] It is by education that inequality can be reduced, "by giving an education which will draw out everything which is in the child, not allowing it to be witheld because of poverty..."[2]

Here one can draw *a distinction between Gandhiji's aim of education and Dr. Annie Besant's.* Though Gandhiji's scheme of education was based on Indian traditions and Indian needs, Annie Besant considered it largely "a fanatical scheme having an utterly inadequate contact with the deeper fundamentals of the nature of real education."[3] She believed that in the present competitive, materialistic world when the weak were being suppressed by the powerful, when power, money continued to remain in the hands of a few, one has to either go forward or backward. Gandhiji's views, according to her, were based on going backward to the simple village life of a spinning- wheel and handloom. He considered machinery to be devilish and wanted to confine people to hand-made goods and not to have machine goods at all. In contrast Dr. Annie Besant's views were best expressed in her own words:

> We do not wish to force the cultured to the level of the illiterate, but to raise the illiterate to the many-aspected life of the cultured. We do not wish to make the rich poor, but to lift the poor so that they may share the comforts and refinements of the life of the highest class; we do not wish to go back to the simpler, more animal, and merely primitive condition, with a few mighty and outstanding geniuses, but to develop all to a level of high intellectual and emotional life.[4]

She laid emphasis on the perfecting of man as the keynote of the coming civilisation where one no longer looked at his fellowmen as fundamentally evil but as fundamentally divine. The new law no longer negative, had for its object not mere prevention of injury to another, but was positive in that it tried to help forward the good of all. Dr. Annie Besant observed:

> What after all is the object of Education? To train the body in health, vigour and grace, so that it may express the emotions in beauty and the mind with accuracy and strength. To train the emotions to love all that is noble and beautiful; to sympathize with the joys and sorrows of others; to inspire to service ever widening in its area, until we love our elders as our parents, our equals as our brothers and sisters, our youngsters as our children and seek to serve them all; to find joy in sacrifice for great causes and for the helpless; to feel reverence for all who are worthy of it, and compassion for the outcast and the criminal. To evolve and discipline the mind in right thinking, right discrimination, right judgement, right memory. To subdue body, emotion and mind to the Spirit,

the inner Ruler Immortal, making the mind the mirror of the Ego, the emotions the mirror of the Intuition, the body the expression of the will.[5]

In order to build the nation, she laid the foundations of a national system of education. One of her lectures, titled, *Education As The Basis Of National Life,* which was delivered by Dr. Annie Besant at Adyar in the Theosophical Hall, on the 23rd of February, 1908. The opening words of the speech were as follows:

Friends,

All over the world at the present time, thoughtful men and women-the men and women who make the public opinion of their day-are concerning themselves with education as being the basis of national life, the foundation of national prosperity ...Now if the importance of a wisely planned and wisely directed system of education is recognised by all the great nations of the world, it surely cannot be undesirable that the Indian public, awakening to a national life, should also interest itself in this matter, and bestir itself in the shaping of an education which shall form a solid basis for the erection of the national edifice.[6]

The British government exerted a rigid control on education through Directors, Inspectors, red tape and making English the medium of instructions. Old Indian values were despised and discarded. Generations of such educated Indian were produced, suitable only for clerical and lower administrative government jobs. Dr. Annie Besant was against all this. She said:

But the East India Company not only drained her of her accumulated wealth and reduced her to poverty, but despised her Learning and her Art, crushed her with ignorance ...It destroyed her self-respect and jeered at her religion and her traditions. It consummated her degradation by imposing on her an Education in a foreign language, till her educated people talked it better than their Mother-tongue...it wanted English knowing men to fill the lower ranks of its administration...[7]

Mere book knowledge or imparting of information is not education in the true sense. The child is not a sheet of blank paper in which the teacher can write what he/she likes. In Dr. Annie Besant's words:

> As man is a spiritual being, manifesting in the external world as Intelligence, Emotion and Activity, the Education of the young must help the inspiring Life to unfold itself, and must train the organs of Intelligence, Emotion and Activity; that is, must be religious, mental, moral and physical. Any so-called education which omits any one of these four departments of human nature is imperfect and unscientific and its outcome will be a human being deficient in one or more of the groups of capacities on the balanced evolution of which the extent of his usefulness to Society depends.[8]

This points out to the fact, that Dr. Annie Besant considered *education to be a means of individual and social development*. The individual is not an isolated being. The individuals in their relationships to one another comprise the society. The working of a social order depends on the efficient working of the individuals who form it. Therefore, the all round development of the individual must take place in the social context. Education must bring out and train the capacities in the individual which will help him to discharge his social duties and responsibilities efficiently.

Dr. Annie Besant held *education as knowledge or growth that was related to the spiritual world on the one hand and to the material world on the other*. It is a process of building of the individual whereby he gathers knowledge about the spiritual and the material world thus enabling him to relate and adjust himself to the two worlds. Thoughout the process of education "the evolving life and its environment"[9] are given importance. "The evolving life" includes the drawing out of all the capacities that the individual has in him, thus progressing him in the chain of evolution. The "environment" includes all the relationships that the individual builds in his surroundings, "the unfolding consciousness recognizing, and therefore becoming related to, a larger and larger environment, the Home, the School, the College, the City, the Province, the State, the Race, Humanity, the World".[10]

Educational Ideas of Dr. Annie Besant

Dr. Annie Besant was basically a religious and spiritual minded woman and on joining the Theosophical Society, this tendency became stronger. She therefore viewed education from this angle. *She regarded education as the drawing out of the hidden potentialities, of the faculties that are latent in man, training of inborn capacities and powers brought over from former lives.* This concept was the result of her belief in the Law of Karma and Reincarnation which have been discussed in the chapter on the philosophical ideas of Dr. Annie Besant.

Dr. Annie Besant affirmed that education should be recognised "as a science, and not a haphazard dragging up of youth, consisting chiefly in forcing into them knowledge from outside, instead of helping them to unfold and utilise the capacities they have brought with them into the world."[11] Like science, education should be imparted in a systematic and methodical way. Through the sense organs, the capacities or faculties that lie within the individual are brought into contact with the outer environment. This results in the acquisition of knowledge. This makes it clear that the quality of acquisition of knowledge is inherent; it does not come from outside but with the awakening of the hidden faculties within the child.

To highlight the Indian ideals in education and to remind the Indians of their past rich heritage, Dr. Annie Besant strongly affirmed the relationship between education and culture.

> Culture is the result on the mind of certain forms of knowledge... it differs from Education in that it is not the drawing out and training of faculty, but is the result of the exercise of faculties on subjects which arouse sympathetic emotion and imagination, broadening the mind, eliminating personal, local and racial prejudices, acquiring an understanding of human nature in its many aspects ...[12]

As a result of education the changes that are brought about in the behaviour, thinking and action of individuals is culture. If education and culture are completely separated during the formative period, the over emphasis on knowledge and storing the brain with facts would result in over-specialisation and one-sided development leading to narrow mindedness and harshness. Dr. Annie Besant was of the opinion that Literature, Art, Beauty were instruments of culture. After studying each child in the educational process, those who have an aptitude and interest in such subjects should be identified and given proper training so that they could contribute to the culture of their land. This was in concurrence with ancient Indian thinking of giving prime importance to truth, beauty, goodness in education. The following quotation of Dr. Annie Besant aptly sums this up:

> Let us make our cities beautiful; above all, let us make our Schools beautiful. Let us surround the children with beauty and joy, and they shall grow into harmonious relations with each other. Let us bring Art to the Schools, the Colleges, the Universities, as of old... Let each of us be a messenger of Beauty, in our language, our manners, our courtesy. All this Beauty is hidden in the Indian heart, in the Indian customs... Your dharma, as Indians is to spread Beauty around you, and not allow yourselves to be distorted into ugliness.[13]

Goals of Education

The supreme goal of education, according to Dr. Annie Besant, is to build the people in the right way. This has two components, (1) leading to man becoming a good citizen that will in turn build the nation and then a free and spiritual Commonwealth of Humanity. (2) to expedite the process of evolution by helping the development of attributes brought forth by the child from previous births. Details are considered under following headings:

1. Character Building

To build the people, Dr. Annie Besant laid stress on building of character. As she herself said:

> The aim of education is to draw out all the faculties of the boy on every side of his nature, to develop in him every

intellectual and moral power, and to strengthen him physically, emotionally, mentally and spiritually, that he may turn out at the end of his College career a useful, patriotic, pious gentleman, who respects himself and respects those around him.[14]

Dr. Annie Besant's concept of the embryonic existence from past life, of powers and capacities in a person which have to be correctly drawn out and developed during the process of education have been discussed earlier. *This mandates that individual needs of the child are of paramount importance, having priority over a rigid educational pattern.*

Dr. Annie Besant had brought up J. Krishnamurti and wanted to give him the necessary environment, which would draw out the faculties latent in him. She believed that J. Krishnamurti was to be the vehicle of the World Teacher and wanted to rear him in such a way that humanity would benefit from the teachings of such a great man.

She stressed certain ideas that might be familiar now but were not considered at all at that time, such as the importance of building up the adolescent body with proper diet, hygiene and the playing of games. She was later to become a pioneer in *Indian Scouting*, a movement, which she started in order to build up character and the attitude of ready service in young men who badly lacked such an outlet for their energies. She formed a cadet corps in the Central Hindu College, which drew much attention wherever it went; the cadets were all dressed in an Indian uniform, drilled in military style and taught to act as a team loyal to one another and to their leaders. She also tried something that was then new to Indian schools, namely, the *prefect system*. All the time, in her institutions, the stress was on character and service and there was the distinctive feature of a complete absence of punishment.

2. Importance of Religion in Education

In order to build the character of the people, Dr. Annie Besant laid stress on religion. "Education was to her a matter of life and therefore of religion. It was based upon religious principles and the religious outlook of the people"[15].

She wanted religion and morality to be an integral part of education. To quote her:

> You cannot build up rational citizens, you cannot build up noble men, men of ability and usefulness to the land that gave them birth, unless you lay the foundation of their education on Divine Wisdom, and train the boy in the knowledge of his duty to God and to man. Religious principles must come first and foremost in every perfect system of education.[16]

Dr. Annie Besant believed that the *core teachings of religions should be properly grasped and translated into everyday living*. Very often, she emphasised that the basic teachings of all religions were the same, that all the great leaders of religion had spoken of the oneness of God, of the unity or brotherhood of humanity and of the moral values that emerged spontaneously from that sense of oneness of life. Religion as the true basis of morality, art, literature, was necessary for the greatness of a nation.

Religious training should be an integral part of educational curriculum and not merely given incidentally in the homes, in informal gatherings or on special occasions. If due importance is not given to religion, the students would treat it as a secondary subject, of lesser importance than those subjects that are within the educational curriculum. Religion should be taught without sectarian bias, thereby laying the foundation for patriotism, nationalism, humanitarianism. Dr. Annie Besant applied the Great Law of living to all spheres of national activity–in religion, education, art, social relations and politics. As C.S. Trilokekar observed:

> Education was to be wedded to religion and was to be graded according to the inner nature of the individual. Art was to be national property. Society was to be but an enlargement of the joint family. Politics was to be based on spiritual socialism in which those who have were to share with those who have not-a welfare state-bound by strong ties of brotherhood and love. Thus was to be welded a nation and its life on the stable rock of spirituality in which religion was to be its inspiration, education was to

be its shaper and moulder, art was to be its beautifier, a happy society was to be its supporter, and government was for the good of all.[17]

3. Role of Ideals in Education

An ideal, according to Dr. Annie Besant is a fixed idea that is continuously held in the mind and influences one's behaviour. One becomes what one constantly thinks and one's character is shaped accordingly. One can remove one's drawbacks and improve, upon the good qualities one possesses to a great extent, these being the residual characteristics of the past life.

Dr. Annie Besant stressed on Indian ideals to be best, for imparting education to the students in India since according to the Great Law which guides the universe men are born into the religion which is best suited to mould their lives and character. Hence Hinduism was the religion both taught and lived in the Central Hindu College. Also a nation has a jivatama; a spirit which is a fragment of Ishwara and which comes direct from God Himself "and according to the peculiarities embodied in that fragment, are the characteristics of the Nation which is built up thereby. No two individuals are alike, and similarly no two Nations are alike. It is the totality of all Nations that builds up Humanity – the human reflection of Ishwara Himself..."[18]

Dr. Annie Besant believed that the foundation of education in India must not be English sentiment but Indian sentiment, because whatever is beneficial for the West is not necessarily so for the East. Also, national education should be in Indian hands and under Indian control as Indians can best judge the character that is expected to be developed amongst boys and girls of the country:

> And as the child has a past, of which his present is the outcome, so has the nation into which he is born a past, which must not be disregarded. Its type, its traditions, its spiritual, mental, emotional and physical characteristics must all be taken into account, and this can only be thoroughly done by those who are also born into the nation. Thus, none who are not of the national

household, however useful they may be as counsellors and helpers, must be allowed to dominate national education. Their help may be gladly welcomed, but they must never be allowed to control.[19]

Indian ideals presented before the children, could develop a love for their Motherland, feelings of patriotism could be aroused in their hearts as they would learn about the great rich heritage of their past and develop a respect for them. To stress the Indian ideals in education, Dr. Annie Besant emphasised the ancient system of Indian education. She believed that with the attainment of political freedom, India would be able to give the required freedom to Education and Culture and the emphasis on mother tongue in the schools and colleges would bring about a feeling of respect for Indian language, literature and civilisation. Also the gulf between the English- educated minority and the middle classes versed in the mother tongue would be removed. Moreover, the students would be able to comprehend the subjects in a better way and express what they had learnt in an effective manner. A sense of national unity would be promoted by writing books on Indian lives, to inspire the readers with pride in a common past, "making them regard all the heroes of the past as a common possession, as the makers of India..."[20] The *Ashram Ideal* was stressed, in which there was a close bond between the teachers and students. The teachers regarded their students as their sons, who taught the students due to their love of teaching and not for monetary benefits. Further the Gurukuls with their close affinity with Nature helped in permeating a sense of calmness, harmony, order within the hearts of the teachers and students.

During the ancient period, education was self-controlled and the government exercised no authority over the educational institutions. The rulers or kings built universities and showered money on them but they claimed no authority. Only the teachers of the institution were responsible for the management of the institutions and were regarded with respect by the students and members of the community connected to the institution. This was in contrast to the

British system of education where strict government control was exercised through a mechanism described earlier.

Dr. Annie Besant's principle of the *freedom of education from governmental control* is not only useful for a country that is not free, but also true for countries that are absolutely free. In ancient India, the caste system had clearly laid down the functions of each caste and affirmed that the Kshatriya, namely the government, the men in power, should have no authority over the Brahman, the men of thought who looked to the department of education as a whole. The teachers attracted students to themselves by the very force of their character and learning; and sent out the young people at the opportune time to the world to play their fitting roles therein; and governments were only grateful and pleased to recruit them in their service for the carrying on of the administration and the fulfilment of the many duties that fall to the State. Dr. Annie Besant believed that if a government wants to give financial assistance, it is welcome to do so, but no educational institution should ask for governmental assistance, for that would lead to welcoming control and supremacy from persons who may be quite ignorant about the workings of such institutions. So long as Dr. Annie Besant and her early colleagues were in charge of the Central Hindu College, not even a minimal amount was asked from the government as assistance. Though Dr. Annie Besant toured extensively, collected subscriptions and contributions for her college from the individuals or organisations who were willing to give, she never approached the government for monetary assistance.

4. Towards developing civic virtues and public spirit

To build the people so that they become good citizens was Dr. Annie Besant's chief concern. Dr. Annie Besant said, "A man who can live usefully and harmoniously with his fellowmen is the essence of the idea of the citizen."[21] Among the virtues that are required to be a good citizen is public spirit or civic virtues. According to Dr. Annie Besant, good men are wanted more than good laws. Good laws are useless unless good men are there to carry them out. Therefore, Dr. Annie Besant reiterated in her 1899 anniversary address to the Central Hindu College, "Our work is the work of planting good seeds that healthy plants may grow. To others we leave the honourable task of the utilizing of the sound trees after we have nourished and trained them".[22] She wanted Indian ideals to be the basis of education and patriotism to be the principle or directive of education. "Public spirit is patriotism in action".[23]

5. Blend of the East and West in education

The aim of the Central Hindu College was religio-secular, where an attempt was made to unite the best of Hindu culture with the best of Western principles of education. It brought the East-West together. Dr. Annie Besant believed that in the contemporary age, with its vast progress in science and technology, no country howsoever advanced, could really live isolated. Therefore, she thought it desirable to maintain relationships between England and India on the basis of mutual help and mutual esteem. She felt that India can serve best by keeping friendly relations with all lands, and by continuing in the Commonwealth of which she wished the British monarch to be the head. In education too, she stressed this need of bringing the East and West together so that they could maintain their own respective strength and greatness whilst sharing the good points of both. The task before the future generations would be to co-ordinate the teachings and the systems of the past with the experience and knowledge of the great discoveries of the contemporary world. While reviving the past glory of the philosophy and the religion of ancient India, importance should also be given to the many blessings of modern science and opportunities should be given to utilise them for the well being of the people of India. As C.S. Trilokekar wrote:

> We therefore see in her (Dr. Annie Besant), equally balanced and combined, the intellect, industry and efficiency of the West with the soulfulness and spirituality of the East, an ever living example of the fusion of both, a pattern and type of man and woman of the times to come[24].

Organisation of Education

The crux of the educational organisation of Dr. Annie

Besant was to bring out useful nationals for building a nation, strong in every respect. Her ideal for a nation, as explained by her in the Presidential Address of the Theosophical Society at Adyar in February 1908:

> What is the ideal for a nation? It must have spirituality, expressed in many-graded religions, suitable for every class in the nation: and if, as here, there are several religions, they must be friends, not rivals, acknowledging their common origin, divine wisdom, and their common aim, the uplifting of the nation. It must have certain moral virtues of a virile kind as well as of the tenderer types. It must have intellect, directed and trained to meet the multifarious needs of a nation–literacy, artistic, scientific, political, agricultural, manufacturing, industrial, commercial, engineering etc. It must have healthy conditions of life, a robust and vigorous manhood, a strong and refined womanhood. These are the things which make up the ideal, education is to bring them to realisation."[25]

All these ideals could be achieved by "national education". In the words of Dr. Annie Besant: "By national education I mean an education which is under national control, which provides for all the children of the nation – a point to which we must revert later – and which is directed with a sole eye to the spiritual, moral, intellectual and physical welfare of the nation."[26]

Details regarding Dr. Annie Besant's organisation of education have been given in the following works: *Education In The Light Of Theosophy*, *Education– Basis Of National Life*, *Principles Of Education*, *Builder Of New India*, Volume II of The Besant Spirit Series titled, *Ideals In Education*.

The national system of education was first of its kind in the history of India. Dr. Annie Besant felt that for the reawakening of India and for the building of a strong nation, an ideal national system of education was very essential. She believed that it could be only through education that the hidden capacities of the Indians could be aroused and a strong nation based on the foundation of spiritualism, brotherhood, patriotism, nationalism could be established.

Dr. Annie Besant through Theosophical Educational Trust set up many schools and colleges which were open to students of every faith, and in which religious instruction was incorporated as an integral part of education. Thus many schools and colleges were established and to bring uniformity in these educational institutions, she chalked out a detailed scheme of national education and drew the attention of prominent men of India.

In the year 1918, after the goal of Home Rule had been accepted by the British government, she launched the National Education Movement with the help of Dr. Arundale because she felt that without education on national lines there could be no true national freedom and that in India, democracy should not grow into government by multi-headed ignorance. In the Commonwealth of India Bill for the freedom of India, which she drafted in 1925, she wrote down the right of citizens to free elementary education, embodying her view that every child born in the land should be able to enjoy that right; he should not only have the necessary physical care, but also the education needed to launch him into the stormy waters of life. The Bill contemplated one or more schools in every village managed by the village authorities.[27]

In accordance with the needs of the child and the laws of nature, *the scheme of national education was divided into three stages–from birth to seven years, from seven years to fourteen years, from fourteen years to twenty one years.* Mother-tongue of the district was to be the medium of instruction. English was to be taught as a second language throughout the Secondary and High schools. The hours at school were to extend from 7 a.m. to 6 p.m., teaching work from 7 to 10 in the morning and 2 to 4 in the evening. Food and rest were to be from 10 to 2, and games and physical exercises, from 4 to 6. The school timings could vary according to geographical location in different parts of India. Rest rather than brain work after the morning meals was emphasised. Religious service was to be performed regularly on a daily basis before beginning the day's work and at the end of it. The different stages of education were as follows:

(i) Birth to seven years

This period was divided into two sub-stages: a) Birth to five years and b) five years to seven years

a) Birth to five years

At this stage, care of the body must be the foremost concern. For this the parents should have knowledge of child psychology. The child may be sent to a *nursery school* from two and a half to five years. Here one finds the influence of Kindergarten and Montessori methods on the upbringing of the child, as well as the Theosophical ideas related to the child's education. Dr. Annie Besant said that the Theosophical parents should regard it their "sacred and responsible charge" to train the physical body with scrupulous care, to train the emotions so that noble and lofty thoughts enter the young mind, to set good examples before the child. The child should be protected from all coarsening and vulgarising influences. Home environment should reflect beauty so that it refines the child's tastes.

An atmosphere of love and not fear or authority should surround the child so that he learns to be gentle, obedient, trustful. Little emotional outbursts should be met by drawing the attention to some pleasant object. Fear breeds helplessness, behaviour problems with an inclination to cheat, whereas love of Truth spontaneously comes about in the absence of fear. From birth, good habits should be nurtured after studying the child carefully. Objects that attract the attention of the child should surround him, so that he develops the power of attention and observation and learns to make his own little experiments and broaden his area of knowledge. At the age of three, opportunities of choice should be offered to the child to draw out his inherent capacities and develop originality. At the age of four, an element of organisation may be introduced into the child's games but nothing should be imposed on him. Above all, the child should learn through play the happiness of living in harmony. Opportunities for doing little services should be given, and the child be encouraged to help others, to be kind to the plants, animals, to everybody, to be neat and orderly.

b) Five years to seven years

This stage of education is the *primary school stage*. There are two classes, Class 1A and Class 1B. Playway method should be the most important method of teaching. Apart from this, learning through observation, story, drama, poem etc. should be encouraged. Through the medium of observation, the child should be encouraged to observe the inter-relations of objects, their number, their shape, their colour, their use. Drawing and modelling should be encouraged as they promote the skilful use of fingers and also develop in the children a liking for manual work. The school room should be littered with objects that arouse their curiosity, and the child feels eager to acquire knowledge about the objects or desire to imitate them, thus stimulating the creative powers. The teacher should not interfere but help him when he gets discouraged by failure. Dr. Annie Besant pointed out:

> The child will learn largely by imitation. He will learn exactitude by discovering that badly made things won't work. He will learn that success waits on obedience to conditions, and that impatience, anger, petulance, do not change the nature of things but only ensure failure.[28]

To sum up, the education pertaining to the first seven years should be as much as possible in the open air, lessons to be short and conversational, carefully chosen exercises and games to be included, simple and nourishing food provided, and last but not the least, the imaginative tendencies of the child should be allowed to develop freely in a way, an atmosphere of love, warmth and freedom to be given. Attention should be given to the building up of a healthy physical body, formation of good habits and inculcation of religious and moral ideals. These are the most impressionable years, and traits developed during this age continue to influence one's life later on.

(ii) Seven to fourteen years

This stage is primarily concerned with emotional development. It is divided into two sub-stages: Seven years to ten years and ten years to fourteen years.

a) Seven years to ten years

This stage of education is named by Dr. Annie Besant as the *lower secondary school stage*. This stage includes classes 2, 3 and 4. Education has primarily four main objectives – religious, intellectual, moral and physical development. Under physical development cleanliness of the body, value of a healthy body, self control, good behaviour is practised. Further the harmful effects of anger, jealousy and other passions on health are communicated to the child. Gymnastic exercises, breathing, elementary manual training is given. A sense of cooperation is promoted through group songs, games, concerted exercises with music.

For religious development the idea of God as a loving Father and the relationship of man with God, the idea of the oneness of life, should be told to the students through stories and bhajans. The idea of serving God through serving and helping others should be shown by telling stories about the lives of great religious teachers and philanthropists.

For intellectual development teaching should be done through the mother tongue. To make the students become familiar with their mother tongue, stories should be narrated by the teacher, pupils told to reproduce what they observe. Elementary knowledge of the classical languages of India, Sanskrit, Pali, Arabic, should be given. In language teaching, rules of grammar should begin not before a genuine interest is aroused in the subject. English should be taught through conversation and easy stories. Nature study taught through observation and experimental methods, history taught through pictures and stories, geography taught through travels and puzzle maps, arithmetic taught by taking note of situations from everyday life, easy problems, Indian money, weight and measures, simple bills. Constant reference to be made about the interdependence of various languages and subjects so that the feeling of helping each other should be developed and service to near ones regarded as service to Motherland. Moral education to be imparted through stories of truth, righteousness, and arousing a sense of patriotism through studying the lives of great sons and daughters of India.

b) Ten years to fourteen years

This stage is called *Higher Secondary School level* by Dr. Annie Besant and included classes V to VII.

For religious development alongwith the chief doctrines of one's own religion, the fundamental unity of all religions should be stressed. Harmful influences of fanaticism, sectarianism, intolerance, should be illustrated through stories.

Intellectual development to be brought about by a more detailed study of languages, history, geography, nature study, science, arithmetic etc. An advanced study of mother tongue, Sanskrit, Pali or Arabic should be given. Simple scientific experiments in a practical from should be added, where the child performs some simple experiments and learns the inviolability of natural law. Nature study, including anatomy and physiology of human body, dissection of plants; physical geography including elementary physics and chemistry; Indian history and historical geography including preliminary outline of Indian political, economic and industrial geography, Indian life in different periods of history such as Chandragupta I and II, Mughals etc, outlines of world geography, higher arithmetic, elementary algebra and geometry to be included in the curriculum. For moral development the virtues of national unity, patriotism, should always be kept in mind and the superficial differences amongst the people of the country should be stressed as well as information on the current political, economic and industrial conditions of the nation provided. Pupils should be taught to help those who are in the lower classes, to be good citizens, to inculcate civic virtues and appreciation of beauty.

Physical development enhanced through exercises and games of various types, carpentry, cooking, household and garden work, use of tools and lessons in first aid. Instruction in the physiology of sex– plant, animal, human, should be given and the need for observing celibacy or Brahmacharya stressed. Dr. Annie Besant believed that it is in the playground that civic virtues like learning to obey their chosen leaders, healthy cooperation, playing with a love for the group and indifferent to one's own self, perseverance, endurance can be promoted.

Summing up, one can say that in the second seven years attention is given to the training of the body and mind, to the acquiring of general knowledge which every educated and well-bred person must posses as a basis for further studies. After fourteen, attention is given to specialisation "During the later part of this second period of seven years, the future vocation of the child should be definitely settled, due weight being given to his own ideas, which he should be encouraged to express freely, so that from fourteen onwards he may specialise along definite lines and prepare himself for his work in the world"[29]

(iii) Fourteen years to twenty-one years

The third stage is primarily concerned with mental development and is regarded by Dr. Annie Besant as *High School and subsequent level stage*. This is divided into two sub stages: Fourteen years to sixteen years and sixteen to twenty one years.

a) Fourteen to sixteen years

During this period, the type of education depends to a certain extent upon the career that the pupil would like to adopt later on in life. As per the different subjects, Dr. Annie Besant has given a list of four types of High Schools.

(i) AN ORDINARY HIGH SCHOOL:

a) Arts Division

Here Sanskrit, Arabic, Pali should be taught with a more specialised course in mother tongue, English, Indian History, Historical Geography and History of the British Empire.

b) Science Division

Sanskrit, Arabic or Pali with a more specialised course in mother tongue, English, Physics, Chemistry, Algebra, Geometry including Trigonometry and Mensuration with the elements of Surveying to be included. An advanced course in Nature Study to be given.

c) Teachers Division

Lessons on pedagogy, psychology, school management to be provided alongwith a course in the principles of physical training. Domestic Science, practice in teaching, Nature Study to be included.

(ii) A Commercial High School

In this category lessons on commercially useful foreign languages, business forms, book-keeping, commercial arithmetic, office methods, commercial law, type-writing and short hand, commercial history and geography to be given. For girls, there should be courses in food supplies and cooking.

(iii) A Technical High School

Here, alongwith mother tongue, English, Physics, Chemistry, Mathematics, Industrial History, Elementary Engineering, Mechanics, Electricity be taught.

(iv) An Agricultural High School

Here subjects to be taught with special reference to their impact on rural everyday life. Mathematics including book - keeping, land surveying, mensuration; experimental science (physics and chemistry) with special reference to Agriculture for boys, Domestic Science for girls; elements of mechanics with special reference to agricultural machines; nature study and gardening; knowledge on the elements of sanitation and engineering be taught. Apart from the above four categories of High Schools, there can be other types, example, for art, music, drawing, painting etc. In all the above categories of High Schools, religious education is an integral part alongwith training in leadership, chivalrous spirit and aesthetic sense.

Under scientific and other related subjects manual training, shop practice, laboratory work may be given which would constitute practical education. To foster social consciousness and qualities of citizenship, debating societies, student's parliaments, social service groups, night schools etc. may be formed, stress should be laid on the value and usefulness to the community and the nation of the special profession for which the student is preparing. Teachers should highlight the dignity of labour.

b) *Sixteen to twenty one years:*

(i) PRE-GRADUATE AND GRADUATE STAGE

The High School stage closes after obtaining the School Leaving Certificate. Following this the student undergoes his studies in a preparatory class for one year, which is attached to his High School. The University has all types of colleges – business, agricultural, arts, science, teacher's training etc –and in the various preparatory classes the students are given such special knowledge as may be required before starting their three years' College course. The students then enter a College by passing an entrance examination which is conducted jointly by University authorities and selected members of the staff of various schools. The graduation course is of three years after which they embark on their postgraduate studies.

(ii) POST GRADUATE STAGE

After the graduation stage, a postgraduate degree course of two years follows which is similar to the contemporary practice.

Dr. Annie Besant's entire pattern of education encompasses aims pertaining to individual, social, national development. Each aspect of an individual's personality – physical, religious, moral, intellectual, social, is given sufficient opportunities for development. She believed that national character can be strengthened only when the students learn the religion, culture of their country whereby they tend to respect their ideals. Therefore, she based her entire educational system on Indian ideals. She said that educational systems must be remodelled according to the needs of the time. Just as western nations remodel their educational system, India too must do that and find out the most suitable model for that time. Dr. Annie Besant held:

> The educationist has to find out the best ways of cooperating with the inner self of the child, of enabling

the faculties *already there* to manifest themselves and to grow, to strengthen all that is good and to starve out all that is bad, to work on the plastic material of the new brain from without, while the soul of the child works at it from within. This is the high office of the teacher, his great responsibility.[30]

Dr. Annie Besant was against the system of examinations as it resulted in rote memory, cramming. She held that the mind does not grow by being gorged with other people's thoughts, but by exercising its own faculties and for this training in observation, discrimination, reason, comparison, judgement is essential. Therefore, she considered that examinations should be conducted in a very limited way and the years of training should be given more weightage than the few hours spent in the examination room.

Also, psychological principles are reflected in her educational ideas as she regarded education to suit the needs, interests and capacities of the child. Psychological principles of growth and development are taken into account while planning the different stages of education.

Methods of Teaching

Against the backdrop of what has been discussed so far, it is now possible to consider some methods of teaching suggested by Dr. Annie Besant. It was not always possible to follow strictly scientific pedagogical principles in every case, and so Dr. Annie Besant was never averse to adopt suitable variations in individual cases.

1. Playway Method

Children from one to seven years should be taught through the playway method. At this stage the foremost aim of education is physical development. Games, exercises are essential for physical development. Reading, writing and arithmetic should be taught through the playway method. The equipment necessary for games should be available in the classroom as well as in the fields. They should be left free to choose their own games so that the various capacities can be developed spontaneously. Stories, poems, dramas are media through which the child is taught to express himself freely.

2. Observation Method

In any scientific method, observation has its due place. For this proper environment should be available in the home, school and society. In such a conducive environment, the child would be able to develop his capacities through his own sense organs. This method of teaching is suitable for all age groups.

3. Lecture Method

Dr. Annie Besant upheld the ancient Gurukul System and advocated lecture method in higher education and universities. This method is recommended in the teaching of subjects like history, language, philosophy, economics, political science etc. In her Central Hindu College, she adopted this method while imparting religious and moral education.

4. Self Study Method

Asserting the importance of hearing, thinking, contemplation methods in Upanishads, Dr. Annie Besant was of the view that it would be difficult for students to grasp the knowledge imparted through lecture method unless opportunities be provided for contemplation and self study. It is necessary for the students to ponder over the facts collected so that they develop an understanding of them. In higher classes self study method is quite useful.

5. Activity Method

Dr. Annie Besant regarded physical education as imperative at all stages. Games, exercises lead to healthy bodies, strengthening of muscles and bringing in the necessary vigour. Music and other arts, agriculture, training in industrial and technical subjects should also be taught through this method.

6. Imitation Method

Dr. Annie Besant stressed the usefulness of imitation

method. Specifically, among children between the age group of one to seven years, this tendency of imitating others is very strong. This method can be adopted in the teaching of subjects like language, grammar, art, music, religious, moral and physical education, in developing good habits like teaching children to respect their elders, to get up in the morning and say their regular prayers, to appreciate the virtues of obedience, brotherhood, punctuality, tolerance, cooperation, service etc. Parents and teachers should help in the formation of desirable qualities amongst children by setting good examples.

7. Experimental Method

Experimental method is vital in teaching not only scientific and technical subjects but also technology, industry, home science. The truths of general principles of physics, chemistry can be tested and verified in the laboratories which make experimental method imperative. This method is more useful in the secondary and higher levels where the student tests his theoretical knowledge and has a criteria for that.

8. Relating every subject to the pupil

By so doing the pupil discovers himself and this leads to individual growth.

Dr. Annie Besant while reminding the teachers of their duties and ideals told them not to be slaves of any particular method. This does not mean that she was against the use of set teaching methods in education. However, she has not propagated any novel teaching method. As she herself remarked, "Parents and teachers should acquaint themselves with the systems of Froebel, Pestalozzi and Montessori, and the investigations of Binet"[31]. In conclusion, one may say that she has recommended a synthesis of the methods mentioned by her–Montessori, Froebel, Pestalozzi and the experiments of Binet, in proportions that the situation (requirement of particular students) calls for.

Concept of Schools in India

Dr. Annie Besant was deeply upset by the way the current

educational system carried out its objectives. On one side the traditional Indian schools were losing their importance, and on the other, English medium government aided and missionary schools were making their place felt in the Indian Society. In such schools the all round development of the students was not taken care of, and attention was paid only to their intellectual development. Here cramming in order to be successful in the examinations was done, and the students accepted and learnt only what their teachers dictated to them which they stored in their memory and emptied it at the examination only to be forgotten later. The aim of education was just to earn a livelihood and not to prepare for life. The atmosphere of the school was over-ridden by fear and not love. The child was to be disciplined through punishment and fear and not through understanding and compassion. There was no question of any self enrichment on the part of the students. The time spent at school was totally under a strict teacher who tried to bring order into his students through coercion, and when these students returned to their homes after their school hours, they were troubled by the huge amount of home work which they were compelled to do. This led to a pseudo intellectual growth without consideration for comprehensive development. Therefore, for building a strong India, Dr. Annie Besant laid stress on the setting up of such schools that would enable the students to be patriotic, to pride in their past glory, to be true to themselves, to have faith and to respect their own religion and culture, to be conscious and hopeful of a golden future and to discover for themselves what is true through education. She wanted to revive the ancient Indian type of education for India without replicating earlier models. She felt that the old pattern should be remodelled to suit the present needs. The Central Hindu College at Benares founded by Dr. Annie Besant was an attempt at this remodelling. In the educational system planned out by Dr. Annie Besant, a detailed description of the atmosphere of a school and its aims are given.

In her "ideal school" sufficient care is given to bring about a student's all round development. Though the ancient forest environment of Gurukuls is not always possible in the contemporary world, schools can still reflect this love of Nature by being situated in quiet, peaceful places, full of greenery. She felt that Nature has its own way of communicating its purity, harmony and order into the inhabitants. Teachers even in government aided schools must have full responsibility for the all-round development of the students. They should get full support from the community and must be provided with all the means that would bring about the fullest development of the students. There should be an atmosphere of love, tenderness, warmth, cooperation, tolerance in the schools. The evils of the prevalent social structure could be removed by the pure, orderly, refined atmosphere that pervaded the Gurukul systems. *Hence Dr. Annie Besant wanted to inculcate the ancient Gurukul culture with some modifications into the current educational system so that it would revive the past glory of India.* She also emphasised the importance of games in bringing about physical and moral courage. In ancient system of education in India, games were given sufficient importance as is known from the epics and other religious books.

Educator/Teacher

Dr. Annie Besant believed that a good teacher must have certain essential qualities. She laid down certain principles that were true for all times. She believed that the *supreme work of education is to recognise that it is the conscience of the child that is primarily to be developed so as to enable him to discern between right and wrong. All must subordinate to this end. Against this backdrop the role of teacher becomes of crucial importance.* It is the duty of the teacher to help the child to do better, that which he *has* to do, not that which he ought to do, or still less, which the teacher would like him to do. What the personality of a teacher should be is best described in Dr. Annie Besant's own words, in her Presidential Address to the All India Federation of Teachers:

> The teacher must be positive, definite, eager, full of ideals, full of endeavour to bring them down into the actual. This is why the vocation of the teacher is so onerous. He must

be worth sharing with his pupils. There must be in him the power to inspire his pupils to become all that they will desire to be. There must be nothing small about him, nothing dead, nothing indifferent, nothing automatic or machine-like, nothing of hopelessness or despair, everything of joy, of assurance. He must be a fire so that his pupils may catch fire.[32]

Dr. Annie Besant followed Madam Montessori's vision of a teacher by saying that a teacher should fan the spark which is already within the student into a flame and not regard them as empty vessels to be filled in with knowledge from above. In an age of global crisis when all values are being broken, the coming generation has to face the great problem of formulating their own values. For discovering what is true, what is really valuable, a teacher has to first discover it for himself, and only then can he make his pupils discover truths for themselves and be happy in the real sense. The teacher while embarking on his mission has to first study the child, and he can do this only in an atmosphere of freedom, where the child is encouraged to express himself freely. Coercion does not help in the flowering of the faculties from within, leading to behaviour problems.

Dr. Annie Besant, therefore, laid stress on individual education where the child is not forced into a groove with other children who the teacher would think to be alike, whereas in truth they are different from each other. Also, Dr. Annie Besant gave her ideas on the essence of good teaching in the following words:

> Instead of having teachers who will have a certain number of children around them whom they teach and of whom they ask questions for the children to answer, you will have the children asking the teacher questions not what the teacher wants them to know, but what the children want to know themselves. That is the essence of good teaching...continually placing before the child all the things he wants to know and wants to learn, so that education may develop the faculties he has, instead of trying to force upon him the faculties he has not. If that were done the schools would become a place of joy and happiness; as it is we transfer them into forcing places[33].

A teacher should have knowledge of child psychology. This knowledge helps him to mould his lessons according to the child's tastes, capacities, growth, thereby leading to development of these faculties along desirable lines. The end of education is to develop the capacities in the individual to the fullest extent. Subjects of curriculum, methods, plans, systems, technique etc. are all subjected to this end.

Dr. Annie Besant had laid down the following requirements for a teacher:

The first is that "he shall be true to himself above all else"[34], he should discover truth for himself and rely on his own opinions instead of accepting others' opinions blindly.

The second is that he should fully realise that every part of the material of education is a means to truth and not truth in themselves. They are not the ultimate truths. He must realise that individuals in the world are exposed to a large number of pressures. There are a vast number of opinion makers who influence their thinking. There is more respect for authority. This mars creativity, originality. The teachers should realise that education is science, and just as science does not hold any dogmatic truths but accepts a thing to be true only when there is an objective proof or evidence, similarly education too must be kept away from authority, dogmas. Therefore, what is true for the teacher is not necessarily so for the students. The students should be helped to find their own truths, however varied they may be from the conventional or prevalent truths. By relating every subject to the pupil himself, the pupil discovers himself and this leads to individual growth. Though one cannot altogether do away with some system, method, one should not cling to a fixed pattern but mould his method to achieve the desired end.

The third is that the teacher should make the student realise that whatever effort the pupil makes towards understanding his self, never goes wasted. He may undergo failures, disappointments but all these are just a step forward towards the ultimate end of self-realisation. As Dr. Annie Besant said: "The object of education is not to shield from difficulty and trouble, from defeat and failure, but to vitalize in all possible ways the will to walk forward at whatever cost"³⁵.

Dr. Annie Besant believed order and freedom to be complementary terms, one supporting, enriching the other. Forcing students to do something or imposing one's authority on the students does not lead to a proper understanding of the student. Dr. Annie Besant propagated rules and laws which are nevertheless necessary in protecting the students from harming themselves out of their own ignorance, or from a lack of common sense, when their capacities have not developed to the full. As Arundale wrote in his article on *Theosophy And The Ideals Of Education*:

> Freedom is necessary for growth, and respectful understanding on the part of the elder. This is what we give. And the freedom must be ordered freedom, constructive freedom, freedom that does not mar the freedom of others, freedom that does not satisfy the lower nature at the expense of the higher³⁶.

The *fourth* is that the teacher should be responsible enough to discover the vocation of a pupil, and this Dr. Annie Besant felt, was greatly neglected in the current educational systems. For this the teacher has to understand each child by studying his tastes and temperaments, and also make the child realise his own strengths and weaknesses. Dr. Annie Besant stressed both theoretical and practical lessons to be imparted by the teacher. *The days of caste by birth are being replaced by the days of vocation by quality, which is the very foundation of the caste system.* The teacher has to discriminate at a very early age the type to which the child belongs.

To sum up, the teacher should have worldly as well as spiritual knowledge so that he can bring about the physical, mental, moral, spiritual development of the pupils. He should inspire the pupils to search, investigate, discover for themselves what is true and thereby give importance to self-experience. He should be able to encourage, stimulate and inspire his pupils. He should be self-dependent, a lover of freedom and originality. He should have knowledge of child psychology so that he can mould his lessons according to the child's tastes and temperaments. He should encourage healthy competition, social consciousness among his pupils and should make them understand that cooperation of the mind and heart is necessary for having a complete and rightful vision of life. The pupil is not just body, but contains within him that immortal soul, the realisation of which is the ultimate end of life, and as education is an expression of life itself, the entire educational process is directed towards attaining this truth, it is a means to attaining this truth and not an end in itself.

Student

Dr. Annie Besant being a serious scholar of ancient Hindu teachings and writings, had based her concept of the student on the lines of the ancient ashrama ideals that prevailed in India. She was convinced that the division of human life into the four stages, that is, Brahmacharya, Grihastha, Vanaprastha, Sanyas was an apt description of ideal human life. Dr. Annie Besant observed:

> The sowing is in the student life wherein the seed of knowledge is planted; the growing to maturity and the ripening is in the life of the householder; the harvesting is in the Vanaprastha stage, wherein active life is over; the grinding to make bread for human feeding is in the life of the Sanyasi, whose work is wholly for others, not for himself.[37]

The important ceremony of the "Upanayana", the giving of the sacred thread, opens the doors to the stage of the Brahmacharya and with it begins control and restraint. The triple thread is worn by the student symbolising control of the mind, control of speech, control of action. As Dr. Annie Besant held:

> The careless freedom of childhood belongs to the body, it is the freedom of the animal; now the child enters on the truly human life, the life of self-mastery and of self-control. If he is for a time to be in subjection to others, this is but to help him to become master of himself; the tender plant

is guarded and supported until it is strong enough to battle alone with the storms of life.[38]

Just as the teachers are required to possess certain qualities, similarly the student too has to possess the four great elements: service, study, simplicity, self-control. Each of these qualities refer to a particular branch of education, and each of these branches of education belong to a particular aspect of an individual's nature.

1. Service

The student's spiritual nature progresses through service, by self-surrender, by self-sacrifice, by abundantly giving out and utilising all his energies to the service of God, to the Guru and to the parents. This spiritual development is helped by religion. The student should be grateful to the Guru from whom he owes so much. It is the inspiration of the guru that stimulates him to seek truth for himself. He must, therefore, be obedient to the Guru, show him respect and trust him and should not resent the discipline he may impose. Likewise he should serve his parents with whatever he has.

2. Study

The second important quality for a student is to study. It refers to the development of the intellectual nature. All right thought, right desire, right action is part of this development. In the broader sense, all these are a service rendered to God and man. The aim of education is to draw out the students capacities and to train and discipline the different faculties. The student should, therefore, acquire knowledge instead of cramming, by exercising his own faculties of observation, reasoning and judgement. By doing so, all his faculties – spiritual, intellectual, moral, physical, are developed. By being far sighted, clear headed, with a broad vision the student can become a guide to himself and also be to those who need help and are not so developed.

3. Simplicity

The life of a Brahmacharya is simple and full of hardships.

He has to sacrifice the comforts of life, be indifferent to luxury, be active, swift, alert, and develop virtues like obedience, physical and moral courage, endurance, cooperation, steadfastness, control of temper, not taking hasty decisions.

4. Self-control

This quality of the Brahmacharya is necessary for physical development. The student has to control his mind, his senses and the body. Dr. Annie Besant believed that through the inculcation of Indian ideals, the student will develop a love for his country. Further, the fourfold scheme of education laying stress on the life of service, study, simplicity, self-control are necessary for an all round development of the student, while giving weightage to the four aspects of education – spiritual, intellectual, moral, physical.

Discipline

Being an exponent of the ancient Gurukul system and an idealist religious minded woman, Dr. Annie Besant believed that discipline was necessary for both the teacher and the student. When she laid down the requisites for a teacher that he should be true to himself, duty-bound, a man of self-control, full of love and warmth for others etc., then she appeared to be a supporter of impressionistic discipline. She said: "The child is not a child save in body. Let the teacher be above all else the friend of the soul and the adjustor of the body to the requirements of the soul, if he has the intuition to be able to find these out".[39] The teacher through his own example can help the pupils to find out the truth for themselves. Since Dr. Annie Besant believed the teacher to be a friend of the student's soul, she felt that whatever the teacher expected the student to become, he should first and foremost reflect it in his own behaviour. The student spontaneously acquires those aspects of behaviour that he sees in his teacher.

For students, Dr. Annie Besant laid stress on the observation of celibacy, and expected the students to follow the rules of the Brahmacharya stage. To be self-disciplined the student has to wear a triple thread denoting control over speech, thought and action. For bodily control, the student has to give away the comforts of life and lead a simple life, full of hardships like sleeping on the floor, wearing simple dress, eating simple food, and not touching any item of food without the guru's order etc. For discipline of the mind the student has to control his thoughts, emotions, and let only good thoughts enter his mind. He has to overcome the animal instincts and devote himself to the service of God and man. For this the students have to follow a regularised daily routine. He has to get up early in the morning, say his prayers, read the Vedas and Shastras and apply into practice whatever he has learnt from the religious books, like expressing his love through service to God, guru, parents and others around him. Service to God is rendered through prayers by expressing one's gratitude for whatever He has given, service to guru and parents through obedience, performing one's duties towards them and serving those around as they share the same life that flows from that one source; and to serve them is like serving God. Therefore Dr. Annie Besant mentioned "service" as the most important quality to be developed among the students. This virtue automatically brings about moral, mental, spiritual discipline.

One finds that Dr. Annie Besant laid stress on impressionistic discipline as well as self discipline. However she is against repressionistic form of discipline and also emancipatory discipline. She expounds freedom to be necessary for studying a child and also for letting his faculties to fully flower from within. If a child is not allowed to express himself freely, his innate urges get suppressed and they later on find expression in all types of undesirable ways which is the main cause of indiscipline in the existing educational systems.

Dr. Annie Besant wanted to discipline not only the students but the whole society through education. When a disciplined student steps into the society, he disciplines the entire society through his behaviour. She laid stress on the ancient ashrama ideal and the "varna" system. Dr. Annie Besant in her 1910 Anniversary Address to the Central Hindu College, had said :

The four divisions of life for instance, the Ashramas, are ever valid : the celibate student under training and discipline; the householder, carrying on the Nation's organization in commerce and industry; the elder, free from household cares, to discharge voluntarily all municipal and national duties and bring the experience of the household and the office to bear on the business of the state; the aged, to live in quiet retirement, counsellor at need, the patriarch of the national household, leaving on younger shoulders the burdens of the Nation, and not a clog on public life.[40]

The "varna" system also has its good points. According to this the Kshatriya, namely the government, the men in power, have no authority over the Brahman, the men of thought, who are entirely responsible for running the department of education as a whole, and are free to chalk out their plans in order to bring about the all round development of the students. In such an orderly type of an organisation, teachers attract students by the very force of their personality and knowledge, and send out the young people at the right time to discharge their responsibilities towards the society. The four groups, namely, Brahman, Kshatriya, Vaishya, Shudra represent the four definite psychological types, and the duties of each one is suited to its constitutional make-up. For instance, the duty of Brahman is to teach, the Kshatriya stands for power, the Vaishya to produce a large number of things and Shudra being the class of servers. The tragedy of the present educational system is that one cannot get the best workers into the teaching profession as they are put into other types of work due to shortage of proper workers.

Thus, the two systems, namely, the Ashrama ideal and "varna" system reflect order or discipline in society. Society is a disciplined organisation of individuals, and its effective working depends upon individuals who have the qualities of self discipline, self restraint, self sacrifice within themselves.

Women Education

The opening of schools for girls like the Central Hindu Girls' School at Varanasi and Theosophical High School, Adyar, show that Dr. Annie Besant was very much in favour of women education. By 1904, Dr. Annie Besant had turned her attention to women education and wrote on the topic, *The Education of Indian Girls*. During the medieval period, before the British rule in India, the Muslim rulers reigned the country for about six centuries and at that time the social condition of women was quite bad. Enough opportunities were not available to women for education and strict purdah system was generally enforced. During the British rule, separate schools were opened for girls, but in these, education was not imparted according to ancient Indian ideals. Therefore, Dr. Annie Besant laid stress on the opening of schools for girls where education was to be given according to the traditional ancient ideals.

The education of girls was very important according to Dr. Annie Besant as it was the girls who would be the future wives and mothers, those on whom the welfare of the family, and therefore to a large extent, the welfare of the nation depended. She cited the example of ancient India and said that at that time the girls were well versed in religion and read the great Indian epics, the Puranas, vernacular religious literature. She gave the names of certain scholarly women of the Vedic period like Gargi, the all-sacrificing spirituality of Maitreyi etc. Girls of such scholarly and spiritual bent of mind would make the Indian homes the centre of spirituality, the strength of the national religious life. Therefore, India should revive her past ancient glory and so educate her women that they become competent to fulfill the complex duties belonging to an Indian family life. She *severely opposed child marriages and laid down free education for girls upto 16 years of age. Her views on women education were rather traditional.* She felt that unlike the west where women compete with men to earn a livelihood, in India activities of women were still confined to the home, the joint family and so giving women a western education would be of little use to her. She laid down a brief period of school life for girls in which they must spend the time to the best of their advantage. Dr. Annie Besant remarked:

> If a woman knows medicine, if she knows the value of foodstuffs, if she knows how to deal with the difficulties of a large household, if she has learnt literature by listening to it, not necessarily by reading it, such a woman is a truly educated woman, whether or not she has passed any examinations or holds any University degrees. And that education was very largely spread among those aged grandmothers and great-grandmothers of the immediate past.[41]

Dr. Annie Besant believed that the national system of education for girls must be one which satisfies the national requirements; and India needed wives and mothers trained in moral virtues, wise and loving managers of the household, able teachers of children, useful advisors of their husbands, efficient nurses of the sick, rather than girl-graduates, trained for the learned professions and government jobs.

According to Dr. Annie Besant the main elements of women education comprised of :

(i) Religious And Moral Education

Every girl should know the fundamental principles of her religion. Characters of great religious leaders should be made known to them through stories. Even though they may belong to different religions or faiths, they should be explained about the essential unity of all religions. Every day the daily lessons of the school must begin with prayers. Girls should be encouraged to ask questions and ponder deeply into philosophical issues, so that opportunities may be given for bringing about women of great intellectual tastes and spiritual bent of mind. They should be made conscious of the prevailing ills of the society. The Indian ideal of womanhood should be conveyed to them through examples and moral instructions.

(ii) Literary Education

Under literary education, girls should be given knowledge

of the Vernacular and their mother-tongue, so that they be able to read and write in these languages. A spoken knowledge of some Vernacular other than one's own may be given, if there is sufficient time for that lesson. Under classical language, knowledge of Sanskrit or Arabic or Persian, according to the girl's religion, is necessary. In doing so, they will understand and learn the ancient religious scriptures. As a second language, knowledge of English is essential, for then they can communicate with their English friends and be able to acquire knowledge of literature, science and technology of other countries.

(iii) Scientific Education

Under this girls should have knowledge of the hygiene, value of food items, cooking, simple medicines like 'first aid' and nursing the sick, adequate arithmetic necessary for keeping of accounts or for calculating quantities and prices.

(iv) Artistic Education

Girls should be given training in some art so that they can usefully utilise their leisure time instead of wasting their precious hours in gossip and useless entertainments. It also enhances their aesthetic sense and brings about a certain dignity and refinement in their behaviour. For instance, they can be coached in music, drawing, painting, needle-work etc. However, the pupil's interest should be kept in mind while selecting any particular art for studies. For girls living in villages, knowledge of some crafts and skills that can be useful in their areas can be given.

Apart from these physical exercises, games should be incorporated in the curriculum for girls and they should be made to realise the importance of dignity of labour. Dr. Annie Besant believed that unless the women of India were educated properly, the nation could not progress. She appealed to the educated women social workers to help in educating the adult working women, to provide them with study material, to educate them in household sanitation and nourishing diet and to enable them to utilise their leisure hours usefully. She felt that men and women should cooperate for the upliftment of India and give each other due respect and status in society. Women should be encouraged to put in practice in everyday life, useful things that they learn from philosophy, literature, science, art.

Mass Education

Dr. Annie Besant believed that inequality can be reduced through education. In the August 1928, *The Theosophist*, Dr. Annie Besant wrote:

> One great rule of our social order should be: Every child who is born into a civilized nation will be certain of the circumstances which bring out of him to the full every faculty which he has brought with him into the world. That is the cornerstone on which I would found the new Society... Education should be free, paid for out of the taxes.[42]

She laid down a detailed system of national education for India. She believed that nation too was like a human being with a body and possessing a divine life within.

Like a human being, the life of a nation was divided into four parts-soul, mind, emotion, body. Religion is a nation's soul, education being its mind or thought, society being its emotion and politics its body. Therefore to build up India, all the four organs should be given sufficient opportunity to develop. It was due to this outlook that she felt that each individual of a nation should get the opportunity to develop all that he possessed from within. Education should not be given with the sole motive to read, write and count, but with the intention of self employment and not just securing a job. Therefore in her national system of education she wanted the villagers to take up training in such vocations which they could skillfully adopt. She wanted them to become familiar with the geographical location and climate of their respective areas so that they could choose the vocation which would be suitable to those surroundings. *Villagers should have knowledge of soil composition, crops, climate affecting those crops, farm equipments, gardening,* knowledge of seed, carpentry, iron mongery, cattle-rearing and hygiene.

Education for the masses involves complex issues as it is concerned with the whole nation. Therefore, responsibility of this branch of education should lie with social welfare bodies who can help in forming cooperative societies and panchayats everywhere. In villages this can be entrusted to village panchayats. Cooperative movements can be started in the villages. Through such an arrangement education can be delivered in a quick and simple way. She believed that if village panchayats organised themselves into cooperative panchayats, one can add one or two more men to look after its educational department. One can have such type of an organisation in small areas, and the cost of it will not be a burden to any particular community. Village panchayats can be formed everywhere, whether the cooperative movement is there or not, and this saves time and money as the case can be looked into by such men of the village who know the problems of that area. With the establishment of such type of self-government that grows upwards in graded ranks and the setting up of cooperative societies, the problem of mass education can be dealt with at all levels, which otherwise would be too widespread to be solved totally by the government in an effective way. Education can be made free by putting the management department of the panchayat into the job of collecting taxes from the public for elementary education. According to Dr. Annie Besant the growth of educational management has to be *from the smallest village level upwards rather than downwards from the government level.*

To quote her own words:

Indian education can only live when it is again rooted in the very soil of the Indian Village. Restore the Village Panchayat or small Republic- that truest of all democracies, give back to the village its land and its power to deal with its own internal problems, and again will there grow up generations of young Indians trained in an education of the hand, the heart, and the head, through which will be expressed the heritage of the Motherland.[43]

References

1. Builder Of New India, p. 448.
2. idem.
3. The Besant Spirit, Volume II, p. 16.
4. Theosophy And World Problems, p. 17.
5. Of Pattern Of Things To Come : Annie Besant's Vision Of The Future Of India, p.10.
6. Annie Besant On Right Citizenship, pp. 18-19.
7. The Besant Spirit, Volume II, p. 56.
8. Principles Of Education, p. 3.
9. ibid., p.6.
10. ibid., p.7.
11. The Besant Spirit, Volume II, p.106.
12. ibid., p.30.
13. Builder Of New India, pp. 389-390.
14. ibid., pp. 425-426.
15. Wake Up India, April-June 2000, p.5.
16. The Besant Spirit, Volume VII, pp. 3-4.
17. Of Pattern Of Things To Come: Annie Besant's Vision Of The Future Of India, p. 2.
18. Builder Of New India, p 288.
19. Annie Besant On Right Citizenship, p. 22.
20. ibid., p. 25.
21. ibid., p. 83.
22. The Besant Spirit, Volume VII, pp. 15-16.
23. Annie Besant On Right Citizenship, p. 12.
24. Of Pattern Of Things To Come: Annie Besant's Vision Of The Future Of India, p.5.
25. Education-Basis Of National Life (pamphlet), p.6.
26. ibid., p.4.
27. Wake Up India, April-June 2000, p.7.
28. The Besant Spirit, Volume II, p.118.
29. Education In The Light Of Theosophy (pamphlet), p. 15

30. Annie Besant On Right Citizenship, pp. 20-21.
31. Principles Of Education, pp. 22-23.
32. The Besant Spirit, Volume II, p.68.
33. Builder Of New India, pp. 448-449.
34. The Besant Spirit, Volume II, p. 68.
35. ibid., pp.71-72.
36. Theosophy And The Ideals Of Education, p. 101.
37. The Besant Spirit, Volume II, p. 78.
38. ibid., p. 81.
39. ibid., p. 72.
40. The Besant Spirit, Volume VII, p. 95.
41. Builder Of New India, p. 417.
42. ibid., p.449.
43. ibid., p. 39.

4
[B] Educational Ideas of J. Krishnamurti

Krishnamurti's educational thoughts flow from his philosophy almost indiscernibly, and mingle with it in a subtle manner at all stages. This renders conceptualisation and appreciation difficult. For purposes of elucidation Krishnamurti's educational ideas have been discussed under the following heads:

I   Preamble
II Some Problems of Contemporary Education
III Krishnamurti's Vision of Education
IV Goals of Education
V   Curriculum
VI Methods of Teaching
VII School, Educator and Student
VIII Discipline

Preamble

Krishnamurti perceives the problem of existence as the fragmentation of human consciousness. The continuous struggle, the endless work, the misery, the sorrow, the confusion, that one goes through in life has actually no meaning. One finds chaos, disorder everywhere. In the outer world there is war, violence, competition, exploitation, division, inequality, crime, ecological disorder, over population, all the harmful effects of industrialisation and so on. In the inner world, that is, within man himself, there is loneliness, despair, jealousy, anger and all other forms of disorder. To escape from the inner chaos man tries to seek some form of permanent happiness and thus gets caught up in some belief, religion, dogma or tries to cultivate humility, though within him there is total disorder. According to Krishnamurti life is a total unitary movement in which there is no division, in which everything is included and, therefore, these aspects of life are to be perceived as one total process. It is the self, the thought that has created this division. It is the fragmented approach to life that has brought about this disorder. Therefore Krishnamurti laid stress on a *holistic vision of life and saw the supreme goal of education to be a radical transformation of human mind and thereby of society.*

Radical transformation of the mind or a real education

Real education is concerned with a transformation in the human mind, a creative revolution in the psyche to enable man to have a holistic approach to life. This is also the key to Krishnamurti's philosophy.

Krishnamurti distinguishes between change and revolution. Change implies the alteration of "what is" into "what should be" which is a reaction of the known, and is therefore a modified form of the known. Reform is considered by him to be a change within the pattern of society, that is, a modified continuity of the same structure in a different framework. Any type of reform begets further reform, it only brings more misery, more destruction. Total transformation or radical transformation is not a change which is the modified continuity of the existing order. Attempts are being made all over the world to bring about a new social order by the slow process of legislation and political action; but such actions are fragmentary as they are based on some ideology. Such changes, according to Krishnamurti, are designed to protect the stability of the state, redressing at the same time the sufferings of the people at large to some extent. It can never totally dissolve the problems of human relationship. Krishnamurti clarified:

> Surely, if political action is separate from the total action of man, if it does not take into consideration his whole being, his psychological as well as physical state, then it is mischievous, bringing further confusion and misery, and this is exactly what is taking place in the world at the present time.[1]

Therefore, action based on idea or ideology is partial; even though it may affect the individual outwardly, it cannot bring about a revolution. Man must be liberated from the fundamental ignorance, the illusion of a separate self in order to enable him not to accumulate, not to possess beyond his needs, not to be greedy, envious, and to seek self expansion. The reformists try to bring about order when they are often themselves corrupt. Living a chaotic, corrupt life, they try to bring order in the world, whereas this is disorder, the result of the fragmentation of consciousness. What requires to be changed is not merely the arrangement, social, political or economic organisation of society, but the bases of such organisations which are oriented and centred around the self and can cause exploitation of society.

Revolution according to Krishnamurti is a psychological revolution–a psychological transformation of the structure of consciousness, a mutation of the mind, the thing that is being transformed totally is the human mind.

This begets the question on what the mind is. The mind is made up of what one has learnt so far, the memory of all one's little experiences, what one has been told by one's parents, by one's teachers, the things that one has read in books or observed in the world around. It is the mind that observes, discerns, that learns, that cultivates so called virtues, that communicates ideas, that has desires and fears. It not only exists on the surface, but also in the deep layers of the unconscious in which is hidden the radical ambitions, motives, urges, conflicts.

Man has attached tremendous importance to thought. The books, the social, political, economic, religious, moral structure, the relationship between man and man, between man and nature, between man and the things created by man are all based on thought. It is thought that brings about all types of confusion, disorder, conflict by creating divisions. "We have been raised in this modern world to do and think what we want. And we have developed this antagonism to anybody who says, 'this is different'".² Man is always wanting, always lacking, always trying to fulfill, to achieve, to become, to be this and not to be that, the "me" is always trying to express itself. It is this self-centred activity of the "me" that creates isolations, divisions, that always tries to seek security in its relationships and such relationships create the society of rifts, chaos, disorder.

Any type of desire only strengthens the self and when one tries to arrive at a result one only operates within the walls of the prison created by the mind, the self. Even the desire to become a great saint or to reduce oneself to a cipher are but desires of the self, and therefore strengthen the self. Therefore, no activity which is geared to a desire for becoming can rid the mind of the self. In Krishnamurti's words:

> The problem of the "me" and the "mine" is one in which we are all involved. It is really the only problem we have, and we are everlastingly talking about it in different ways; sometimes in terms of fulfilment and sometimes in terms of frustration, sorrow. The desire to have lasting happiness, the fear of dying or of losing property, the pleasure of being flattered, the resentment of being insulted, the quarrelling over your god and my god, your way and my way – the mind is ceaselessly occupied with all this and nothing else. It may pretend to seek peace, to feel brotherly, to be good, to love, but behind this screen of words it continues to be caught up in the conflict of the "me" and the "mine", and that is why it creates the problems which you bring up every morning in different words.³

A mind that understands the whole structure of acquisitiveness, of greed, of ambition and breaks away from it, is in constant revolution. Such an action may create a new culture, a better social order, a different world, but the mind is not concerned with that creation. Its only concern is to discover what is true and it is the movement of truth that creates a new world, not the mind which is in revolt against society.

Such a transformation takes place in the whole of the mind and not only in thought. *Thought is only a result and not the source.* There must be a radical transformation in the mind which is the source of the conflicts and divisions. Mere modification of the result, that is, thought, cannot free man from his anxieties, fears, worries, conflicts. It cannot lead to the development of the whole human being. The goal of education is to deal with this vital change, that is, development of a fresh new mind which will destroy the old ways of thought, totally free the mind from working within the narrow groove of tradition, beliefs, ideology and habits.

Thus, the concern of education, according to Krishnamurti, "is to free the mind of the me."[4]

Holistic approach in relation to education

This psychological revolution as pointed out by Krishnamurti has often been questioned by his audiences. They have often asked Krishnamurti how a psychological revolution brought about in the minds of a few, lead to a better world, a new world. To this, Krishnamurti had replied that first *you* undergo this transformation and then think about this. According to Krishnamurti, there is no distinction between the "I" and the "we". He has often repeated the phrase: "The world is you, you are the world."[5]

In a dialogue with Professor Allan. W. Anderson in 1974, Krishnamurti pointed out to the implications of the word "whole" and "individual", saying that the word "whole" meant "not only sanity, health but also holy"[6], and the word "individual" signified "undivided, indivisible, in himself."[7] Therefore, the individual is actually a human being, "who is totally, completely whole, sane, healthy and therefore holy."[8] Unfortunately, human beings all over the world lead the same miserable life of conflict and division, torn by their various problems of life. Thus they lead a divided, fragmented, contradictory life.

The society, the world is the result of one's relationship to others. The various events in the world have been brought about by the actions, feelings, thoughts of man. Whichever culture man is born in, he is a product of that culture, and that culture in turn creates the world. *The outer is the result of the inner and the inner is the product of the outer.* There is no division between the two. Hence *there is no difference between the individual and society.* The human being is the society, he is the collective as well as the individual, he is the one who brings about this world of divisions, chaos, conflict, wars. Therefore, change in the very psyche, in the minds of human beings is essential. "...It isn't society first, or the individual first, it is human change which will transform society. They are not two separate things."⁹

Here one can draw a distinction between the basic principles of communism and Krishnamurti's views. Communism believes in change in society and thereby in man, whereas with Krishnamurti it is the other way round, communism believes in state control as the supreme authority and the proposition that those who do the work must directly receive the profits of their labours.

Krishnamurti held that the human mind, conditioned as it was, would have to be re-conditioned to accept the totalitarian doctrine, and that reshaping and re-patterning human thinking and behaviour, did not free the individual from ego, competition, conflict.

Krishnamurti is concerned with the total development of man, with the totality of life. He says that it is the daily living that one has to explore-the daily living with its agony, with its boredom, with its loneliness, with its fear, with its unseeable future. To do that one has to look within oneself and one cannot go within oneself, without understanding the outward movement of life, that is, understanding one's relationship to the world. The outward movement of life is the same as the inward movement:

> The outward movement is like the ebb, the tide that goes out, and the inward movement is like the flow, the same tide that comes in. If the two-the outer and the inner-are

divorced, if the two are separated, then you have conflict, you have misery.[10]

A mind that has undergone radical transformation will view life holistically, which includes not only acquiring of technical knowledge but a deep understanding of the whole problem of living, the whole existence of mankind. Such a human being feels responsible for everything– responsible for education, responsible for politics, responsible for the way he lives, responsible for his behaviour. When a human being feels this total responsibility – that he is responsible for the chaos, the misery, the violence in the world then he looks at the problem as it is, as a fact and does not translate the problem according to his conditioning. Then the fact itself will have the answer, one does not have to bring the answer to it. One sees that the problem is self-created, that the person and the problem are one, that they are not two separate processes. Then the human being responds to the problem, to the challenge adequately, completely without the "me" and the past operating. The educational goals of Krishnamurti flow from this philosophy. In order to understand these goals better it is appropriate to first consider some problems of contemporary education and Krishnamurti's vision of education.

Some problems of contemporary education

Today educational structures all over the world are being questioned. There is a growing realisation that the existing educational systems have created a gulf between the individual and the complex, contemporary society. The ecological crisis, the increasing poverty, the continuous violence are forcing man to face the realities of the human situation. Man is disappointed with political, religious and intellectual leadership. Humanity is living on the brink of the third world war, which is capable of complete destruction of civilisation. The major challenges facing mankind today have been reviewed by several learned persons, notably P. Krishna[11] and maybe briefly mentioned as:

a) Divisive tendencies

The human beings all over the world are divided into

groups, racial, national, religious, linguistic, economic, political, professional, and each individual identifies oneself with one's group and is ready to defend the ideology of that group or to die for it, or to fight for that ideology and stand against anyone who deviates from that ideology. This has become the greatest single cause of insecurity today, leading to violence such as wars, terrorism, rioting and militancy. A person who has received the highest form of contemporary education appears to be no different from the illiterate in this sphere of activity. Contemporary education is certainly deficient in solving such present day problems, prompting us to seriously consider an altogether different vision of education. Such a vision becomes all the more important in view of the fact that the dangers caused by fissiparous tendencies in the past have magnified enormously, and one can visualise the awesome picture of total annihilation of mankind by nuclear weapons etc.

b) Environmental crisis

Pollution, destruction of the earth's resources and environment is another major problem facing mankind today. Depletion of the ozone layer, air pollution near ground level, acid precipitation, heedless exploitation of depletable ground water supplies, pollution of rivers, lakes, deforestation, soil erosion, nuclear fall-outs, enormous pressure of exploding population, genetic engineering and experiments in the laboratories of biochemists, are threatening distortion of the sources of life itself. The basic cause of most of these is the lack of right relationship between man and nature - man treats nature as a resource to be exploited, he does not return to nature what he takes. The rapid pace of development in science and technology has given a boost to industrialisation. Industrialised and technologically advanced nations are competing for economic supremacy and trying to monopolise international trade. In the past, man, animal and nature lived in harmony and perfect balance. By today's pace of industrialisation and the consequent genesis of pollution, the exploitations of nature's wealth, man has created for himself a situation where he stands on the brink of disaster. Even children are regarded as a commodity of the family, keeping in mind the wealth they will bring to the family by earning a profitable livelihood. Nature is regarded as something meant for the use of mankind, man being the masters.

c) Inequitable distribution of power

To be able to do things forcefully and effectively may be described as power. There is no inherent evil in this. The evil lies in the wrong use of power, where this is used for exploiting the weak, where this is used to stifle voices of protest, where this is used to impose one's will on the other, or where on a larger scale this is used in the form of dictatorship. It is evident that power could prove to be a dangerous weapon of destruction, unless human beings are able to radically transform their relationship with power. The right use of power must therefore, be an important concern of education. The relationship of the "me" and "the other" and its proper appreciation would inculcate a spirit of equality, friendship and democracy, where improper use of power becomes redundant.

d) Dissensions within the family

The family is a fundamental unit of human society. It exercises the most profound influence over its members. Its influence in infancy determines the personality structure of the individual. Psychologists like Freud and Erickson have proved that a child exhibits the same characteristics and mental tendencies in adult age which he acquires in the family. Today the size and functions of the family have been reduced. The striking problem that confronts the modern family is its instability. The marriage bonds have weakened. The worst sufferers are the children and consequently juvenile crime, delinquency is on the rise. This implies that one's outlook on life is not right and there is a need to find out where mankind has gone wrong.

e) Prejudiced and rigid outlook

The human mind over the years is being conditioned to respect nationalistic ideals, religions, systems, beliefs, leaders and hero myths, searching to find a place of security. This creates further antagonism, insecurity. This in turn leads to a static society, incapable of moving ahead. It is therefore, of paramount importance to create an inquiring mind, a mind that is willing to undertake the task of discovering for itself what is true, not only in the field of science, but also in social, moral and religious questions, in fact, in every aspect of life.

According to the Report to UNESCO of the International Commission on Education for the 21st Century (*Delors Commission*), the problems facing education today are, "the global vs. the local; the universal vs. the individual; tradition vs. modernity; long-term considerations vs. short term; the need for competition vs. the concern for equality; and the 'age-old tension between the spiritual and the material'."[12] There has been a tremendous advancement in science and technology, but man is very much bound by individualism leading to compartmentalisation at various levels on various considerations.

Looking into the problems facing mankind one must stop to ask oneself what it is that one has done wrong. In today's world, can success be equated with content and happiness, or is it usually related to material possessions? What is the present vision of education? When one ponders deeply into the aims of present day education, one finds that, regardless of a few minor differences, education all over the world is only concerned with the acquisition of knowledge, skill in order to enable one to earn his livelihood, to produce a human being who is productive but devoid of love and compassion. It makes one imitative, worship authority, encourages comparison, enables one to build an image about oneself which inevitably leads to a hurt mind, a violent mind, does not makes one sensitive to the whole movement of life, to Nature and thus makes one more and more artificial, superficial, destructive. As Krishnamurti puts it that one never thinks, "let's find a way of living which is whole and therefore healthy, sane and holy"[13]

Krishnamurti's Vision of Education

Keeping in mind the drawbacks of present day education,

Krishnamurti regards "educating the mind differently as the function of education."[14]

To educate the mind differently entails the question of *"how"* – that is, by what method one can educate the mind differently. In his educational thoughts, Krishnamurti has not prescribed any rigid methods. He holds that rigid methods destroy spontaneity. They make one imitative. To pursue a rigid method implies struggling after an ideal, of "what should be" instead of the "what is", thus preventing an understanding of "what is" and thereby creating conflict, and all inward conflicts have their outward manifestation in society. Krishnamurti said:

> Any method which classifies children according to temperament and aptitude merely emphasizes their difference; it breeds antagonism, encourages division in society and does not help to develop integrated human beings. It is obvious that no method or system can provide the right kind of education, and strict adherence to a particular method indicates sluggishness on the part of the educator. As long as education is based on cut and dried principles, it can turn out men and women who are efficient, but it cannot produce creative human beings.[15]

From this one can conclude that the technique does not create the vision. It is the vision that creates the technique. Here one can see a *difference between Montessori Method and J. Krishnamurti's vision.*

Both Madam Montessori and J. Krishnamurti have pointed out the need for educating the whole human being and not merely the intellect. Based on this notion of education, Madam Montessori stressed self-education and developed certain techniques, materials like "didactic apparatus" which controlled every error and the child was able to correct himself. Though Madam Montessori had advocated the spontaneous development of the child through full liberty, which meant the absence of any restraint that would mar or stifle the inborn power of the child, her emphasis on "didactic apparatus" can make a teacher who does not share her vision use this incorrectly, thereby inculcating a sense of competition, lack of sensitivity and imagination among the children, thus blurring the very vision of educating the whole human being and not merely the intellect. These very features set her approach apart from that of Krishnamurti.

At this stage it will not be out of place to mention some thoughts of Ivan Illich who expressed radical opposition to the conservative type of schooling. In his view education ought to be a liberating force in which the individual explores, creates and freely uses his initiative and judgement to develop his faculties and potentialities to the maximum. No matter how modern teaching implements are or how professionally skilled the teacher may be, the pupils are nevertheless held in captivity as regards the curriculum which they have to follow and the hours which they have to spend in school. They are made to pursue rewards and recognitions like certifications, diplomas and degrees. He regards schools as repressive institutions which indoctrinate pupils, stifle creativity and imagination and enforce conformity and stupefy students into accepting the interests of the powerful. The pupil has little or no control over what he learns or how he learns it and he has called this "the hidden curriculum" where an authoritarian teaching regime makes him follow fixed teaching plans. Real learning according to him is not the result of instructions but of direct and free involvement by the individual in every part of the learning process. According to him "most learning requires no teaching". The apparent similarity to this extent with Krishnamurti's educational ideas will become clear as they are discussed later. It is pertinent to discuss at this stage some salient features of "Deschooling". The basis of this idea is that teaching skills come best from those who practice those skills in daily life, such as learning carpentry from a carpenter or learning to speak a dialect by living with those who speak it. Education should not be a commodity which would prepare the student for a mindless role and to whom passive consumption of goods and services of industrial society becomes an end in itself. Trained to accept that those in authority know what is best for him, the individual becomes dependent on the directives of the government's bureaucratic organisations and professional bodies. Illich maintains that such a mind set cannot provide the framework for human happiness and fulfilment. By putting forward the concept of Deschooling society, Illich has suggested abolition of the present system of education. However unlike Krishnamurti he is not averse to a teacher or instructor and not against methods. As alternatives, he suggests, firstly, 'Skill Exchanges'. As has been indicated earlier, instructors teach skills they use in daily lives to others. Secondly, Illich proposes 'Learning Webs'. This consists of individuals with similar interests who meet around the problem chosen and defined by their own initiative and proceed on the basis of creative and exploratory learning. At this stage it may be mentioned that both "skill exchanges" and "learning webs" imply dissemination of something known by a person or group of persons to students or people anxious to learn from them. At a later stage "Dialogues" of J. Krishnamurti offer an interesting comparison as these imply beginning from not knowing to the development of a subject on which people express views, and learn at the same time.

Main educational concerns of Krishnamurti were factors that would enable a person to live life creatively. These concerns have been extensively discussed by many learned persons, notably P. Krishna of Rajghat School. They conclude that life has vast dimensions much larger than can be measured. Life cannot be measured in economic terms such as the gross national product or per capita income. It entails a quality which encompasses love and compassion while being rational and intelligent. This involves a spirit of enquiry, recognising that every movement has a sense of beauty, sensitivity, humility, and above all, an awareness of limitations of intellect. Krishnamurti's emphasis was on human development rather than economic development, on the happiness of the individuals as a whole in which physical well being and comfort were small but nevertheless necessary parts. *The crux of this is to work with joy avoiding comparison with others.* Krishnamurti's educational ideas emphasise that children should be taught to work for the joy of working, not for reward, as otherwise reward would be the only stimulus for work, and absence of reward would lead to boredom. Enjoying everything that one does, without concern for the result is the art of living. Such a person works creatively and not for personal ambition. In essence the teacher and the taught should together work for such a meaningful type of living, there being no scope for any didactic apparatus in such a relationship.

According to Krishnamurti, in order to change radically, the individual cannot work within the old framework of discipline imposed from outside. Therefore, he has to be totally free from any form of compulsion, discipline, system, or method. To help the individual to be free from his own self-centred activity with all its fears and conflicts, and to discover the truth, there has to be no method, because when one sticks to a method, then the method becomes more important, and the human being who has to be educated is measured and classified according to the method. *Freedom is at the beginning, not at the end, and the various forms of discipline only guarantee freedom at the end.* One has to be free from any form of compulsion, authority in order to enquire into the truth of any system. If there is no freedom at the very beginning then one is bound to end up with a system and therefore, with a mind which is incapable of subtlety, swiftness, sensitivity. In the absence of any method, what should be the values which one should try to imbibe through education? This brings one to the goals of education.

Goals of Education

As mentioned earlier, the supreme goal of education according to Krishnamurti, is the transformation of the human mind and thereby of society. From this supreme goal certain other sub-goals ramify. The holistic approach of Krishnamurti precludes any watertight compartmentalisation of the sub-goals. These have been enlisted for purposes of discussion, bearing in mind that there are many overlapping areas.

1. To help one to look at oneself in the right manner:

Radical transformation of the human mind is not possible unless one learns to look at oneself in the right manner, to accept one's capacities and limitations with complete humility, without pretence, with complete scientific detachment.

One is only educated to learn about the outer world and to somehow deal with its problems. Therefore one grows up knowing so much about the external world, but being ignorant of the activities of one's mind, desires, ambitions, values, outlook on life. An individual may be skilled in his job, but he may not know that the pursuit of pleasure does not lead to happiness. If he knows this, the pursuit of pleasure drops away of its own accord, without any effort or control. It is due to one's ignorance about oneself that one cultivates virtues, practises austerities. Practising generosity, simplicity, non-violence, does not in itself transform the consciousness of man, does not produce kindness in oneself, for then it becomes something to be achieved, some means through which one seeks self satisfaction, it is a process of becoming, and though one practises all these virtues outwardly, he remains violent within. It is only by observing the causes of violence in oneself and removing them, not through will or effort, but through understanding that there is an end to violence. Goodness must be spontaneous, otherwise it is not goodness. Any change in the outward behaviour of man, brought about through effort, compulsion, discipline, conformity, imitation, does not imply a true change in the consciousness of man and is therefore, superficial and contradictory. Through observing, inquiring, investigating, one realises that there is essentially no difference between one human being and the other, and that all share the same problems of fear, insecurity, all lead the same miserable life of conflict, violence, sorrow, loneliness. It is ignorance that gives so much importance to such superficial differences between human beings like the difference in belief, in wealth, in knowledge, in ability, whereas every individual shares the same human consciousness. All these superficial differences are only acquisitions, and if one strips a man of his wealth, status, possession, knowledge, and looks into his consciousness, one finds there is no real difference between one human being and the other.

Real education is not merely to pass examinations or to write down what one has learnt by heart, "but to help you to see the walls of this prison in which the mind is held."[16] Any type of reform brought about in the society is like bettering the conditions within the prison, and it does not solve the problem. The reformers never say, "Break through the walls of tradition and authority, shake off the conditioning that holds the mind".[17] It is the mind that has created the present civilisation. Freedom lies outside the walls of the prison, outside the centre created by the mind, outside the pattern of society. In order to be free of that pattern, to go outside the walls of the prison, one has to know the whole content of one's mind. In short, a great deal of awareness is needed. This is brought about by internal realisation of consciousness, not through pursuit of gods, gurus and doctrines.

2. *To bring about a non-mechanistic way of life, which will give equal emphasis to the scientific and the religious quests:*

All through human history, the two great quests of mankind have been the scientific quest and the religious quest. The scientific quest is a search for understanding the laws of nature, and through such understanding, acquiring power to harness nature. The religious quest is a search for understanding man's relationship with himself, with humanity, with the infinite, with death, with God, with the universe. Due to a fragmented approach to life man lays emphasis on specialisation in a particular field, whether it is scientific, philosophical, religious, business, technological, neglecting the vast field of life. One gives more emphasis to the scientific quest and neglects the religious in the educational process. Consequently, education of today makes man more and more mechanical. It is concerned with the acquisition of knowledge, with specialisation in a particular career. It is due to the tremendous scientific and technological progress that certain tasks which were earlier being done by the human mind are now being performed by machines like computers, calculators, and other electronic equipments. This has given man more leisure. In order to escape from this mechanistic way of life man takes recourse to all forms of diversions. Sometimes he turns towards the religious quest in the hope of discovering something new, but the religions too have become insufficient, immature, mechanistic. They emphasise the so called inner world according to their own traditions, ideas, beliefs, dogmas. They function within their own narrow ideas, identify themselves with their beliefs, and thus become more and more isolated and self centred. It is here, that Krishnamurti asks one to bring about a non-mechanistic way of life, to create a mind that is simultaneously scientific and religious. Such a mind will have the clarity, objectivity, precision, fearlessness, impartiality, and at the same time has a sense of beauty, wonder, sensitivity, humility, love, compassion and an awareness of the limitations of the intellect.

3. *To rise above narrow nationalism and to consider the good of the world as a whole:*

Looking to the present state of chaos, one needs to have a global mind through education. Krishnamurti believed that both nationalism and organised religion are fundamentally divisive, as the sense of identity they foster is exclusive. The goals of education must give priority to the earth rather than the nation. All human beings are the citizens of one world and must feel this. What affects one part affects the whole. It is essential to have a mind that feels for the whole world and not just one country. One must learn to live in harmony with one's environment, with the natural surroundings. This comes about when one feels totally responsible for the present state for chaos.

It is ignorance that divides one man from another, not the difference of wealth, possessions, status, caste, colour or creed. Krishnamurti has frequently repeated the phrase "You are the world" in his dialogues and talks. Instead of spending large sums of money on armaments, Krishnamurti's vision of education looks beyond national interests to secure the interests of the planet and in the process also secure the interests of marginalised peoples within the nation.

4. *To improve the quality of the human being, rather than trade or commerce:*

The word 'education' implies to train, to nourish, to rear.

Rearing implies a number of things including guiding, trimming, disciplining and grooming for the harmonious development of total personality. The meaning encompasses the mental, the moral, the physical, the emotional, the spiritual, in fact, all facets that lead to the development of the whole human being, and endows education with the responsibility for gearing optimum growth in all these facets.

Education of today regards individuals as raw materials for economic progress. To live creatively and happily education should cease to be concerned with merely producing specialists. Some amount of specialisation may be inevitable, but one is a human being first and engineer, doctor, lawyer, scientist afterwards. Specialisation must not be at the cost of understanding what it means to live fully. Human beings differ in their abilities, but are not superior or inferior. They must be respected irrespective of their abilities. This results in flowering of the human mind.

5. To develop a mind that seeks for itself unfettered by theories propounded by others:

Education is not merely the imbibing of knowledge, information, technique, but the cultivation of an inquiring mind, a mind that is not concerned with bringing about a change or reform in the social structure, but a mind that is totally devoid of authority, totally free, that is not afraid, that has no division, no preconceived notions from which to begin, that lives in order to find out for itself what is true, that is learning all the time, learning from everything day to day life offers. Such a mind is a light to itself. Such a mind will penetrate into the question of what is religion, and not merely accept the established religions with their beliefs and rituals. According to Krishnamurti such a mind is a religious mind. As Krishnamurti put it: "Religious education in the true sense is to encourage the child to understand his own relationship to people, to things, to nature."[18] A religious mind, as Krishnamurti pointed out, perceives the false, and by the very seeing of the false, there is the negation of the false. To bring about an inquiring mind, an atmosphere of freedom is essential. Freedom helps one to find out for oneself what is true.

To live freely and without fear is the function of education, and to create such an atmosphere in which there is no fear requires a great deal of thinking on the part of the students, teachers, parents. If inquiry is suppressed by past knowledge, memory, information, by the authority and experience of another, learning becomes a repetitive, imitative, mechanical process devoid of anything new. The child must be free to make mistakes and learn without the fear of being rebuked. His mind would then be rational, flexible, and not attached to an opinion or belief.

6. To bring about co-operation and not competition

According to Krishnamurti, learning implies the love of understanding and of doing a thing for itself. Learning is not brought about through comparison. "Comparison brings about frustration and merely encourages envy, which is called competion."[19] A mind that compares is an immature mind. It is only capable of measuring, and comparing who or what is doing better everyday and, therefore, wastes its energy. To understand the movement of life which has no beginning and no end, one must have freedom and therefore, energy, which is not to be wasted by creating a space between oneself and the observer and the thing he observes, which in reality is his despair. The moment one compares there is a compromise with "what is" and, therefore, an enormous wastage of energy. Comparison denies love, denies the understanding of oneself. It is measurement between oneself and another, between what one has been and what one will be, and this measurement leads to the genesis of divisive tendencies and conflicts in life. One has to learn for the sake of learning and not for the sake of success. With great success there is also great sorrow. If one begins to understand what one is without trying to change it then what one is, undergoes a transformation. Krishnamurti said, "I think one can live in this world anonymously, completely unknown, without being famous, ambitious, cruel. One can live very happily when no importance is given to the self; and this also is part of right education".[20]

Reward and punishment, whatever be their form, only make the mind repetitive, imitative, dull. Giving medals and cups in matches shows who can run faster than the other, who is victorious. But the question should be directed to whether the players enjoyed the game. Giving rewards enables the child to work for a reward and not for the joy of working. Such a mind is encouraged to work only when there is a reward, otherwise it remains in a state of boredom. One must enjoy everything one does, regardless of the results it offers. The sense of competition that the present day education emphasises leads to envy, jealousy and rivalry, and brings about division and destroys love and friendship. In his talk with Allan Anderson, Krishnamurti said:

> Sir, don't you think that our minds are so commercial, unless I get a reward I won't do a thing. And one's mind lives in the market-place. I give you this, you give me that. We are so used to commercialism, both spiritually and physically, that we don't do anything without a reward, without gaining something, without a purpose. It must all be exchange, not a gift, but exchange. I give you this and you give me that; I torture myself religiously and God must come to me. It's all a matter of commerce.[21]

One must understand that all species on earth are inter-related and inter-dependent. Co-operation, a sense of sharing, is to be encouraged through education, so that one works not for personal gain or reward but for the welfare of the whole community.

Children should be made to realise that perfection and not greatness should be the aim. When a child does a thing as perfectly as it is possible for him to do, then he will feel happy and that happiness is the creative state-not merely doing something better than another. The best thing that a child could see is the beauty of a life which is completely selfless. One cannot teach this to the child but one can make the child feel the harmony that it brings in the lives of everybody, to make him discover the disharmony that ambition, the feelings of "great" and "small" bring. The words "great" and "small" do not exist in Nature. In Nature there is just perfection. There is no struggle between one tree and another for greatness. One is as perfect as the other. The words "great" and "small" are creations of the mind, of thought, and this in turn creates conflict and chaos between human beings. Krishnamurti is in favour of the removal of all hierarchical distinctions in the school. The head of an institution is on exactly the same level as the smallest child in the school. There is difference on the basis of function but not on the basis of status.

7. To bring about a learning mind and not an acquisitive mind:

According to Krishnamurti there are two forms of learning. One is acquiring and accumulating a great deal of knowledge through experience, books, education which may be used in skilful action. Another is that form of learning in which one never accumulates, never registers anything apart from that which is absolutely necessary. In the first form, the brain acquires, accumulates knowledge, stores it up and acts according to that stored information. In the second form one only registers that which is absolutely necessary whilst the rest is allowed to drain off. The mind is not cluttered and influenced by accumulated psychological reactions. There is no psychological building up of the "one", that is, giving importance to one's name, one's experience, one's opinions and conclusions. The mind may use a discovery through knowledge and technique, but the discovery itself is something original, which suddenly bursts upon the mind irrespective of knowledge; and it is this explosion of discovery that is essential. As Krishnamurti once cited the example of a great mathematician:

> A great mathematician once told of how he had been working on a problem for a number of days and could not find the solution. One morning, as he was taking a walk as usual, he suddenly saw the answer. What had happened? His mind, being quiet, was free to look at the problem and the problem itself revealed the answer. One must have information about a problem, but the mind must be free of that information to find the answer.[22]

8. To bring about the awakening of intelligence

The awakening of intelligence is more important than

the cultivation of memory. The whole cannot be understood through the part, and mere efficiency cannot understand the whole of life. To find out the areas where knowledge and technical skill are necessary and where they are not, and even harmful, requires intelligence, the development of which is brought about through education. Intelligence comes about when one is in a state of constant learning, never concluding.

What can be taught is limited but learning is endless. The greatest things in life cannot be taught, but can be learnt. The feeling of love, respect, beauty, friendship, co-operation, cannot be taught, but like sensitivity, can be awakened; and this is an essential aspect of intelligence. The ability to discern for oneself what is true and what is false is also intelligence. It is important to bring about a mind that neither accepts nor rejects an opinion or a view too readily, but stays with the question. While talking to the students and staff at Brockwood Park, Krishnamurti said:

> Education being not merely the acquisition of technical knowledge, but the understanding with sensitivity and intelligence, of the whole problem of living - in which is included both death, love, sex, meditation, relationship and also conflict, anger, brutality and all the rest of it - that is the whole structure of human existence.[23]

9. To bring about flowering of the human mind:

Each individual is unique and therefore, opportunities must be given through education to let him fully flower. It is only in freedom that one can learn. Krishnamurti wrote: "The flowering of the mind can take place only when there is clear perception, objective, non-personal, unburdened by any kind of imposition upon it. It is not what to think but how to think clearly."[24]

10. To bring about creative human beings:

According to Krishnamurti creativeness can come only through understanding the total process of oneself.

Creativeness is different from capacity. To paint pictures, to write poems and become famous is not creativity. It is merely the capacity to express an idea which the public likes or dislikes. For Krishnamurti, creativeness is a state in which the self is absent. When one accepts what one is, without condemnation or justification, then in that understanding of "what is" there is action, and that action is creative reality, creative intelligence, which alone brings happiness, tranquility, beauty, love.

To be sensitive is to love. By being sensitive to the whole movement of life, by being sensitive to everything around, to the birds, animals, people–one's behaviour naturally becomes open, unselfish, caring. The moment one is sensitive there is a spontaneous desire not to destroy, not to hurt. There is "the complete abandonment of the 'me', the self, the ego."[25] The mind of such a human being is totally devoid of self-fulfilment, disappointment, achievement. Such a mind is totally silent, quiet, has no hurt, no image, no desires. It is creative in itself. As life has no pillar to hold on to, but is like a river endlessly moving on, a mind that is creative has no resting place.

To conclude, for holistic development of the individual it is important that there is a deep understanding of all the faculties of the human being and that they are developed in a balanced way. It implies that in order to cultivate one faculty one must not impair another. This means one cannot use fear and punishment to make students work harder, since that destroys inquiry, intelligence, initiative. When one educates not for economic development but for human development, then one must be concerned with the happiness of the individuals as a whole, in which physical well-being and comfort are a small but necessary part. Far more important is the ability to work with joy, without comparing oneself with others. If one is insensitive, there is constant boredom and to escape from it, a constant pursuit of pleasure.

To learn the art of living there is no set method. It comes with one's understanding of life and of oneself. Intellectually adults may know more than the child but in the larger issues of life one faces the same difficulties as the child–

problems of boredom, worry, fear, habit, conflict, desire, frustration and violence. One needs to learn along with the child, not merely teach, that is, both the teacher and the student should learn together.

If one cannot use reward or punishment, or competition to make students learn, then what other incentive should be used to do so? It is only by making education a joyous process, by making education lively and interesting for the child. To broaden the child's vision the beauty of life should be revealed. According to Krishnamurti:

> Seeing what is happening around the world, will you in your daily life, find out something that is really true, really beautiful, holy, sacred? If you have that, then politeness has meaning, then consideration has meaning, has depth. Then you can do anything you like, there will always be that perfume. How will you come to this? It is part of your education, not only to learn mathematics, but also to find this out.[26]

In this kind of holistic education, ethics begin with the perception that the ideal, the "what should be", is irrelevant. Krishnamurti held that wherever there is fragmentation there is bound to be conflict. True morality is not just a matter of creating good habits, but a question of bringing about true individuality, where the individual while learning the various skills, disciplines, learns about the psychological realm and is thus able to relate his inner human nature to his outer action and deeds. Self knowledge and the discovery of moral action by each individual lead to a responsible education, an education that is in itself ethical. It is in discovering the capacity to be alone, independent and non-divisive, that one begins to learn to live together, and a measure of wholeness enters into one's relationships.

Curriculum

No specific books have been prescribed by Krishnamurti in the form of a curriculum. Krishnamurti is concerned with reading the text of life. To learn in the real sense is to learn throughout one's life and there is no special teacher to learn from. One learns from everything in life and, therefore, there is no guide, no philosopher, no guru. What is important is to be one's own teacher and pupil. It is essential to be in a state of constant learning. A teacher comes into being when one stops to explore the whole process of life. However, such a teacher is not a dynamic teacher but a static one. Such a pupil and such a teacher are both academically dead human beings.

An extract from the article *Birthday Tribute To J. Krishnamurti – His Life Was Filled With Beauty And Fragrance* by Radha Burnier, the International President of the Theosophical Society illustrates:

> Krishnaji did give a little indication of what his beloved was. "My beloved is the open skies, the flower, every human being." In his life this was the truth. This was not just a grand statement; his was a life which at no moment showed any thought of something being important and others not; a feeling that some are low and others high. He said it was his practice to listen to everybody always. "I desired to learn from the gardener, from the pariah (untouchable), from my neighbour, from my friend, from everything that could teach, in order to become one with the Beloved." To the end, he listened carefully with attention and with affection, to everyone, without distinction of high or low. He responded with what might have appeared to others as impractised generosity. Watching, listening to the scientist, the intellectual, the politician, everybody, he saw into the core of things, as a reading of his *Commentaries On Living* and other writings makes clear".[27]

The art of learning is a continuous process in daily life, not a process of addition or gathering. One cannot store up learning and then act from that storehouse. Learning is the capacity to think clearly without distortion, to start from facts and not from beliefs and ideals. It implies the love of understanding and the love of doing a thing for itself.

According to Krishnamurti school is a place where one learns about the wholeness of life. Whilst academic excellence is absolutely necessary, real learning is not limited to that. To celebrate the joy of learning is to take learning out of the classroom and into life. It means to awaken the child to discover that the knowledge and information they gain are only a small part of their education and that they are learning from life and not just from books.

Methods of Teaching

Methods in the case of Krishnamurti are in fact an absence of methods (Non Methods) or at best creating a milieu, conducive to the right type of education since according to Krishnamurti the latter is subtly imbibed from the atmosphere of the school or campus. It has been opined by several persons who have known and understood Krishnamurti's idea of education that his concern was to bring about a kind of education that would enable the new generation capable of dealing with the issues of life as a whole. He was concerned with the establishment of right relationship to everything. Seeing the disruptive tendencies like nationalism, organised religions, creating chaos in the world, new kinds of schools and new philosophies emerge, but all the while one runs away from the fact that one does not know what to do to change either oneself or the world. Education today fails to deal with the source of this fragmentation and chaos. Krishnamurti has, therefore, appealed to the educators to see the harm that conventional education does, by deeply conditioning the mind. To take up a wholly new and different kind of education, he asked the educator to be a scientist of awareness, to be one who develops sensitivity and intelligence in the child. For this he has not prescribed any set method. At the very beginning, Krishnamurti questions the wisdom of seeking a method which would tell one how this problem is to be solved. The mind that is interested in the "how" is obviously not interested in the "what", that is, the mind that is concerned with how to arrive at a conclusion is not concerned with what the problem is. To Krishnamurti solution lies in understanding the problem. A method involves a goal to be achieved, and that requires effort or will, an action based on idea, and this mars spontaneous discovery; then the mind starts functioning in grooves according to a fixed pattern of action.

(1) The milieu of observation

School is a place where the teacher and the student explore together, not only the outer world but also their inner world of thinking, feeling, and their own behaviour. By so observing they begin to discover their own conditioning and how it distorts their thinking. Therefore, Krishnamurti stressed the importance of observation where the teacher and the student learn to observe the world not from any particular point of view or conclusion, without necessarily being told what to do.

R.E. Mark Lee, expressing views on Krishnamurti's advice to teachers, has written in his article *The Art Of Listening, Looking And Learning* that to foster attention, Krishnamurti has asked the teachers:

> ...to help the child to listen to noises far away and then those that are closer. Exercises can be developed with minimum teacher prompts, to make a child's ears sensitive and alert to ambient noise and the sound of the phenomenal and natural world. Listen far away, listen closer, and closer still, until finally the ear can hear the beating of the heart. This can be generalized to an unconscious level, where a child is listening while paying attention, but is not drawn away by the sounds that are not relevant at the moment. It is when the child is not attentive to all the sounds that he gets distracted by others, by loud noises, and allows the noises to divert attention.[28]

A child who has been raised to listen with attention will grow up to grasp the true meaning of things, to hear a lie and discern truth. Real listening dispels the false.

(2) The milieu of relating subject to the child or the "me"

Krishnamurti has asked the teachers to imagine how the child's interest can be affected if it is realised that the child is a product of geography and history and has a hand in shaping them. For instance, Alok Mathur in his article *From Local Studies Towards A Global Outlook – A New Geography For 12 Year Olds'* has described vividly how he has put in practice the thoughts of Krishnamurti regarding teaching of the child. He says: "Obtaining detailed local maps where available and using them in the geography class, is a sure way to developing map skills. It would also arouse interest in the multitude of natural or man-made features that constitute the local region".[29] At a later stage he has mentioned, "Again examples of settlements from the local region and the kind of impact felt on surrounding landscapes may be given. In this context, issues of urbanization, rural-urban migration over exploitation of resources, pollution, degradation as well as regeneration of lands may be touched upon through examples".[30] Similarly, science can be taught in a way that the spirit of questioning and observing is awakened.

Krishnamurti also asked the teachers to find ways and means of relating the subject to the "me". For this he tells the teachers not to start teaching the subject as soon as they enter the classroom but to start some conversation on some larger issues before teaching the subject, or to ask the class to carefully listen to sounds or observe closely some form. This would help gather a certain quality of attention, which would then be directed to the subject. Krishnamurti said:

> A sharing, taking a journey together, and therefore, an infinite care on both sides; which means: how is the teacher to teach mathematics, or whatever it is to the student and yet teach it in such a way that you awaken the intelligence in the child, not simply about mathematics? And how do you bring this act of teaching in which there is order–because mathematics means order, the highest form of order is mathematics – how will you convey to the student in teaching mathematics that there should be order in his life? Not order according to a blueprint. That's not order.[31]

Krishnamurti had once said that if he were a house master, he would build a close relationship with each child and be concerned with everything–how one walked, talked, behaved and so on. He would ask the child in a friendly way to keep her body and her room scrupulously clean. That type of responsibility wakes one up to his own life style. Also, love for nature like caring for plants, going for nature walks, learning about birds and insects, must be developed in the children. He felt that nature, through space and silence, affects the mind in unknown ways, and brings about a certain resilience and strength.

(3) The milieu of sharing

Sharing as a part of the learning process involves thinking together and learning together at all levels, between student and student, student and teacher, teacher and teacher, student, teacher, parents and with everything else such as nature and another person. Schools are places of learning, of sharing where both the teacher and the student learn together, where both see together what actually is without interpreting it according to each other's conditioning, to see together one must be free to observe, free to listen and this freedom can only come about where there is love. As Krishnamurti put it:

> To see together – which is sharing together – we must both of us see; not agree or disagree, but see together what actually is; not interpret it according to my conditioning or your conditioning; but see together what it is. And to see together one must be free to observe, one must be free to listen. That means to have no prejudice. Then only, with that quality of love, is there sharing.[32]

In this context it may be mentioned that students differ in speed and ability to learn subjects. An attempt to tackle this situation has been made at some schools of Krishnamurti where classes of mixed age group have been introduced. Krishnamurti was of the view that children learn better by observing older children and, therefore the younger segment would learn faster. The criticism that the older segment would suffer in the process may be nullified by making this segment the junior one in another class.

Sensitivity and openness can be brought about in the child where there is the feeling of togetherness, of love, when the child feels that he can be what he is, without being compelled in any way. Then the child does what he likes, but in what he likes, he finds out what is the right thing to do. Krishnamurti has explained the meaning of the word "communion". He says it means "to communicate, to be in touch, to transmit a certain feeling, to share it, not only at the verbal level, but also at an intellectual level and also to feel much more deeply, subtly."[33] It is this communion that is essential, when the teacher and the student psychologically feel themselves to be at the same level, and not the teacher as someone superior, imparting information to the students authoritatively.

This feeling of togetherness has to be there among the teachers comprising the school. Therefore, Krishnamurti insisted on a core group that would jointly take decisions regarding the school. This is how a feeling of total responsibility can be brought about. Total responsibility comes about when one responds adequately to the situation in which one is placed. It is "the feeling of being at home".[34] A home is a place where there is no fear, where one is open, happy, creative, active, where there is mutual trust, generosity. If each member of the school has this feeling of total responsibility in his heart, each will then create an atmosphere of absolute order without criticising or being mindful of what the other does.

(4) The milieu of dialogues:

Krishnamurti said that people should not blindly accept or reject what he said but that they should look at it, listen to it, experiment with it, question its relevance in their life and work, discuss their views freely. He felt that intense and open dialogues were to be encouraged in the schools.

The dictionary defines "Dialogue" as a conversation between two or more people and also as an exchange of opinions or ideas. Krishnamurti gave it a much deeper meaning and pointed out its importance as a means of discovering the truth. A dialogue is very different from what one normally calls a discussion or debate in education. A discussion is usually between people who hold definite points of view and who wish to emphasise each other's points of view or compare their outlooks. They begin with knowledge, encourage an exchange of ideas and end in more knowledge and more ideas. Since it is confined to ideas and knowledge, it does not lead to the realisation of a deeper truth. On the other hand, a dialogue as a mode of discovering the truth begins with "not knowing". In not knowing, not identifying oneself with any point of view or ideology, not trying to convince each other of anything, all are prepared to investigate the truth together. It is like two friends deeply interested in examining any issue in life and coming to a deeper understanding of it. As Prof. P. Krishna has written in his article *Dialogue As Inquiry*:

> Krishnaji likened a dialogue to a game of tennis in which the question is like the ball tossed from one court to another, each player returning it with his comment or observation. This goes on till both the players disappear and the ball is suspended in mid air. That means the observers (participants) with their particular knowledge, view points, opinions etc. disappear and there is only observation of the issue taking place.[35]

Dialogues are held on many issues. For instance, in the teaching-learning process, the teacher, most often, is at the centre of the classroom, initiating every activity in the classroom and students becoming passive recipients. However, some questions come out of this situation. Was it possible to create a situation where children could also do work based on their own initiative? Could there be a design that freed the teacher from being the centre of attention, so that he or she could focus more on observing the student and his or her learning process? There are study centres which form an integral part of each school. In these study centres, teachers, parents and students deeply inquire into the fundamental questions of life. Krishnamurti himself felt that learning and inquiry should go side by side otherwise nothing new would be born. A description of the study centres has already been given in the *Life And Times Of J. Krishnamurti*. Here it can be said that without a meditative quality, this type of an educational work may not be of very great significance. This work requires continual inquiry and not some quick agreement or disagreement with the teaching. One must persistently and critically examine it from different directions and actually test it in one's daily life.

School, Educator and Student

This is a line-extension of methods of teaching where an attempt has been made to identify the extent of participation of the school, educator and the student, in what is an intricate and indeed inseparable interaction.

School

Krishnamurti thought of schools as a place where the teacher and the taught would live and learn together, where a spirit of equality prevailed, where function of the students and the teachers would differ but not their status; where there was no scope of fear of being rebuked for mistakes in the student's mind. Krishnamurti believed that in such an environment a true spirit of enquiry in the child's mind, unstifled and unbridled, would be aroused by awakening his sensitivities, thereby enabling him discern the right from the wrong, a quality that develops by learning from one's mistakes. Krishnamurti stated that from the ancient times, man had always looked for something beyond the materialistic world, something immeasurable, something sacred, something timeless that cannot be destroyed by circumstances, by pressures, by human actions, and the intention of the schools was to investigate into this. He saw the schools as a *"sacred place" where deep religious enquiry can be pursued.*

Krishnamurti was concerned with creating a deeply religious atmosphere in the schools. His view of religious atmosphere does not mean cultivating moral values pertaining to kindness, co-operation, love, respect etc. without grasping their true meaning. Nor does it mean following a guru or a teacher in order to illumine oneself spiritually. To understand nature and be close to it, to appreciate what was happening from moment to moment and to closely observe these movements of nature by keeping an open mind and letting all that nature has to say flow into it freely without any bias or prejudice, and to understand oneself in relationship to all this, was being religious. He held that the school should view everything else, such as academic learning and acquisition of skills, as secondary to this primary purpose.

Krishnamurti held that schools are places where the student pursues academic excellence, learns about the importance of knowledge as well as its limitations. He is helped to observe the outer and the inner world. Apart from academic excellence, great stress is laid on co-curricular activities. The teacher and the student relate to each other without fear. Together they try to explore not only what has happened historically but also what is happening now in the outer world, as well as their own ways of thinking, behaviour and motivation. Working, functioning and living in nature demands and alertness of the senses and the ability of looking afresh at what is going on around one. It is of crucial importance for youngsters to develop, a different quality of relationship with the natural world. Nature moves in different ways, never fixed, always new, revealing deeper patterns and principles. To engage fully with this involves looking and listening, an agile body and a quiet non-judging and yet intensely alert mind. This takes time to develop and most children come upon this gradually if given some playful guidance and space. All of this is of value, wherever one is, in manual work, academic study and so on. Moreover, close touch with nature gives opportunities for direct experience and first hand awareness, which is often ignored in education, especially as the child grows older. Contact with the primary gives way to abstract learning, often with detrimental results leading to disconnected, disoriented learning. This is one of the reasons why youngsters grow up with no sympathy for their immediate environment, nor for things or people. Therefore, in these schools gardening, nature walks, bird watching, quiet assemblies are encouraged in order to establish a relationship with the earth and all life on it. By listening to the songs of the birds, the music of the winds, children learn to listen with care to another human being.

Bringing about a quiet mind, a silent mind, *a sense of leisure and space,* is another function of the school. Space itself can create a sense of order and in relationships one needs to look and ask if he has the right space, which means not to be identified with another or be extremely critical of one another. Does one have time to look at each other or is he too occupied with agendas, activities, studies? Therefore, Krishnamurti emphasised the importance of self knowledge, learning to observe oneself in the right manner. According to Krishnamurti:

> A school is a place where the educator and the one to be educated are both learning... Leisure means a mind that is not constantly occupied with something, with a problem, with some enjoyment, with some sensory pleasure. Leisure implies a mind that has infinite time to observe: observe what is happening around one and what is happening within oneself; to have leisure to listen, to see clearly. Leisure implies freedom which is generally translated as doing as one desires, which is what human beings are doing anyhow, causing a great deal of mischief, misery and confusion. Leisure implies a quiet mind, no motive and so no direction. This is leisure and it is only in this state that the mind can learn, not only science, history, mathematics but also about oneself; and one can learn about oneself in relationship.[36]

This is in concurrence with dictionary meaning of "scholé", which means leisure, and from which the word "school" is derived. Space itself can create a sense of order and so the design of the campus, houses, classroom etc. reflect this in the schools set up by Krishnamurti; overcrowding is avoided in the schools. There are two types of spaces – outer physical space and inner psychological space. The outer space of a person or society becomes an expression of the inner space. The outer space in its own way influences the inner space of the user.

Sounding a word of caution regarding computers, Krishnamurti said:

> ... When technology and computers with robots dominate

and become part of our daily life, then what is to happen to the human brain which has been active so far in outward and physical struggle? Will the brain then become atrophied, working only a couple of hours or more? When relationship is between machine and machine, what is to happen to the quality and vitality of the brain? Will it seek some form of entertainment, religious or otherwise, or will it allow itself to explore the vast recesses of one's being? The industry of entertainment is gathering more and more strength and very little human energy and capacity is turned inwardly, so if we are not aware, the entertainment world is going to conquer us.[37]

To help one to unfold is an important function of the school, and this can come about with the *right relationship between the teacher and the student*. Most children come from homes where they have been educated to respect status and so when they come to schools they are used to that fear which respecting status entails. Therefore, it is necessary that in the schools a real atmosphere of freedom be created; and that can come about when there is function without status, when there is a feeling of equality.

To enable the schools to function democratically, Krishnamurti insisted on setting up a core group that would take consensual decisions through dialogue and discussion. There was to be no authority in psychological sense of the higher and the lower. There was to be only functional authority and not authority pertaining to status. The schools were to move in a direction decided collectively and not by a single person. Moreover, every teacher is given the opportunity to openly voice his or her feelings, in case of disagreement, without repercussions and to learn about responsibility, working together. In the absence of an open atmosphere, doubts and fears crop up and occupy psychological space and mar an institution's functioning. Functional authority had to be exercised with competence as no school can establish order and efficiency without it. Only in exceptional cases would the head of the school take overriding decisions.

The school was not to be *just an organisation*. What made the place fresh, alive and different was *the spirit of self-awareness* on the part of the individuals. Krishnamurti had tried hard to *convey the feeling that all the Krishnamurti Schools are one*. A school does not become "one school" by creating a common authority at the top, but through a meeting of minds. Living, working and questioning together, a oneness, a feeling of learning together can grow from grass-roots upwards. Krishnamurti, in his writings and discussion with teachers, has indicated that the school is for the teacher and the student to learn together. The operative word is "together". The schools are thus *experiments in living*. The word "experiment" itself implies that a campus life of Krishnamurti Schools are still in a trial stage, where the educational philosophy of Krishnamurti is being collectively interpreted through dialogues, and practised to the extent that is possible under constraints of prevailing circumstances of the day. The goal of attainment of academic excellence is the impact of an eventual confluence with the conventional pattern of education, as also is the spirit of competition which this would invariably create, inspite of a philosophy to the contrary. Competitive matches which are held with other schools is yet another example of such a situation.

In a way, one can say that the foremost function of the schools is to see that the *coming generation is not ruined by the superficiality and mechanistic way of life of the modern civilisation*. One can conclude with the following extract from the speech delivered by Achyut Patwardhan:

> Once I was in Rishi Valley school and I was asked, "What is it that this school is trying to do?" and I said, "It is a very simple thing. We tell our students here, 'You may be intelligent or not intelligent, clever or not clever, but with whatever brain you have, for God's sake, don't destroy yourself.'"[38]

Educator

A right kind of school according to Krishnamurti has a two fold aspect of education, that is, *learning not only* in the field of the conceptual but also learning in the field of "what we are". While it is one of the educator's functions to impart a good intellectual training to the student, this function is contained within the wider responsibility of educating "to be what one is". This can be done only to the extent to which the educator has applied himself to the function of inquiring deeply into the workings of his own mind, to look without prejudice to whatever is happening outside as well as to the nature of his own thoughts, of "being what one is".

There must be a *cultivation of the totality of the mind and not merely the giving of information*. In the process of imparting knowledge, the educator has to invite discussion and encourage the students to inquire and to think independently. Such clarity of mind leads to the development of character. According to Krishnamurti : "To think for oneself, to find out what is true and stand by it, without being influenced, whatever life may bring of misery or happiness-that is what builds character."[39]

A teacher who knows that a mind free of authority is a free mind, that disorder is caused by fragmentation of thought, will be able to make the child understand this. So an atmosphere of "learning together" has to be created. As Krishnamurti put it:

> I say it is possible when the teacher, the educator realize that he is hurt and the child is hurt, when he is aware of his hurt and he is aware also of the child's hurt, then the relationship changes. Then he will in the very act of teaching mathematics, or whatever it is, not only be freeing himself from his hurt, but also helping the child to be free of his hurt. After all, that is education: to see that I, who am the teacher, am hurt, I have gone through agonies of hurt and I want to help that child not to be hurt and he has come to the school being hurt. So I say, "All right, my friend, we both are hurt, let us see, let's help each other to wipe it out".[40]

In the *relationship of learning together* between teacher and student *the feeling of "total responsibility"* for what is *happening in the world has to be communicated to the child by the teacher and he cannot do so–unless he feels this "total responsibility" himself.*

It is natural that different children respond differently and at their own respective pace. So finding the common and distinctly different factors, and reaching out to them accordingly with patience and affection is very important on the part of the teacher. The entire schooling system of today is based on comparisons and competition. Parents, teachers, students are all aware of the position in class. This breeds fear, jealousy and anger, although, being better in a subject or skill does not make a better human being. Educators must be convinced of the futility of comparisons. They must be concerned with the total development of the child, helping him to realise his own highest and fullest capacity, not that capacity which the educator has in mind as an ideal. The spirit of comparison prevents the full flowering of the individual. *Motivating the child through love and not through competition* should be hinted at. Love must begin with the educator. As Krishnamurti pointed out:

> So the educator must be concerned from the very beginning with this quality of love, which is humility, gentleness, consideration, patience and courtesy. Modesty and courtesy are innate in the man of right education; he is considerate to all, including the animals and plants, and this is reflected in his behaviour and manner of talking.[41]

Sensitivity and openness can be aroused in the child by the educator when he sees that the child feels at ease in school. This *sense of security is different from dependency.* Dependency comes about when the educator feels himself superior to the child and becomes authoritative. That leads to fear and conformity. By feeling secure in his relationship with his teachers the child feels that he can be what he is, without being compelled in any way, the child will do what he likes but in the very act of doing what he likes he will find out what is true morality, he will find out the right thing to do. His behaviour will be open and he will be receptive to his teacher's suggestions.

In the cultivation of an inquiring mind, the teacher's emphasis should not be on concentration but on attention. Forcing, or urging the child to concentrate narrows down listening, and attention. Concentration does not result in attention, rather it creates in the mind a habit of excluding sounds, and hence stifles attention. Attention is a state of inquiry not based on self advancement or selfish motives. Attention is not something that can be learnt but a teacher can help to awaken it in the student by creating an atmosphere of freedom where the student is free to focus his mind at any moment on any given subject, and it will not be brought about through the compulsive urge of acquisition or achievement.

Since the educator is concerned with the total development of the human being, it is essential for the educator that all facets of the pupil should be given due importance. *Cultivation of an inquiring mind and emotional sensitivity should go side by side with the development of a healthy body.* For this the educator has to see that the student keeps his body clean, takes regular exercises, has the right type of food and adequate sleep. Also, the educator must understand the consequences of sexual urge and should be able from the very beginning to meet the child's natural curiosity. The educator must be able to make the pupil realise that no problem is separate from the self. The problem of sex arises when there is the lack of affection in oneself. This makes one seek affection from others. If one has deep affection in oneself for everything –not just one, but for everything – love for the trees, the birds, the flowers, the fields and for human beings then this becomes a totally different issue. It is due to lack of affection in oneself that one craves for affection from others which finds expression in sexual relationships, constant companionships, which in turn breeds fear, jealousy, anger. Therefore, Krishnamurti has recommended co-education. He believes that it is love that really matters. To just separate boys and girls will not solve the problem if there is no love. A mind that is merely concerned with itself, its own activities, remains ugly, limited, incapable of understanding what beauty is. To be religious is to be sensitive to reality, to the whole of existence and without this sensitivity there is no beauty, no love, no goodness.

Every teacher is concerned with all aspects of the school. The school offers a place for the teachers to work and grow. Dialogues are held frequently where innumerable issues are discussed. Attempts are made not to find an easy agreement but to find an honestly discussed solution. The key question is, how do teachers share and together attend to the education of the young and to the needs of the school? *Teachers are required to openly discuss their doubts* and apprehensions so that no misunderstandings arise. Every teacher regards the school as his home and is not expected to do only that task that has been allocated to him. A staff member may also be assigned non-teaching responsibilities.

Krishnamurti's views on the right type of an educator will remain incomplete without emphasis on two aspects. Firstly, *it is the relationship that counts.* It is the relationship that provides the teachers with the right perspective for adopting appropriate strategies in his educational process. Secondly, *teaching is not limited to a profession.* It is something much deeper. By making teachers undergo training, one limits teaching to a profession, that one can be "trained" to teach. A trained teacher may be equipped with the necessary knowledge and direction that is essential, but not with creating an atmosphere of freedom that is required for making the students feel safe to explore and without which there can be no learning on his part. If a teacher feels that teaching is something dynamic and that he cannot start from a fixed point and proceed to a definite point, he will begin with this vision and then use the techniques that he finds suitable. For this, dedicated teachers are required who will awaken the capacity in themselves to meet the students at their level of understanding and take them beyond.

Student

The aim of education at present is reduced to producing efficient and capable young people who can feed the various professions to maintain the existing order of society, which is increasingly being identified with the government that employs the majority of the intellectuals. Education is therefore a means of earning a livelihood and becoming good citizens in order to be a part of the bureaucratic world conforming to the pattern of a consumerist society, incapable of functioning freely, and therefore seeking to merge with sectarianism or religious groups in quest of security. The present system of education is inadequate in producing persons of intelligence and spiritual insight.

Krishnamurti asks the students to be *discontented with everything*. To be discontented means to be *dissatisfied with one's prejudices, beliefs, fears without seeking a result through discontent*. Let this flame of discontent burn within each student, so that finally this leads to clarity, a questioning, inquiring mind, and it is this inquiring mind which can find out what it is to be sensitive, what is love, what is meditation. Krishnamurti observed:

> While we are young, it is the time to be discontented, not only with ourselves but also with the things about us. We should learn to think clearly and without bias, so as not to be inwardly dependent and fearful. Independence is not for that coloured section of the map which we call our country, but for ourselves as individuals; and though outwardly we are dependent on one another, this mutual dependence does not become cruel or oppressive if inwardly we are free of the craving for power, position and authority.[42]

Krishnamurti asks the students to develop an *integrated outlook on life*. Integrity does not come by putting the parts together, but there is integrity if the process of fragmentation is fully comprehended. This implies self-knowledge and enquiring into oneself. One must *observe oneself in relationship*, that is, how one thinks, feels, behaves without condemning, justifying, concluding. As in a dialogue, one begins without entertaining any opinion, ideology, religious belief, and is only committed to acquiring a deeper understanding of the situation, similarly one can live all one's life with the *mind in a state of continuing dialogue – a dialogue with oneself, with others around us and with*

Nature. It is a mind that is not attached to any opinions or religious beliefs, one that is not seeking satisfaction or judging on the basis of its likes and dislikes. To such a mind, every experience, every talk, every book is a source of deep question.

Krishnamurti tells the students *to feel very seriously about everything*. When one is serious about everything, little things do not matter in life. When men grow older, they lose this feeling of sympathy, tenderness for others. Therefore, they want to fill their inward emptiness with all sorts of entertainments like drinks, drugs, inventing religions. These religions too become full of superstitions, rituals. "Religion born of fear becomes ugly superstition".[43] Again, to understand fear as a fact one has to go into it deeply, till the fact itself reveals what is involved in it. The moment one is totally devoid of fear, one becomes sensitive to everything and sensitivity means love.

From this one concludes that the *crux of Krishnamurti's advice* to students would be to *keep an open mind*, free of fear, with a keen sense of inquiry and sustained stamina leading to discovery, to be unbiased by information or images which may have been formed earlier. To *inculcate a spirit of love* so that he does not fall prey to competition and therefore, a false sense of fear.

Discipline

The human mind is perpetually harassed by several thoughts that are destructive and ought to be suppressed. Success in this area is in common parlance known as discipline. Such destructive thoughts, of which desire can be taken as an example, is a form of energy always waiting to be unleashed. Convention demands that this energy is completely stifled at the appropriate time. A person who is able to do this is said to be disciplined. Nevertheless in the process of this suppression there is bound to be resistance, fear and conflict with the authority that imposes such a control, be it from within oneself or some outside authority. Therefore, Krishnamurti is against organised religions, prayers, yoga, imposed self discipline, that lead to concentration. The exclusive concentration on an idea makes one choose that idea because it seems to be true, noble, good as it gives one pleasure, reward or achievement. One wastes his energy in the process of choosing an idea and discarding the other, and is thus incapable of bringing about a transformation in one's relationship. The various forms of discipline, of control only strengthen the self further. Krishnamurti observed: "If change is through conformity to a pattern projected by the mind, through a reasonable, well studied plan, then it is still within the field of the mind".[44].

To make this clear Krishnamurti has given the example of non-violence. He said that there are individuals who in order to get rid of violence, have used a concept, an ideal called non-violence. With this ideal they feel they could effectively combat the cult of violence. To get rid of this trait of violence one has to understand in depth what it exactly means. This enables the person to have a realistic vision of the problem and he is therefore able to combat it more effectively by taking recourse to appropriate measures which need not necessarily be choosing the opposite, such as non-violence for violence. One's conditioned mind, one's way of life, the whole structure of society in which one lives, prevents one from looking at the fact, and be entirely free from it immediately, spontaneously.

However, this does not mean that Krishnamurti advocated indiscipline. As a matter of fact he is for a higher discipline, the discipline that is not brought about by an external or an internal authority through fear; but which is inherent in the understanding of life as a whole and of one's relationship to it. *For this one needs freedom. It is in freedom that one can learn. By understanding one's conditioning, one's fixed opinions or judgements, one is free to observe, how disorder is brought about through conditioning, through fragmented approach to life and with this understanding one rejects this disorder. Then there comes about a deep sense of inner order which is true discipline. True discipline comes with "choiceless awareness",* without a desire to quickly form an opinion or come to some conclusion, with the discernment of what is true and what is false, and the false drops away by itself without any effort or will. So, discipline, according to Krishnamurti does not mean the cultivation of virtue, but the discernment of distractions, which of its own accord, naturally and spontaneously, brings virtue into being.

To Krishnamurti the various forms of discipline only guarantee freedom at the end, but freedom is at the beginning and not at the end. One has to be free of any system, belief, any form of compulsion in order to inquire into the truth of any system. Krishnamurti spoke of discipline that increases human energy not that discipline that thwarts it. When one is really interested in something and gives his complete being to it, that energy creates its own being. Krishnamurti pointed out: "As a river creates the banks which hold it, so the energy which seeks truth creates its own discipline without any form of imposition and as the river finds the sea, so that energy finds its own freedom".[45]

In the schools of Krishnamurti, emphasis on the full freedom of the child to learn to observe, to think and to discuss with teachers who do not have a superiority complex, leads to tremendous vitality and energy which in turn bestows on the student his own abilities of discerning and disciplining all such forms of energy. The very process of interaction with fellow students, nature, environment and his own thoughts, encourages a sense of discipline in the student, which automatically brings about a sense of orderliness.

References

1. Commentaries On Living, III series, p.45.
2. Beginnings Of Learning, p. 121.
3. This Matter Of Culture, pp. 134-135.
4. Letters To The Schools, (15th February, 1979) Volume-1, p.37.
5. A Wholly Different Way Of Living, p.12.
6. ibid., p. 8.
7. idem.
8. idem.
9. ibid., p.11

10. Talk in New Delhi on 4th February, 1962. The Collected Works Of Jiddu Krishnamurti, Volume 3.
11. Education For The Transformation Of Consciousness. *Journal Of The Inter-University Centre For Humanities And Social Sciences*, pp. 26-29.
12. Educational Reforms In India For The 21st Century, p.14.
13. A Wholly Different Way Of Living, p. 184.
14. ibid., p. 173.
15. Education And The Significance Of Life, p.22.
16. This Matter Of Culture, p. 66.
17. idem.
18. Education And The Significance Of Life, p. 37.
19. On Learning (Pamphlet), p.3.
20. This Matter Of Culture, p. 132.
21. A Wholly Different Way Of Living, p.138.
22. This Matter Of Culture, p. 124.
23. Beginnings Of Learning, p. 55.
24. Letters To The Schools, (1st September, 1978) Volume I p. 8.
25. A Wholly Different Way Of Living, p. 125.
26. Beginnings Of Learning, p. 100.
27. Northern India Patrika, llth May, 2001.
28. Journal Of The Krishnamurti Schools (4th May, 2000), pp. 6-7.
29. Journal of the Krishnamurti Schools (3rd March, 1999), p. 41.
30. ibid., p.42.
31. A Wholly Different Way Of Living, p. 63.
32. The Awakening Of Intelligence, p. 86.
33. Krishamurti On Education, p. 74
34. Beginnings Of Learning, p. 29.
35. Patrika, Sunday Magazine (February llth, 1996), p.3.
36. Letters To The Schools, (1st October, 1978) Volume-I, p. 12.
37. Letters To The Schools, (Ist Feb., 1983) Volume - II, p. 55.

38. In Honour Of Dr. Annie Besant, p. 23.
39. This Matter Of Culture, p. 177.
40. A Wholly Different Way Of Living, p. 159.
41. On Learning (Pamphlet) p. 16.
42. Education And The Significance Of Life, pp. 41-42.
43. Krishnamurti On Education, p. 30.
44. The First And Last Freedom, p. 136.
45. This Matter Of Culture, p. 161.

4

[C] Educational Institutions of Dr. Annie Besant and J. Krishnamurti, visited by the Researcher

The Researcher visited the educational institutions at Kamachha and Rajghat, Varanasi, and collected data through personal observations and interviews, and a descriptive account of these institutions is given below.

I- Educational Institutions at Kamachha, Varanasi

The educational institutions at Kamachha, Varanasi comprises of :

1. Annie Besant Shishu Vihar
2. Theosophical School for Boys
3. Vasant Kanya Mahavidyalay

1. Annie Besant Shishu Vihar

Annie Besant Shishu Vihar was set up by Dr. Annie Besant in 1934 at approximately the same time when Rajghat Education Centre was established at Rajghat. It is a nursery co-educational school for the age group, two to seven years, comprising Lower KG, Upper K.G., Classes I and II. It is run by the Theosophical Society. Here fees is very low, just Rs. 135/- per month. A proper environment is provided to draw out the hidden potentialities of the children. Apart from the school building, it has a children's park and playground. There is a small number of students in each class paving way for individual attention. There is one teacher per class and no subject teachers. All teachers are ladies. The classrooms are attractive and airy. The children sit on the floor; have low desks on which to keep their books. Each student maintains a diary of his/her daily activities in school. School timings are from 8 a.m. to 12 noon. National festivals are observed. Also many cultural programmes are organised. Attempt is made to make the children familiar with the Indian culture and develop group feeling, respect for man and environment. There is a continuous all round process of assessment of students, comprising of teachers' observations, periodic minor tests and general performance in studies and co-curricular activities of the students. No formal examinations are held. All these fall in line with Dr. Annie Besant's ideas about the child's environment for the first seven years.

The above information has been gathered from Dr. Sarala Agrawal, Director of Annie Besant Shishu Vihar, whom the Researcher had the privilege to interview. The Researcher's impressions were that in this section, Dr. Annie Besant's concepts of freedom from rigidity in learning in the early years of childhood, together with encouragement for physical development, were being put into practice.

2. Theosophical School for Boys

This was set up by Dr. Annie Besant. Now it is government aided but managed by the Theosophical Society. Here classes are from III to XII. Boys who either pass out of Shishu Vihar or come from some other primary school get admission in the school on the basis of entrance test. There is only Arts Faculty at the Intermediate level. Since this institution is government aided, it is bound by the syllabus of U.P. Board of education and follows the conventional methods of teaching.

3. Vasant Kanya Mahavidyalay

The Researcher met the Principal of the College, Dr. Smt. Kusum Mishra. This College is solely for girls. It is upto graduation level. At the Intermediate and Graduation stage there is only Arts Faculty. It is affiliated to the Banaras Hindu University and is government aided, though run by the Theosophical Society. Upto Intermediate level it is tied to the U.P. Board.

There is a big Theosophical Society Study Hall which is common for all the institutions. Here religious discourses are held thrice a week at a fixed time. A Theosophical Library is located in the campus where books can be borrowed by interested people. All these educational institutions have vast open spaces with plenty of greenery around. There is an amphitheatre where cultural programmes are organised. 'Shanti Kunj', the home of Dr. Annie Besant is located in the campus.

One finds glimpses of the aims of education as had been enunciated by Dr. Annie Besant, in these schools/colleges. These in a nutshell aim at forward thinking with a past orientation. There are activities like National Social Service (NSS), programmes like 'Sanskrit Shivir' where scholars from different areas participate; inviting people from various fields round the year to come and give a talk, thus promoting the study of literature, philosophy; tours to nearby villages or drug rehabilitation areas; honouring teachers on Teachers' Day and bringing about some modifications in the teaching work; pondering over new perspectives in teaching; seminars and tutorials etc. At present Smt. Bina Singh is in charge of activities like 'Kavi Sammelan', dance and music competitions. Manju Sundaram teaches Sanskrit in the College.

The impressions of the Researcher after visiting the educational institutions at Kamachha and talking to teachers and students, was that the educational ideas of Dr. Annie Besant in different phases of a child's life, such as the first seven years, were to a great extent implemented in the Annie Besant Shishu Vihar, the reason being that this was run entirely by the Theosophical Society, without any government aid or specific directions. In the Theosophical School for Boys and Vasant Kanya Mahavidyalay, although the guiding principles of Dr. Annie Besant were kept in mind, extraneous influences such as a curriculum prescribed by the U.P. Board of education and conventional lines of assessment have to a considerable extent, modified Dr. Annie Besant's approach. This is not to say that Dr. Annie Besant's concepts have been totally nullified, because adaptation to contemporary methods in life and education formed a part of Dr. Annie Besant's teachings. For extraneous reasons, the science faculty, on which Dr. Annie Besant had laid great emphasis, has not developed in this institution. Dr. Annie Besant's ideas of mingling the good of the east and the west, of different cultures and people, is to some extent served by Vasant Kanya Mahavidyalay through their programme of inviting scholars from different fields and from various parts of the world to speak on various subjects.

II- Rajghat Education Centre, Varanasi

The Rajghat Education Centre comprises of the Rajghat Besant School, Vasanta College for Girls, Vasantashram, Rural Centre and Krishnamurti Study Centre/Retreat. The campus stretches over four hundred acres and overlooks the confluence of the Varuna with the Ganga.

Rajghat Besant School- *Structure and Functioning*

The Rajghat Besant School is run by Krishnamurti Foundation India. B. Sanjiva Rao wrote the following about it :

> The children's school building at Rajghat was begun in 1933. Rabindranath Tagore generously sent his own architect Surendranath Kar, who designed the building... Thought and care are evident at every step. The whole atmosphere of the building has a certain mystic quality about it. There is a sense of Eternity, of a blessed Peace, in the entire structure. The Ganga and its flowing waters are visible from most of the windows and on moonlight nights the light effects are exquisitely beautiful.[1]

The school is a residential, co-educational, English

medium one, affiliated to the C.B.S.E. Board. There are four hundred students studying in the school from standard II to XII, among whom sixty are day scholars. Since the number of students is very few as compared to other schools, the classes are not crowded, making it possible to give individual attention to each student.

There are separate hostels for boys and girls and for small children, which are spacious and comfortable. In each hostel, a House Parent looks to the needs of fifteen to twenty students. The school has its own catering arrangement under the supervision of a Catering Manager and provides a well-balanced, nutritious vegetarian diet which also includes dairy products. Cleanliness is maintained in the canteen.

Some important features of the educational philosophy of this school are:

1. to awaken the intelligence of the child and cultivate in him/her a love for nature and for all forms of life.
2. to create an atmosphere of love, order and freedom.
3. not to condition the child in any particular belief, religious, political or social, so that his/her mind may be free to ask fundamental questions, inquire and learn for itself.
4. to help the child have a balanced development of body, intellect and emotions.
5. to motivate the child to work without reward, punishment or comparison, and achieve academic excellence.
6. to create confidence in the child to face the challenges of life.[2]

The task of teachers at Rajghat Besant School is somewhat more difficult than those of other Krishnamurti Schools. This is because students of other Krishnamurti Schools come from a different background with an English orientation, as these schools are mostly situated in the South and Pune. Rajghat Besant School receives inputs from the U.P. and

Bihar belt where students have a Hindi background. Initiation of students into the thoughts of Krishnamurti is easier in English as his philosophy has on many occasions relied on one word to convey different meanings.

However, this school shares with all the other schools of Krishnamurti the following characteristics, viz., large campus with immense natural beauty, a friendly, caring relationship between teachers and students; simple, nourishing vegetarian diet; austere but comfortable living quarters; spacious and welcoming classrooms; well-equipped libraries and laboratories; a small teacher-pupil ratio; dedicated teachers. The junior and middle schools have a flexible and innovative approach by which teachers plan out the curricula in their subjects of interest. Co-curricular activities include arts, crafts, music, games and sports, hobby-clubs like gardening, hiking, photography, first-aid and computers. In order to develop a healthy attitude towards life and nature, students are encouraged right from an early age to care for plants, keep their surroundings clean and beautiful and learn the dignity of labour by doing manual work.

On Saturday mornings there are Krishnamurti discussions for teachers. In these discussions practical things in context to the day to day school life are taken up. These issues are discussed in line with Krishnamurti's views.

Books like *Thinking Together* have been introduced in the school to promote discussions in the classroom between pupils and their teachers. This book deals with Value Education. As Value Education cannot be taught intellectually, cannot be moralised or preached but can be perceived and understood when one observes oneself in the matrix of relationship, this book, therefore, though dealing with values such as responsibility and sharing, co-operation and integrity, questioning and self-reliance, does not try to sermonise. The passages of the book are read out in the culture classes set apart once a week alongwith dialogues, and it is in these dialogues with the class that much of what is relevant to children in their own lives are revealed, and this helps the teachers to understand the children in a better way.

There is an assembly held before the actual commencement of the classes at 8.15 a.m. The whole school gathers in the assembly alongwith the teachers, Principal, Rector etc. There is a chanting of devotional songs by all, followed by a short period of silence which uplifts the soul to a higher level of tranquility, and there is an experience of total peace in the mind. This stillness augurs well for the learning experiences carried out during the rest of the day.

The assembly also contributes towards the integration of teachers and pupils in creating an atmosphere of harmony and mutual goodwill. The relationship between teachers and pupils is thus characterised primarily by informality and freedom. At music assemblies teachers and pupils are both passive participants, but not so at the talks and lectures and joint presentations when they are active participants. The spoken component of the assembly is wide ranging in scope and may consist of talks by visitors, teachers or pupils, the performance of short plays and skits by pupils and teachers, and the playing of taped music occasionally. These assemblies are held separately in the junior and senior schools and their contents differ. Their intention is however, the same; apart from the plays that are staged primarily for entertainment, they are intended to inform and instruct the audience on a variety of topics.

Multi Level Card System

To encourage critical thinking and to deal with individual differences, teaching is not done with the help of prescribed text books but multi level cards are prepared by the teachers themselves for classes II to VII. As the school is affiliated to CBSE Board, students of classes VIII upwards follow the courses prescribed by the Board but till class VII there is a flexible curriculum made by competent teachers. In a horizontal division like text-book teaching, all children study the same text, and it becomes difficult to cater to the individual needs of each child. Multi level cards system is a unique way in this respect. There are 4 levels of cards for each class. For instance, Class II will have 1, 2, 3, 4 levels and Class III will have 3, 4, 5, 6 levels.

Each level has a minimum of six sub levels and a maximum of ten. Last two levels of the previous class overlap with the first two levels of the next class, as shown by the following diagram:

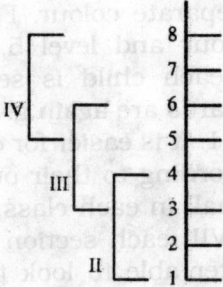

Children who are not able to master the last two levels of the previous class can again begin with these two levels in the next class.

In order to relate the subject to the child and to enhance their power of observation, the teacher first introduces the concept through oral lessons, questioning the children about subjects that they know. For instance, while taking up "Nouns" in the English grammar periods, the teacher asks the students what they see in the classroom. They come up with names of such objects as blackboard, chalk etc. The children then know that blackboard, chalk are names of objects, and nouns pertain to names of persons, places, and things including living and non living. After they are familiar with this concept, they are made to understand the differences between proper nouns and common nouns. "Describing words" or adjectives are taught by taking the children outside the classroom and asking them to pick up anything lying on the ground like a flower or a leaf and describing how it feels. The describing words are the adjectives. Definitions of nouns or adjectives are difficult to be memorised or understood by small children. Therefore such oral lessons and active involvement on the part of students are very helpful. In classroom situations as well as in outdoor projects, the child is helped to come directly into contact with facts. To be sensitive to everything around, the child is encouraged to observe form and colour, handle materials, feel the texture of objects, of softness and hardness, weight and size, and so on. Once the concept is introduced, the multi level cards are picked up by the students and they start working on it. The cards are colour coded, each level having a separate colour. For example, level 4 may be of yellow colour and level 5 of red and so on. The performance of each child is seen by the teacher and accordingly the cards are again given; some may need level 2 and some level 1. It is easier for children to cope up when they proceed according to their own level. As the number of students is small in each class, there being one section from class II to VII, each section having 22 children, the teachers are better able to look to individual differences.

Self study

Self study in also encouraged in the classes. A child having completed the required levels of cards is free to pick up any book kept in a "book box" in each class and read. Each new subject is introduced to the whole class together, and the teacher waits till the subject is understood by everyone. A child who grasps it earlier than the rest of the classmates, can continue with further reading. Moreover, there are children who are avid readers and there are library periods where the children can pick up and issue a book of their liking.

Arousal of interests of students

Though there is no system of reward or punishment, the colourful and catchy cards arouse the interests of the students, and they run and pick up a different card as soon as one card is finished. As they think more and more, their interest level also increases.

The school has teams in football, hockey, cricket, basketball and tennis which play only "friendly" matches with teams from neighbouring towns and districts, or between teachers and pupils of the same school. Matches with other schools, although not encouraged, are not totally avoided. This is done to avoid competition as other schools may not enter into the rhetoric of "friendly" matches.

While games are not organised around competition, the matches played induce a spirit of competition into the game. This may be due to the widespread notion that matches in sport may be "friendly" but are always about winning or losing. The spirit of sportsmanship, which implies playing by rules to win a game, rather than "fighting" to defeat and humiliate the other side, may however, also prevail and influence the participants' attitudes. These matches between schools and other friendly games help to generate and sustain a spirit of enthusiasm and interest in students, promoting the urge to perform their very best. Just as Krishnamurti was not averse to the conventional type of education, alongwith a value based education; similarly, these competitive matches, as also organising functions like flag hoisting, are to be taken as a blend with the social milieu within which the school has to function.

Integration of Various Activities

There is an integration of various activities like redefining the learning process, environmental awareness, guest lectures or workshops, sports and games, cultural events and co-curricular activities, educational excursions.

Assessment of the pupils

The assessment of the pupils is not according to marks. Reports cards are based on observations done in the classroom. Every month or at least twice in a term, there is a meeting of all the subject teachers of each class, and each child is discussed. The class teacher keeps noting down the remarks meant for each child of his/her class, and according to this she continues to observe the progress of students in her own class.

Such types of report cards do not encourage competition amongst the students, but highlight a novel and elaborate system of assessment. In the reports, the teachers comment on the "achievement" and "effort" of the pupil in each subject, apart from making general remarks.

Class VIII and upwards have examinations as these students have to face the C.B.S.E. Board. As gathered by the Researcher in her talks with the staff members, their reports give a comprehensive picture of the pupil's personality and performance. The report cards of pupils in the senior school contain their grades, remarks by subject teachers on the pupils' performance, remarks on activities, health and house behaviour, and a general remark by the Principal or Headmistress.

Teacher-Student Relationship

The teacher student relationship is a relationship of sharing where the teacher and the student both learn together. The teachers are the Hostel Parents too. The students have no hesitation in approaching their teachers. They have their meals with the teachers and also get time to come up with their problems in the night, before going to bed in the hostels. Sometimes the teachers too play games with the students during their playtime.

Daily life

There is an orderly schedule. There are fixed periods for study, games, rest, meals etc. Each period is of forty minutes. The relative emphasis on various subjects and activities is reflected in the number of periods allotted to each. In addition there are classes where they discuss social issues, current affairs, problems at school etc. The inclusion of arts and crafts and music in the curriculum is part of the school's policy to develop the creative and aesthetic elements in the pupil.

However, this orderliness of following a daily routine is not a departure from Krishnamurti's ideas. As members of a family live together, have a particular time for their meals, prayers etc., similarly, the students, teachers and other members of the staff live together in a responsible way in the campus. Though the children are exposed to an atmosphere of openness, flexibility till Class VII, they are trained according to a conventional pattern from Class VIII onwards. This type of an academic programme cannot be avoided as the school is affiliated to CSSE Board, and the children have to appear for the Board examinations. However, the students at this stage, having been brought up in a different type of atmosphere in the lower classes are ready to face the challenges and pressures of everyday life, and are able to find out what is right for themselves.

Involvement of Parents

Parents visit the school at least once a term and interact informally with teachers. Sometimes parents actively involve themselves in the task of education by supplying the school with video cassettes on some educational topic or selecting relevant materials like poems, stories etc. Parents-Teachers meetings on a formal basis are held twice a year.

Admissions

The main entry points for pupils are at Classes II, VII and XI. An elaborate process of selection which consists of a brochure containing information on the school is sent to parents who are also required to answer questions regarding the pupil's background, such as, the pupil's earlier education, academic record, hobbies and interests, and in particular, his home and social background. A selection committee then selects pupils who are eligible for registration. Finally, the registered pupils are called for an interview and test, after which selected candidates are admitted.

The effort to keep the school "non-sectarian", "national" and "international" finds expression in the criteria of "regional representation" and "various religious backgrounds". Children of parents working abroad are also considered so as to have a good mix of pupils in the school.

Finance

The school does not get any aid from government and is purely autonomous. The sources of funds are from school fees, estate of the schools, dairy and some donations. The school fee includes tuition fee, board and lodging fees which is about Rs 40,000 to Rs 50,000 per annum.

Management Committee

The school has a Management Committee consisting

entirely of school staff which includes the Rector, Principal, Senior School Headmistress, Junior School Headmistress, and a few members who are also members of the Foundation. They deal with all matters of the school and receive inputs from various sub-committees. The pupils present their problems through representatives on the School Council which meets the senior teachers and members of the Management Committee, at least twice a term. Thus, the pupils have a forum where they can discuss their problems and present their views.

Selection of Teachers

When teachers are selected care is taken to see their academic record and co-curricular activities. It is not necessary for teachers in the junior section to have qualified their B.Ed. However, once appointed, they have to complete their B.Ed. within three years. Due importance is given to humbleness and clarity of their thoughts. It is not necessary that one should have knowledge of Krishnamurti's teachings. It is imperative that the teacher should be dedicated, earnest, eager, enthusiastic, intelligent, humble and good natured. Sometimes the selected teachers are given an opportunity to stay in the school for sometime and get accustomed to the atmosphere. In the event of their not being able to do so, they are free to resign.

Workload of teachers

Usually the teacher's work starts at 7.30 a.m. and continues till 4.30 p.m. They generally have three or four periods of teaching in a day, but in between they are occupied in different types of co-curricular activities. As most of the teachers reside in the campus, they can willingly give more time to students for educational and personal guidance. For teachers with young children, special facility of free education is available in all classes; for them, arrangements also exist for students of K.G. and Class I.

Teacher, Staff Interrelationships

The relationship between teachers, teacher and principal,

is based on how one "actually is", and there are no intricacies or complexities or misunderstandings involved, as all these are cleared from time to time if they so arise. Pay scales are same for teachers irrespective of the class they teach. This creates a feeling of equality and keeps the teachers away from jealousy, and competition.

Study Centre/Retreat

The Krishnamurti Study Centre/Retreat is a place of great natural beauty, tranquility, serenity. The atmosphere lends itself to the intention of such centres, that is, the study of oneself in the light of Krishnamurti's teachings. The Study Centre is located in the building in which Krishnamurti lived during his annual visits to Rajghat. In these cottages people stay, study and meditate.

The Study Centre has a library with a good collection of books on religion, philosophy, science, a large number of Krishnamurti books, audio/video tapes, the Archives, a Silence room, a lending library to enable people to borrow books, a bookshop selling books and audio/video tapes of his works. Apart from offering the usual facilities of a Krishnamurti Study Centre, it has a cell for translations and publications making available books in Hindi, Bengali and Urdu.

The Researcher had the pleasure of meeting and interacting with Miss Hema Rao in charge of the Study Centre at Rajghat.

Vasanta College for Girls

Vasanta College for Girls was started in 1913 by Dr. Annie Besant with very few girls for the sake of promoting women education. This college being previously situated in Kamachha, was later shifted to Rajghat and is now run by the Krishnamurti Foundation India. This college comprises of the faculties of arts, social sciences, commerce, education. There is s hostel, Vasantashram, for the college girls who come from outside Varanasi. According to the Principal of the College, Dr. Vijay Shivpuri, "Though the College is affiliated to the Banaras Hindu University and is bound by the syllabus and examination standards of the University, it still has the vibrations of Krishnamurti's teachings. We are proud to say that we are the only College run by Krishnamurti Foundation, others are just schools".

A culture textbook pertaining to Krishnamurti's teachings is given to each student who enters the college. There are students', forum where topics related to the teenage group and pertaining to authority, fear etc. are discussed. Also there are Krishnamurti gatherings in the Rajghat Besant School, which teachers are encouraged to attend if they are not tied up to other activities. Teachers are also free to go and study at the Study Centre. Above all, there is an atmosphere of love, affection pervading throughout the college. There is a B.Ed. department for the training of teachers and quite a few students, who have received their training here, have been employed as teachers, at Rajghat School. Ex-students of the college, contact their teachers informally when they get time.

This information is based on personal interview by the Researcher of Dr. Vijay Shivpuri, Principal of Vasanta College.

The Rural Centre

The Rural Centre consists of a Village Primary School, a dairy, a farm, a hospital on the eastern side of Varuna. The school has about six hundred children. It has a Principal, a Headmaster and about eighteen teachers and an educational assistant. An educational director, Mr. Saklani is in overall charge, whom the Researcher had the opportunity to interview. Classes are from I to V. The aim of the school is to develop a complete human being. To impart a holistic type of an education, involvement of parents, teachers and students is sought, but still much has to be done. For women of the village sewing and embroidery classes have also started. To develop the sensitivity of the students and a love for manual work, clay modeling and wood work are taught to the children of village school by students from Rajghat Besant School. The teachers of the Rural Centre are generally B.A. or B.Ed., and they stay in the campus of the Rajghat Besant School.

The rural centre does not get aid from the government.

It gets financial assistance from the Foundation. A minimal amount of fees is also taken from the students who study here. Also, donations are accepted. Previously an American organisation, named, "Asha" which looked to the educational needs of the poor gave financial support to the institution. Financial constraints allow only conventional forms of teaching and examination; however, a Krishnamurti orientation, which means total freedom without fragmentation and image formations, even of Krishnamurti and his teachings, is given to all this by the teachers who live in the Rajghat campus and by the students of the Rajghat Besant School.

The purpose of the visit by the Researcher was to see for herself the working of a Krishnamurti school and first hand impressions and findings have been recorded. Emphasis has been given to the successful creation and preservation, by the school, of a type of environment which encourages freedom, and proximity to nature. This is in concurrence with the view that values are passively and subtly imbibed by all who live and interact in the campus. The Researcher saw that in Rajghat Education Centre, emphasis was given towards the development of a good human being, and when Krishnamurti's teachings were not clear to the teachers in their learning process, they were discussed in staff meetings and taken up only after clarifications. The school is basically meant to help both the student and the teacher to flower in goodness, which implies understanding of correct behaviour, action, relationship. According to some staff members and ex-students, whom the Researcher had the occasion to meet, the pupils who passed out of this school, or had the opportunity of receiving their schooling here for sometime, definitely found a change in their way of thinking. They felt that they had become more mature serious-minded and had a broader outlook.

References

1. The Story Of A Project For New Education, p.11.
2. Rajghat Besant School (prospectus), p.2.

5
Comparison, Conclusions, Suggestions

In this concluding chapter a gist of comparison of some salient features of the educational ideas of Dr. Annie Besant and J. Krishnamurti has been given, and the relevance of both these thinkers in contemporary times has been discussed. Some suggestions have been offered, on the basis of this discussion, towards a paradigm for value education.

Comparison

Comparison of Dr. Annie Besant's and Krishnamurti's educational thoughts reveals a curious blend of ideas which at times seem to be wide apart, showing total confluence on other occasions, and treading grey areas very frequently. This is not unexpected. Krishnamurti's long association with Dr. Annie Besant and Theosophical Society certainly made imprints during his impressionable years. Later Krishnamurti had experiences (during meditations) which brought about an inner transformation in him and subsequent blossoming of his philosophy, that of radical inner transformation (of the mind). This radical transformation was a spontaneous process in him during his meditations, when his mind was silent and yet observing. The "what is" began to have meaning for him and drew him away from "image formations" of Theosophical Society. He became his own teacher and pupil, and he felt that there was no specific method of knowing the "what is" or the Truth. He therefore talked of Truth as a pathless land. The genesis of convergence and divergence in the educational ideas of Dr. Annie Besant and Krishnamurti thus become apparent.

Dr. Annie Besant, was born a devout Christian, turned into an Atheist due to circumstances, propagated the ideals of the Freethinker, actively supported groups that questioned God as commonly visualised, only to join the Theosophical group later, in answer to an inner voice, and then became interested in Hinduism, which she studied deeply and finally embraced as her religion. It was but natural that this should bring her to India, a country which she loved, for which she lived and worked and finally called her "Motherland". She willed her mortal remains to be consigned to flames according to Hindu rites[1]. *In contrast, Krishnamurti had no such religious upheavels or turmoils.* He has neither clearly denied nor accepted God in conventional form. He was essentially a seeker of truth and he believed, "Truth is a pathless land", which every individual has to reach in his own way. He was against preachings and teachings, against religious or any other groups and indicated that such formations were the refuge of the insecure.

Both Dr. Annie Besant and Krishnamurti believed in the betterment of man and the world, although their ideas of attaining such betterment were different. Whereas Dr. Annie Besant had clear-cut concepts regarding the reviving of Indian heritage and culture by freeing it from the yoke of British dominance, by arousing a spirit of nationalism, religious fervour and pride, and thereafter to work for betterment of the world, Krishnamurti had a philosophy of holistic approach, the core of which was upliftment of the individual. He believed that society was made from the individual and individual was society. Without defining any approach, Krishnamurti negated the importance of self, the "I", and by doing this removed comparison, competition and fear.

Whilst Dr. Annie Besant's views were pride in the past, unshakable faith in the future and hard work in the present,

Krishnamurti held that the most important moment was "now", the present– the past converged on it and the future emerged from it. Attempts at separation would be a futile exercise.

Blueprint of Educational Ideas:

1. Nationalism and Religion in Education

When Dr. Annie Besant arrived in India in 1893, the country was under British rule. She sensed that the education system introduced by the Britishers alienated Indians from their cultural heritage, made them materialistic and denationalised them. The people were being carried away by the glamour of western civilisation. She, therefore, laid down a broad plan for India's renaissance and developed a spirit of nationalism among the people of India, so as to fight back the British domination. To carry out her mission, she believed that the key to success was to educate the people in the right manner. She felt that in the scientific age, it was necessary for the moral conscience to develop before knowledge advanced further, and educating people in the right way would mean creating right individuals for the future, which would lead to man becoming a good citizen of a free and spiritual Commonwealth of Humanity. She was not averse to incorporating in her system the commendable features of western education which imparted pure knowledge without ulterior motives.

To build a nationalistic ideology she chose to arouse the spiritual insights of the people and took recourse to ancient Hindu scriptures, delivered lectures on the Ramayana and the Mahabharat, wrote text books on Hindu religion and ethics which were called the *Sanatana Dharma series*, and translated *The Bhagavad Gita* into English. She toured all over the country delivering lectures, drew a group of thoughtful and influential people of the land around her, and with their help managed to set up schools and colleges in various parts of the country. She stressed on Hinduism being taught to Hindus as according to "the Great Law which guides the universe, men and women are born into the religion which is best fitted to mould their lives and characters"[2]. Therefore Hinduism was the religion both taught and lived in the Central Hindu College at Benares. Also, according to Dr. Annie Besant "religion only becomes an inspiration when the heart loves what the lips dictate"[3]. Further, she felt that India's work was to uplift the world through the truths embedded in her religious system. She wrote that Hinduism was the only ancient civilisation to survive continuously into modern times, and that it was open to all the religions of the world. She quoted Lord Krishna's words from *The Bhagavad Gita:* "However men approach Me, even so do I welcome them, for the path men take from every side is Mine, O Partha. (iv, II)"[4].

To put into practice her nationalistic ideology, she laid the foundation of a national system of education. She felt that national education should be under national control, which meant in Indian hands, for it was the Indians who could best judge the character that was expected to be developed amongst the youth of the country.

In order to build the people in the right way, Dr. Annie Besant laid stress on character formation, made religion an integral part of education. She held that the basic truths of all religions should be properly grasped and translated into everyday living. Religious training should be given without sectarian bias, so that it paves the way for unity, creates useful citizens, a nobler outlook. In her religious training, Indian ideals of education were emphasised. Thus she laid stress on Brahmacharya, Ashram Ideal. She felt that Indian ideals would develop in the students, a love and respect for their Motherland and would inculcate a spirit of patriotism in their hearts. Moreover, she felt that whatever is beneficial for the West is not necessarily so for the East.

In contrast to Dr. Annie Besant, Krishnamurti had a vision which went beyond nationalism from the very beginning, towards the transformation of the human mind as the main purpose of education. Whereas Dr. Annie Besant first wanted to build a strong nation by building the people, and later proceeded to build a strong Commonwealth of Humanity, Krishnamurti wanted to transform the whole human society by transforming the individuals. He saw the problem of existence rooted in the structure of the human mind which is fragmentary and incomplete. Unless each individual underwent a radical transformation the world would not change and to undergo a radical transformation at the individual level, meant a radical transformation of the human mind. It is the individual that comprises the society, and unless the individual changed, no reform, howsoever good, can transform the society, as any type of reform is a modified continuity of the same structure in a different set up, it only results in the confusing demand for further reform. Whatever happens in the world is the result of the behaviour of man, which in turn occurs due to the inner psychological states of man. Therefore, he points to a revolution that must take place in the whole of the human mind and not merely in thought. Thought is only a result and not the source. There must be a radical transformation in the source and not mere modification of the result. It is with this important change that one should be concerned –that is, freeing the mind from the old ways of thought, from traditions, habits, images.

To bring about such a psychological transformation within each person, Krishnamurti did not take the help of any religion or belief or the terminology of any particular philosophy. He felt that such words pertaining to any system of thought would be tainted with the authority of the system to which they belong. What was important for him was to build a communion between himself and his audience, so that they could take a journey with him through self awareness, free from mental pre-occupations and discover the truth for themselves. It was a dynamic movement in inquiry. Instead of delivering lectures, he held dialogues which began with a state of "not knowing", a state in which there was an absence of views, hypotheses or assumptions. He then led the investigation with others, watching the flow of the dialogue and analysing the issue. At some point, an insight would come that thought is an inadequate tool to understand the complexities of the psyche or to investigate into the nature of the immeasurable.

To carry out an education that would lead to a radical transformation of the human mind, Krishnamurti did not resort to any system or method. Therefore, unlike Dr. Annie Besant, he did not propound a national system of education; he felt that method destroys spontaneity. It lays down a path which one must follow and then the path, the technique becomes more important than the vision. It is the vision that creates the technique and not the other way round.

Krishnamurti felt that both nationalism an organised religion divided man from man. By fostering a sense of identity, that one is a Hindu, or a Christian, or a Muslim and so on, one gives rise to divisive tendencies. One defines oneself and rejects others. This results in conflicts. Freedom from conflict is not attained by cultivating an ideal which may be any Indian ideal, or an ideal of brotherhood or an ideal of non violence, but in coming face to face with the actual, with the "what is", with the psyche in conflict. According to Krishnamurti, religion is the understanding of Truth which is not a projection of the mind, and religious education is the understanding of oneself in relationship to everything. A mind that is sensitive and understands the "what is", recognises the false as false and by so recognising, the false drops away of its own accord and true relationship is automatically established.

2. Goals of Education

In addition to awakening a spirit of nationalism, and later to become a useful world citizen while preserving his national moorings, the purpose of Dr. Annie Besant's education was for life, leadership and livelihood–to educate a person with a view to enable him to become a useful citizen and to fruitfully engage himself in earning a livelihood on the basis of the knowledge acquired by him during his education. Looking at it from a Theosophical angle the primary purpose of education would be to provide the fullest opportunity to the individual for increasing the speed of his evolution by growing as much as possible in this life period, in everything that increases his human and noble qualities and eliminates the lower qualities of his nature. The purpose of Krishnamurti's education was to encourage independent thinking on the part of the pupil, so that he may form his own impressions and thereby understand the Truth. This implies that the mind would be ever alert as Truth according to Krishnamurti flows in and out every moment, and the significance of this has to be grasped by the pupil himself. Knowing the Truth would lead to inner transformation and a better individual and society.

3. Teacher or Guru

According to Dr. Annie Besant the supreme work of education was to recognise that it is the conscience of the child that is to be primarily developed, to enable him to discern between right and wrong, and to this end the teacher must devote all his energies. The teacher must have the power to inspire his pupils and at the same time not exert authoritarianism. The teacher has to allow the child scope for originality and independence. While teaching children, the teacher should have knowledge of child psychology which would enable him to mould his lessons according to the child's tastes, capacities, growth, thereby leading to ideal development of the child, bearing in mind that Dr. Annie Besant believed that the child was born with qualities brought forth from previous lives. The teacher must be true to himself and must be careful to keep education away from authority and dogmas, and the students must be helped to discover their own truths. The teacher should be able to encourage the students to move towards self realisation and not be disappointed by failures. Dr. Annie Besant's teacher is nevertheless an idealist teacher who helps the students to follow an ideal. It is interesting to recall that while Dr. Annie Besant considered the role of a properly motivated and devoted teacher necessary, one must not lose sight of the fact, that when it came to the supremest form of acquiring knowledge the "Brahma Vidya", Dr. Annie Besant has proclaimed that this has to be learnt by the person himself. No teacher can ever impart this knowledge to him.

J. Krishnamurti, on the other hand, did not believe in a guru in the conventional sense. The teachings of a guru according to his philosophy would only result in a fragmented mind with image formations in the mind of the pupil. In psychological learning, there actually can be no teacher. Each human being must inquire alone into the beauty and complexity of life, and be free to discover love. A teacher comes into being when one stops to explore the whole process of life. Such a teacher nevertheless is a static and not a dynamic one, as the process of learning is continuous throughout life. This implies that the qualities of a student's mind should be the free mind, active and alert from moment to moment, grasping the truth without previous images, to be in a state of constant learning. In the schools run by Krishnamurti Foundations, the teacher has a functional status and not an authoritative one, the teacher and the students are encouraged into a "togetherness" where they learn and share together. The function of the teacher is to remove obstacles in the path of the students for realising the truth.

In contrast to Dr. Annie Besant, Krishnamurti feels that a teacher who is an idealist is like a specialist who pursues a part and not the whole. Such a teacher cannot bring about total integration in the student. "To study a child one has to be alert, watchful, self-aware, and this demands far greater intelligence and affection than to encourage him to follow an ideal"[5]

However, Krishnamurti's vast body of writings, talks and tapes have come to be called "the teachings", a term to which Krishnamurti himself did not object. Krishnamurti had once remarked:

> We thought of using the word "work"–ironworks, big building works, hydroelectric works, you understand? So I thought "work" is very, very common. So we thought we might use the word teaching. But it is not important-the word-right? ... It depends upon you, whether you live the teachings or not.[6]

4. Curriculum

Dr. Annie Besant's curriculum takes into account each aspect of an individual's personality, and these are given sufficient opportunities for development. In this way, she resembles the Naturalists. In as much as her curriculum includes subjects that are helpful in earning a livelihood,

Dr. Annie Besant's views are similar to Pragmatists. So far as curriculum is subjected to attaining self realisation, she is closer to the Idealists. By stressing the importance of scientific subjects, she is similar to the Realists. Therefore, her outlook was one of synthesis. *Her emphasis was on attainment of knowledge, which would lead to arousing of consciousness* and the formation of an integrated personality–*a knowledge based curriculum.* This does not imply that basic moral concepts were of secondary importance in the attainment of knowledge.

As far as Krishnamurti is concerned, there are no prescribed books given by him. He laid emphasis on reading the text of life. It is imperative to make the children understand that though academic excellence is vital, it is only a small part of their education, and that one should learn about the wholeness of life. Krishnamurti believed that in education, consciousness is the epicentre from which extensions move towards knowledge which is at the periphery. In other words, *his curriculum is consciousness based moving towards knowledge.*

Both Dr. Annie Besant and Krishnamurti recognised the need to blend their forms of education with the conventional one as practised in other schools particularly in the higher classes.

5. Methods of Teaching

Both Dr. Annie Besant and J. Krishnamurti believed that teaching methods should be such that they adapt to the child and not the child to the methods. Nevertheless the paths chosen by them to reach this end point are different. The guiding principle for Dr. Annie Besant was her belief in Theosophical convictions. Dr. Annie Besant believed that each child has a soul, which is a manifestation of reincarnation in a new garb. Proper care be given to the child so that all his faculties that he has brought forth from his previous lives are developed to the fullest extent. She detailed different types of teaching methods for children pertaining to different age groups and capacities, viz, play way, observation, lecture, self study, activity, imitation,

Comparison, Conclusions, Suggestions 219

experimental, relating every subject to the pupil. All the methods recommended by her were nevertheless, a judicial synthesis of the views of Montessori, Froebel, Pestallozi and Binet, as she herself wrote in the book, *Principles of Education*, pp22-23. This shows that her methods conform to an ideology.

Krishnamurti on the other hand, suggests different types of teaching methods which are neither rigid nor do they conform to any ideology. He encouraged the child to be his own teacher, to find out for himself the truth by being close to nature and having an active mind as discussed earlier. Krishnamurti was never guided by any religious beliefs or sentiments, and never committed himself on Reincarnation. He pointed out that fixed methods, revolving round fixed patterns of thought, took away the freedom of mind. He nevertheless spoke about entities, which for sake of flexibility have also been called methods, like Observation, Relating subject to the child or the "me", Sharing, Dialogue. All these methods apart from helping the individual to gain information or knowledge helps to free the mind from self-centredness with all its fears and conflicts. The shift of emphasis from acquisitive learning to accelerated learning places the learner closer to the heart of things and to his own "proper study" of himself.

6. School

In Dr. Annie Besant's "ideal school" sufficient care is given to bring about students' all round development. She laid stress on setting up such schools that were totally free from governmental authority, that would enable students to be patriotic, to take pride in their past glory, to be true to themselves, to have faith in their own religion and culture, to be conscious and hopeful of a golden future and to discover for themselves what is true. Games were to be an integral part of school life.

According to Krishnamurti a school is a place where the educator and the one to be educated are both learning. Schools have to be such places where a new climate can be created in which freedom of thought can flourish. Krishnamurti also believed in all round or holistic development of the student. For this purpose a small teacher-pupil ratio is necessary. The schools function democratically and Krishnamurti insisted on setting up a core group that would take consensual decisions through dialogue and discussion. The school is not to be just an organisation but actual experiments in living. The school has to function in such a way that the coming generation is not ruined by the superficial, and mechanical way of life of modern civilisation. For perpetuation of such thoughts extraneous interventions and influences, for example, from government or any other body was discouraged by Krishnamurti. These advantages of Krishnamurti schools demand vast sums of money, and tuition fees happen to be very much higher than most schools, thereby precluding the entry of many deserving students. To neutralise this disadvantage, rural education centres have been set up near the main schools to cater to the needs of poorer students. Students from the main schools lend a helping hand in the teaching process of these schools. This is in concurrence with Krishnamurti's views that even if a dozen people change, they would in turn change the world. Study Centres are open for prolonged hours including evenings to enable people to study and meditate after their working hours, supporting Krishnamurti's educational thoughts of learning being a continuous process. While the milieu in Dr. Annie Besant's schools encouraged Brahmacharya spirit and therefore was against co-education, the same is not seen in Krishnamurti's school where the classes are co-educational.

7. Student

Dr. Annie Besant held that student life spans the Brahmacharya phase of human life. She refers to four great elements: service, study, simplicity, self-control, which were essential for every student to possess. This was necessary for all round development and gave weightage to the four important aspects of education, viz., spiritual, intellectual, moral and physical. A prior stage of free play for the first seven years of the child's life precedes the stage of Brahmacharya or student life.

Krishnamurti pointed out that a student has to keep an open mind, free from the weight of opinions, biases, prejudices, fears etc., and be serious about everything so as to have a keen sense of enquiry and sustained stamina leading to discovery.

8. Discipline

Dr. Annie Besant believed that discipline was necessary for both student and teacher. A teacher should be true to himself, duty bound, a man of self control, full of love and warmth for others, and such that the student can emulate. For students she laid stress on observation of celibacy and expected the students to follow the rules. The students were to lead regular and clean lives and give service to guru and parents through obedience and performing one's duties towards them. To serve them would be like serving God. "Service" therefore is an important quality to be developed as this virtue automatically brings about discipline. Dr. Annie Besant wanted to discipline not only students but the whole society through education. This is in concurrence with her concept of guided freedom whereby the student is given an environment of freedom in which he gives vent to his imaginative flights, comes out with original ideas and new values and self discipline. However, this freedom is not allowed to be at the expense of others or to satisfy the lower instincts at the cost of the higher. *Dr. Annie Besant felt that an individual who was determined to lead a spiritual life must daily devote sometime to meditation, and meditation according to her meant a concentrated mind, a mind shut out from the world.*

Krishnamurti also believed in discipline being an essential part of education, although his idea of discipline differed from Dr. Annie Besant. Krishnamurti said that a mind that is disciplined leads to clarity of observation. Only when the mind is empty can it observe in such a way that the observer and observed become one. For this Krishnamurti speaks of attention when there is no frittering away of energy as there is no compulsion, no resistance. Attention is not something to be forced on the mind, for the moment there is force there is always a counteracting resistance opposing the force, and there is no attention though there may be concentration. However in concentration the observer is established and the mind is not empty in the sense that Krishnamurti envisages. It leads to image formation, fragmentation of ideas, attention directed to one single object, excluding all others. So a disciplined mind according to Krishnamurti has to be an empty mind which is capable of complete attention and as such there is no loss of energy. An empty mind which is attentive and receptive to the flow of thoughts from moment to moment is the free mind capable of observing holistically all happenings, allowing the truth to stay and the false to wither away. This, according to Krishnamurti, was the essence of meditation in contrast to the concept of concentration by Dr. Annie Besant. These are reflected in the respective educational ideas of Dr. Annie Besant and Krishnamurti.

9. Spreading of Education in Women and the Masses and advocating Vocational Education

While Dr. Annie Besant has laid considerable emphasis on these three aspects of education, enunciating the methodology of propagation, defining its effectiveness and enumerating their benefits, Krishnamurti on the other hand, has a centrifugal approach of transformation of the human mind from self to society, which obviously includes vocational education, women and the masses.

10. Cooperation and Competition

Both Dr. Annie Besant and Krishnamurti are strong proponents of cooperation. While a healthy competition according to Dr. Annie Besant is desirable and indeed an inseparable component of cooperation, Krishnamurti differs from this and says that competition can lead to comparison, fragmentation and conflict. In this context it may be pointed out that even in Krishnamurti schools, friendly matches and debates etc. may be said to lead to healthy competition, but this is taken as a part of cooperation itself and is unavoidable in the social context of real life. Krishnamurti has himself referred to his schools as "experiments in living" which have not yet been able to fully implement cooperation in every sphere of life.

To Conclude

In proceeding to the conclusion the researcher briefly recalls here the educational scenario in India since ancient times, to highlight the fact that this has been one of dynamic cultural continuity, leading to the present day social order. During the period of Dr. Annie Besant and Krishnamurti there were other seers and thinkers in India who contributed immensely to Indian education. The views of some such seers have also been briefly examined to place the present study in its proper perspective. Education in ancient India was spiritual in nature. The Upanishadic doctrine about "Brahma" –the all pervading, by knowing Brahma alone, one knew everything, aimed at the development of inner consciousness of man. It taught the way of oneness with the Absolute (Brahma) by the destruction of ignorance, which is the cause of all worldly suffering. With the advent of Buddhism, educational system continued to be mainly religious, and the chief aim of education was to attain Nirvan or salvation. Emphasis was given to purity of character. Education was given in monasteries, where the bhikshus were educated by monks. Medieval education began from the early part of the eighth century A.D. with the start of the Mohammedan invasions. The education of this period aimed at the propagation of Islam, extension of knowledge and achievement of material prosperity together with development of character and moral well being. With the advent of British rule, education was imparted with the motive of meeting the demands of a foreign rule. Then began the search for new values in education. Efforts were made to instill the national spirit in a system that would be modern as well. It was, therefore, felt that a new educational philosophy, giving emphasis to science and spirituality, would to a great extent suit national requirements. Some great Indian thinkers of the time have shown the way.

Swami Vivekanand had laid emphasis on equal exchange of learning which was based on the belief that nations cannot rise simply by running down their past. A generation must have faith in its spirit and with an unencumbered soul, partake of and give knowledge. His educational philosophy was firmly rooted in *Vedanta* that emphasised the education of the "whole man" and prompted the unity of mankind on both the national and international levels.

On the subject of education both Mahatma Gandhi and Tagore developed a balanced view. The general aim of education for them was the harmonious development of personality. Both pleaded for simplicity and naturalness in education. Both were spiritualists in education and regarded education to be an expression and preparation of life. In Shantiniketan, Tagore emphasised that the ideal of human unity can be realised best and most successfully through educational activity. Educational activity, through the creation of an atmosphere of mutual understanding and appreciation, can help in the formation of a cooperative society. Tackled in the proper spirit, Gandhiji's Basic Education helps the growth of the whole personality of the child as it satisfies the natural urge of the child for work. Also peace can be established through self realisation, human interaction, socialistic democracy, non violence.

Sri Aurobindo's education was for the development, modification, and transformation of consciousness in human beings. He propounded *Integral Yoga* which is the art of harmonious and creative living. It is not bound down by scriptures or an external teacher, but seeks its guidance from the master within. In ordinary yoga a single power or group of powers of human beings like knowledge, devotion, action etc. is made the means. In Integral Yoga, however, all powers are combined and included in an all out effort directed towards complete transformation of bodily existence. Like Integral Yoga, integral education is synthetic in its approach and aims at harmonious development of all aspects of human personality. In his integral scheme of education both educator and educand were unified in a common bond. The teacher does not impart knowledge to the student, he shows him how to acquire knowledge from himself. Aurobindo tried to modernise education in India by synthesising old values with new ones.

Dr. Annie Besant's approach was on creating the right individual for the future. Such rightness was all encompassing and touched the entire fabric of society which

Comparison, Conclusions, Suggestions

in turn would develop the nation. She held that mere development of individual nations, though important in its own may, was not in harmony with the future of world politics. Nations had to group together forming a federation, working together for the good of all. Harmony is the most important essence and element of any society and it can only be secured by each unit working together as part of the whole, for the welfare of the whole. In such a society each individual would grow to its full stature, would be able to express his faculties and capacities to the fullest extent and thus would be able to help others along their own lines.

Krishnamurti laid total emphasis on the individual and said that various divisive tendencies working through his thought created conflicts for him in the psychological area. This had to be actually understood, and this actual understanding could alone lead him to the truth where he would be free from conflicts and division and therefore would be virtuous and religious, the observer and the observed becoming one. Such a man could then be educated in other disciplines of study which would be of benefit of all.

All these thinkers other than Krishnamurti had stressed teachings of Hindu scriptures like Vedas, Upanishad, Bhagavad Gita etc., but Krishnamurti never quoted any scriptures nor has he claimed to have read any[7]. He spoke of "what is" as being the only reality, and that was dynamic in nature, in the sense that it was changing from moment to moment. To understand such reality was to discover truth which was un-chartered and which could not be anchored.

All thinkers mentioned were overt supporters of Indian culture. However, Krishnamurti although born of Indian parentage stated repeatedly that he had no nationality and belonged to no culture or group. What he hoped his audience would learn he himself lived. All thinkers were concerned with enrichment in the quality of life and society, for the achievement of which they recommended a value based education. There were differences only in concepts and approaches.

Contemporary Relevance

In education, salients and retreats in relevance respond to the contemporary scenario. Some values remain, others recede, and yet others resurge with a force of rejuvination proportionate to requirements of the times.

For a better appreciation of relevance of Dr. Annie Besant and Krishnamurti it will be useful to first review the present day scenario.

Present day scenario :

Present day scenario can best be described as a situation brought about by a crisis of values. Selfish interests of individuals and groups are powerfully projected and made to masquerade as values. Man today is deeply conditioned and is therefore unable to see the "what is". He is thus insecure and seeks refuge in what he believes is a value, such as groups, religions and movements. This is the reason for the prevalent chaos of today. Be it man's cherished ideals and beliefs, his culture, language and thinking or his raw sufferings of hunger and pain–they have all been exploited by the unscrupulous for their own narrow gains. Society as a result, has become attuned to conditioning by the wrecker, and tribulations of the oppressed continue only to reach a flash point when a severe backlash like riots, murders and even wars break out.

Education today is highly specialised and very demanding, leaving little scope for a total overhaul of the mind structure and complete change in direction. The prime movers appear to be money and muscle, while the mind remains fragmented. Children grow up in such an environment, their parents are often confused and helpless. There are talks of a holistic education, to inculcate values in the curriculum of study, but these have failed to change the mind set of image formations, conditioning and of use of power to subjugate.

Society therefore finds itself at critical crossroads. Only an academic interest in values will not remove the ills, nor will plain extrapolation of ideas from seers help. A deep study of values and their judicial synthesis with the conventional pattern of education appears to offer a ray of hope.

Relevance of Dr. Annie Besant

From the days of Dr. Annie Besant, when the British hold on India was threatening to ruin the Indian psyche completely, and there was a need to dislodge it urgently, to more recent times when the market is the prime mover in education, and science and technology are the driving force, educational patterns in India have undergone many changes. In the process some "values" have been put on the back burner, others have been given priority while some have defied the changing times and continue to be relevant even today.

When Dr. Annie Besant arrived, India stood totally devastated of her political, financial and cultural freedom. The primary challenge before Dr. Annie Besant was to encounter British dominance in these spheres, and she rightly chose the path of proper education, based on India's ancient culture and teachings of sages and holy books to achieve this.

A detailed unfolding of the blueprint of her educational ideas has been discussed and several important aspects which were eminently suitable to national interests of the times have been highlighted. In many schools *role of ideals in education is still encouraged through description of lives of great people in text books of children, observing national functions* etc. Her emphasis on culture, art have not lost any relevance. Being a strong believer in Karma and Reincarnation, she maintained that qualities brought forth from previous lives should be encouraged to develop to its fullest extent. The *Delors Commission Report*, while talking of the fourth pillar of education, that is "Learning to be",[8]. has added that no talent in a person must be left untapped and attributes like memory, reasoning power, imagination, physical ability, aesthetic sense, aptitude to communicate, must be identified and allowed to blossom. This reinforces the relevance of Dr. Annie Besant's thoughts. Her ideas of *incorporating the best of west with the best of east* will always remain relevant. This would ensure that a spirit of nationalism would take deep roots in a person and then gradually spread towards making him a world citizen. This would further ensure a respect for cultures and customs of other parts of the world while preserving one's own. The relevance of these thoughts have remained even today and have been mentioned in *Delors Commission Report* under "Tensions to be overcome"[9]. and topics like global vs. local, universal vs. individual, tradition vs. modernity have been talked of in this context. Emphasis has been given on spiritual vs. the material and need for moral and religious values which while having faith in one's own religious values would understand those of others.

It is but natural that the organising of education will alter with times but it cannot be denied that Dr. Annie Besant's concepts about *women's education* and *mass education* remain as relevant if not more today than they were in her times. Her *gradation into stages of education* in schools and colleges, categorisation into commercial, technical and agricultural high schools, accent on vocational, graduate and post graduate training broadly remain unaltered. The *methods of teaching particularly in the lower classes*, the *qualities of a teacher and student* that she defined have not altered much over the years. *The Delors Commission*, while taking cognisance of increasing pressure on curricula, has placed emphasis on a basic education that teaches pupils how to improve their lives through knowledge, through experiment and through the development of their own personal cultures.[10]

The concept of the *Gurukul system too is being re-examined* and its merits assessed in the conditions of the present day. Further students are being encouraged to get involved in *rural upliftment schemes*. The *Delors Commission* referred to earlier also talks of this under "Learning to live together" and "Learning to do."[11]

Initially Dr. Annie Besant's institutions began with these concepts, but as more contemporary ideas took over some of these were gradually relegated to the rear. *With the attainment of independence the concept of a nationalistic ideology was altered. Now the aim was no longer to disengage the foreign strangle hold, but to integrate the people of the land so that India could be recognised as a nation at the international level.* Students would cease to look for greener pastures in other lands and "brain drain" would be stopped. This has a further ramification today when violence and terrorism have raised their ugly heads and fissiparous tendencies need to be checked. The message of Dr. Annie Besant regarding national integration in this sphere still rings loud and clear with all its relevance. Further, her declared love for one's own religion alongwith the *concept of integration of the best of all religions*, should serve to cement bonds of tolerance and friendship, and end violence. The educational thoughts of Dr. Annie Besant regarding character building, discipline and its many ramifications, such as the scouting movement, prefect system which was pioneered by her, are very relevant even today.

Circumstances such as the need to acquire newer types of knowledge, and government financial grants, alongwith its impositions and restrictions, have to some extent blurred some of Dr. Annie Besant's relevance. With the onset of global transactions, the demand of specialised skills in certain areas like software and hardware, in pure sciences, in economics, in management of finances etc. has grown both within and outside India. This makes it imperative for the students to be trained in the latest techniques of problem solving, production, servicing and management. Further, the education system is now predominantly government's responsibility and consumer oriented. These have diluted Dr. Annie Besant's concepts. As circumstances can partially alter priorities, the attainment of independence by India has imposed some changes in the blueprint of Dr. Annie Besant's educational ideas, but it cannot be denied that even after more than eight decades have elapsed since the formulation of her educational policy, most of it remains totally relevant.

Relevance of J. Krishnamurti

The relevance of Krishnamurti in today's context is a *holistic approach to life*. It is not that conventional holistic approach which the educational planners, teachers strive for today, by way of an all round scholastic development. The holism of Krishnamurti encompasses the whole of life, which is like a text-book from which a person learns continuously, without a break, throughout life. To illustrate this difference it is noteworthy that the *Delors Commission* has talked of a wholesome education under "Learning to know"[12], by saying, emphasis has to be given on combining a sufficiently broad general education with indepth study of selected subjects. This according to the Commission provides a person impetuous to lifelong study. The Delors Commission has distinguished between continuous studies and repeated resumptions of studies necessitated by the person's requirements. The dimensions and differences of Krishnamurti's views on a holistic approach to education are now easier to perceive. Under prevailing turbulent conditions in society, the relevance of Krishnamurti's holistic approach goes even beyond those visualised in the Delors Commission Report, to the extent that it covers the whole of life rather than academic excellence alone.

Krishnamurti often uttered the following words, "you are the world." The very words emphasise each individual's responsibility to the social order. All the endless problems of man are in the psychological field. What man is within is projected out, and this creates a society of strifes, chaos, wars. The contents of human consciousness are qualitatively the same in every individual, and therefore the quality of consciousness remains unchanged in the society as a whole. This in turn implies that the society, and indeed the world, is not separate from the individual. Total radical transformation in the psyche of every individual, therefore, holds the key to the transformation or betterment of society. *Psychological transformation as Krishnamurti visualises, goes far beyond psychological changes involved in traditional character building.* The person transformed in the manner of Krishnamurti will have a quality of character much better and finer than that which is developed through traditional methods.

Education is the key factor in social transformation as it produces the kind of individuals that comprise the society.

Comparison, Conclusions, Suggestions 231

Rules and laws only keep the individual under check but do not transform him.

An educational institution imparts both formal and informal education. The formal education is the curricula taught in classrooms, culminating in the award of degrees. *The informal education is what is imbibed from the atmosphere.* It is the learning that takes place from the experience of living in the campus. The atmosphere of relationship of people pursuing their studies in a climate of freedom from fear and comparison, proximity to nature, filled with the joys of learning, by itself, creates a fountain head of values, which imperceptibly flow into all those who comprise the campus population. This in turn subtly shapes their minds and brings about an inner transformation, having greater significance and relevance than all knowledge gathered by conventional education, designed primarily to pass examinations.

The atmosphere in the campus therefore becomes the most important medium of education for communication of values. The creation and nurturing of such a network of relationship in the campus is thus of cardinal importance and supreme relevance in the present day context. What begins in schools and colleges will eventually extend to the entire human society. There will be respect for values, and orderliness in the world. This relevance is best brought out when the *Delors Commission* places great emphasis on one of the four pillars of foundations of education, that is, "Learning to live together"[13] by developing an understanding of others and their history, traditions and spiritual values, and on this basis creating a new spirit of recognition of our interdependence, and common risks and challenges of the future.

Some drawbacks of the present day system of education such as, reward and punishment, competition, jealousy, learning by rote, mad rush for degrees and qualifications, and ambition to become rich through education and specialization, lead to constant struggle and conflict, and affect the quality of one's mind and his life.

The question that arises is that does one continue to

be educated in such a way that his life becomes a battle which he has to fight every moment, and his vital energy is uselessly drained out. This is what is happening to everyone today. *From Krishnamurti's ideas on education one can see that the first step here is to observe what is happening without any disturbance*, to observe oneself in relationship to everything without any preformed images. Krishnamurti was of the view that to live is to be in relationship, and one absorbs truth as it is in the process of living. *One may consider this as a starting point for the education of today. As one moves further one may see that the system based on reward and punishment has to be done away with.* Can one have a system where a student learns a subject from which he derives joy, and that joy alone motivates him further? Here the following account of the Russian writer, Sinyavsky deserves mention:

> A beautiful distinction was drawn by Sinyavsky between motivations prompted by "a desire to seem" and motivations prompted by "an urge to be". When I am prompted by a desire to seem, I perhaps wish to appear superior to others in the eyes of the world or of the appraisers who hold the rewards in their hands. Rewards and punishment induce me to be a performer. But when I am prompted by an urge to be, I cannot be up for sale. It is not my performance before my appraisers that bothers me then but what I am in the eyes of God, if I have a God, or, more austerely, in my own eyes, if I have no God. When I study physics, economics, law or literature, do I do so to be rewarded with a higher designation or a higher scale of pay, or do I do so for the joy of understanding and of sharing that understanding?.[14]

It is important that the educational institution should arouse in the teachers and the students alike the "urge to be" and not the "desire to seem" To such an extent Krishnamurti's ideas on education are very relevant today, and probably is the only way to bring about a change of heart in man, which in turn could make the world a better place to live in.

To bring about a radical transformation in the human

mind, Krishnamurti set up schools which are not merely places for accumulating knowledge, but places *for learning a way of life which is not based on pleasure, on self-centred activities, but on the understanding of the depth and joy of correct action, behaviour relationship.* Such a school has a relationship of sharing, of togetherness, of cooperation between the teachers and the pupils. As both the teacher and the pupil are in a relationship of learning together, there is no need of the imposition of order from above, and it comes of its own accord. *Nothing is forced, but values of love, order, freedom are imbibed by those who live in such an atmosphere which has nothing to do with duty, and is therefore free of the burden of guilt and tradition.* Psychological transformation and its beneficial effects on the mind become evident when a student of Class VII proceeds on to formal studies of Class VIII, and merges into the mainstream of national education. The first seven years enable him to develop a free thinking mind, as visualised by Krishnamurti. Such a mind is better suited to tackle difficulties that the student may encounter later, not only during the course of his study but later in life also.

A person having undergone a psychological transformation as Krishnamurti visualised, can in turn encourage others to a similar transformation. It is, therefore, essential to see to the *quality of education that is being imparted and not the quantity.* Education has till now concerned itself with material progress and advancement. Human beings feel that they can solve their problems through greater knowledge, wealth and power, through scientific and technological advancement. What is required, however, is greater cooperation, greater sense of sharing and togetherness.

Krishnamurti often said that *a dozen persons undergoing total psychological transformation could change the world, and that learning was reading the text of life–a lifelong process.* To this end all educational institutions of Krishnamurti have satellite centres where students from the institutions go and transmit Krishnamurti's ideas to larger groups who are unable to afford an expensive education. For those who are unable to attend during school hours for various reasons, and for those who are busy earning a livelihood and are no longer young, there are study centres where people can meditate and learn to read the text of life.

Krishnamurti accepts that technological advances are necessary and such evolution is not harmful to the extent that undue emphasis is not given to it. Though computers are useful to learning, over emphasis or over use of computers leads to more and more of accumulated knowledge being used in the technological field. Krishnamurti's view of the Internet is that, although it serves a great source of world information, and is indeed necessary in a world of advancing technology, one must understand that this has the disadvantage of disrupting normal family life and harmony, often blunting the finer feelings and sensitivities which are an essential part of it.

It is, therefore, necessary to have an inquiring mind, a mind that understands a thing as it actually is, and having thus understood is ready to solve the problem. Therefore, *Krishnamurti stresses that an education that gives emphasis to the whole movement of life cannot be based on a system of ideas or a blueprint for action.* A system implies authority, conditioning the individual in some special manner and making the individual act according to that conditioning. The individual's dependence upon the source of authority breeds fear and insecurity. In order to awaken critical thinking in the pupils, it is essential to make them *free to make mistakes and learn for themselves, without the fear of being punished.* This would lead to the development of a rational, flexible mind not tethered down by any opinion, belief or tradition.

All Krishnamurti schools open up new avenues for the teacher and the taught and to a whole new way of life which results in the production of a balanced and right thinking citizen, contributing to the formation of a healthy society. It is worth adding here that with the formation of such a society some evils that plague the world today, such as, commercial rivalry, environmental crisis, jealousy, groupism, terrorism, narrow minded parochialism, and even a false sense of selfish nationalism would completely disappear. Organisations like the United Nations, World Trade Organisations and several others, profess to bring about unity in the society and the world, but have not been able to do so because the individuals have not yet changed. A great relevance of Krishnamurti's educational thoughts in contemporary context lies in attempts to bring about a change at the individual's level. At this stage it is pertinent to revert back to "Tensions to be overcome" of Delors Commission Report. The Report discusses tension between competition and equality of opportunity. It has called this a classic issue where the pressures of competition have come in the way of providing equal opportunities to all human beings. The Commission has proposed that education should be lifelong and reconcile three forces – competition, which provides incentives; cooperation, which gives strength; and solidarity, which unites.

Commenting on the capacity of human beings to assimilate the extraordinary expansion of knowledge, the Commission has recommended some new subjects of study, which are, self knowledge, ways to ensure physical and psychological well-being, ways to an improved understanding of natural environment and preserving it better.[15]

Examining the above recommendations of the Delors Commission, one cannot fail to see, inspite of some differences, the closeness to the relevance of Krishnamurti in today's context, specially in areas where he has talked of promoting cooperation rather than competition, and considered learning a lifelong process, alongwith his emphasis on environment and nature.

Finally in connection with the relevance of Krishnamurti it may be said that the real extent of his influence on contemporary education cannot be measured quantitatively, but perceived qualitatively. To this extent there may be an element of conjecture and speculation, *what clearly emerges however is that, with one's experiencing a sense of freedom, there is unknowingly a sense of cleansing of perception, understanding the truth, and the taking place of a subtle inner transformation.*

Suggestions for Improvements in Education

Taking cognisance of relevance of educational thoughts of Dr. Annie Besant and Krishnamurti, it is time to make a reappraisal of our present system of education. For this there is a need to look at the situation as a whole, that is, not in a fragmented way by considering merely national and international issues. Education has to develop an attitude which would be universally good. One must not lose sight of the fact that education is a process of development of the future generation and cannot be contained within the classrooms. Opportunities for development of curiosity, creativity, motivation have been generally withheld due to fragmented curricula, authoritarian methods and the hierarchy of examinations.

Innovations need not be thought of as something totally original. Almost all innovations comprise rearrangements of principles and ideas in novel ways.

Learning best occurs when it progresses by the student's own efforts. The teacher is there to set the problem and the pupils solve them; but the teacher must watch and help the pupils when they begin to get discouraged by failures. *If knowledge is to acquire genuine meaning, it must be experienced, it must be gained by oneself.* In Dr. Annie Besant's scheme of national education, the first seven years are set apart for the free development of the imaginative tendencies of the child in an atmosphere of love, warmth, freedom, and judicial guidance of the teacher. These are the most impressionable years when traits develop, which continue to influence one's life later on. Krishnamurti also agrees that this type of a learning with certain modifications discussed earlier could extend upto class VII. When considering any improvement in our present day pattern of education, serious consideration and high priority, must therefore, be accorded to this pattern of education during the first seven years.

Heuristic learning offered in the beginning gets formalised as the child steps into the higher classes, and results in a thorough understanding of concepts previously learnt. Children invited to explore in junior laboratories, through their own experiments, test the laws learnt. In an atmosphere of openness, devoid of rewards, punishments, authority, proceeding at their own pace through self-effort and group interactions, not imitating but questioning things, helps in the development of all the faculties in a balanced way. This enables the student to lead the process of learning because of the curiosity that is aroused in them during the process of heuristic learning. The teachers should cooperate with one another in forming specific learning patterns that inter-relate with each other. A continuous process of assessments should be done and given due weightage in assessing performance at the terminal level, emphasising the attainment of those characteristics that define the human being of tomorrow. The merits of this phase of education imparted in the manner observed, leaves no room for doubts. Nevertheless, it is regrettable that only very few schools have given this any importance. This phase of education should be firmly implemented, even if it be under some constraints, in all schools.

When considering an integrated application of education, that is the formal and informal, due importance is to be given to the fact that a student receiving an informal education upto a certain class (for example, class VII) eventually joins the mainstream of formal education. This in a way is a phase of transition, but with the students background of closeness to nature and his prehistoric heritage with it–earth and nature orientations–he is better able to grasp the events of history, the facts of geography and the laws of the sciences. What has taken root through informal education in the earlier standards blends fruitfully with formal education later on, leading to a better understanding of human relationships, a perpetual appreciation of man's common heritage and attachment to nature. All this would add a new dimension to the understanding of all subjects. This concept is illustrated by quoting Radhika Herzberger in her article, *Education And Nationalism:*

> Humanities will teach that all people on this earth, whatever their race or social status, have a common ancestry and a shared pattern of pre-history. History will encourage an impersonal understanding of the past and

detachment from national prejudice. Physics will promote conservation of energy. Biology will teach children to value the diversity of nature. Chemistry will examine ways of repairing the damage human beings are doing to the earth. Schools will find ways to help regenerate their local environment. Children will be taught to see themselves not through their national, religious, caste or class identities, but as human beings. As human beings they will learn to live together on a finite earth.[16]

It is of cardinal importance that the teacher helps the student in this phase of transition, so that the latter does not feel alien to the milieu of mainstream education after an almost complete freedom prior to this. The learning process should continue to be one of joy.

A second look at the old Ashram ideals will not be out of place. The medium of value education being the environment from which values are imbibed, it becomes necessary that teaching institutions should as far as possible have such surroundings which reflect closeness to nature. The teacher, like the Gurus of the Ashram, should be dedicated and do more than mere teaching work. A small teacher to pupil ratio will ensure better interaction with pupils. Such a pattern should comprise at least a part of the regular school curriculum, or should be undertaken during the vacations by way of summer school camps or satellite education centres.

Similarly Rural Service Camps maybe organised as compulsory part of the regular curriculum. Students here will learn the dignity of labour and come in touch with a cross section of society. They could also fan out in the interiors to spread mass education. Student groups should also be exposed to relief works in areas of human misfortunes such as floods, earthquakes, accidents, riots and plight of refugees in relief camps. All this will arouse love and sensitivity for fellow beings and even animals and plants – values of the purest type will be imbibed. International exchange programme for students can bring abut a wider internet of exchange of ideas and identities, giving the relationship a global interface.

It is obvious that efforts at improvement in education by incorporating values in it must necessarily function under certain constraints such as time, finances and the right amount of dedication. Further the functioning routine of society itself, which has certain impositions, come in the way of the freedom of value based education. The greatest effort in this direction would be to remove expeditiously all these impediments.

A few suggestions are offered :

(1) Education improves by incorporation of values.

(2) Value based education needs deep thinking as values including eternal values have been described differently by thinkers. This has been mentioned by the researcher in her findings.

(3) Judicious incorporation of values in correct proportions with the mainstream education will bring about a qualitative change.

(4) This incorporation calls for a close examination of values in their proper perspective and cannot be of a generalized nature. The peculiarities of the situation must identify the priorities. Infact it raises the question – what type of values should be incorporated in the curriculum? would this be of conventional understanding or would it be from the lexicon of Krishnamurti or can there be a judicious mixture of both, and if so, in what proportions.

While considering suggestions for further study, some limitations of the present work may be mentioned :

Limitations of the study

The nature of this study imposes the following limitations:

1. The present study is not in an area which can be measured and quantified.

2. Material has been drawn from primary and secondary sources. The former is not always adequate and the latter is not always free of bias.

3. Both Dr. Annie Besant and J. Krishnamurti belong

to periods which partially overlap, not only between themselves but also with other seers and thinkers, for example, Mahatma Gandhi, R.N. Tagore, Vivekanand and others. This has imposed constraints on some details, in order to prevent this pesentation from acquiring unwieldy proportions. The comparison has been restricted to Dr. Annie Besant and J. Krishnamurti without much cognisance of other contemporary views.

4. The study of general philosophy of Dr. Annie Besant and J. Krishnamurti has been restricted to areas which are directly related to their educational thoughts.

5. Improvement in the educational pattern has been suggested to the extent where educational ideas of only Dr. Annie Besant and J. Krishnamurti have been incorporated. An ideal paradigm for value based education should include thoughts of other thinkers also.

Suggestions for Further Study

The following suggestions for further study are now being offered:

1. Both Dr. Annie Besant and Krishnamurti have talked of value oriented education. Other great thinkers have also expressed similar thoughts and have set up well known educational centres, special mention may be made of Tagore and Aurobindo where they emphasised learning from a particular way of life. It might be fruitful to make a study of these philosophers and their experiments and compare it with the institutions of Dr. Annie Besant and Krishnamurti.

2. It might also be worthwhile to review in greater details the current mainstream educational policy, and to compare this with the educational ideas of Dr. Annie Besant, Krishnamurti and other contemporary philosophers. Mainstream education today is based not on the inculcation of values, but on the inculcation

of competence and efficiency. Such a study would try to find out where and why the mainstream fails to generate values.

3. Another interesting study can be, to find out whether Krishnamurti's mind was conditioned, and if so, to what extent, whether the flowering of his teachings were due to Dr. Annie Besant's influence in his early life.

4. Studies can be undertaken to compare Dr. Annie Besant with other thinkers of the freedom struggle, who lived at that time and with whom Dr. Annie Besant had political interactions, like Rabindranath Tagore, Madan Mohan Malviya.

5. A comparative study of Krishnamurti's institutions in India and Abroad can be undertaken.

References

1. A Short History Of The Theosophical Society, p. 510.
2. The Besant Spirit, Volume VII, p. 65.
3. idem.
4. Hints On The Study Of The Bhagavad Gita, p. 99.
5. Education And The Significance Of Life, p. 24.
6. An Introduction To The Life And Work Of J. Krishnamurti (1895-1986) - Unconditionally Free, p. 10.
7. The First And Last Freedom, p. 13.
8. Learning: The Treasure Within, Report to UNESCO of the International Commission on Education for the Twenty-first Century, p. 23.
9. ibid., p. 17.
10. ibid., p. 18.
11. ibid., pp. 22-23.
12. ibid., p 23.
13. ibid., p 32.
14. Education And Values, Journal of the Inter - University Centre for Humanities and Social Sciences, Vol. VII, No. 2, Winter 2000, p. xiii.

15. Learning: The Treasure Within, Report to UNESCO of the International Commission on Education for the Twenty - first Century, pp. 17 -18.
16. Journal Of The Krishnamurti Schools, March 1999, No. 3, pp. 10 - 11.

Bibliography

Books

Aggarwal, J.C. (2000). *Educational Reforms In India For The 21st Century*. New Delhi: Shipra Publications.

Anderson, J. & Durston, B.H. (1970). *Thesis And Assignment Writing*. Sydney: John Wiley & Sons.

Archambault, Reginald D. (Ed.). (1965). *Philosophical Analysis And Education*. London: Routledge & Kegan Paul.

Bakshi, S.R. (1990). *Annie Besant: Founder Of Home Rule Movement*. New Delhi: Anmol Publications Pvt. Ltd.

Besant, Annie. (1893). *Death And After*. Adyar: The Theosophical Publishing House.

Besant, Annie. (1905). *Karma*. Adyar: The Theosophical Publishing House.

Besant, Annie. (1905). *Reincarnation*. Adyar: The Theosophical Publishing House.

Besant, Annie. (1906). *Hints On The Study Of The Bhagavad Gita*. Adyar: The Theosophical Publishing House.

Besant, Annie. (1907). *The Wisdom Of The Upanishads*. Adyar: The Theosophical Publishing House.

Besant, Annie. (1908). *An Introduction To Yoga*. Adyar: The Theosophical Publishing House.

Besant, Annie. (1908). *Education – Basis Of National Life*. Adyar: The Theosophical Publishing House.

Besant, Annie. (1912). *Education In The Light Of Theosophy*. Adyar: The Theosophical Publishing House.

Besant, Annie. (1912). *Man And His Bodies.* Adyar: The Theosophical Publishing House.

Besant, Annie. (1912). *The Laws Of Higher Life.* Adyar: The Theosophical Publishing House.

Besant, Annie. (1912). *The Masters.* Adyar: The Theosophical Publishing House.

Besant, Annie. (1920). *The Doctrine Of The Heart.* Adyar: The Theosophical Publishing House.

Besant, Annie. (1920). *Thought Power: Its Control And Culture.* Adyar: The Theosophical Publishing House.

Besant, Annie. (1922). *Meditations: On The Path And Its Qualifications* (comp.) E.G. Cooper. Adyar: The Theosophical Publishing House.

Besant, Annie. (1924). *Civilisation's Deadlocks And The Keys.* Adyar: The Theosophical Publishing House.

Besant, Annie. (1931). *The Seven Principles Of Man..* Adyar: The Theosophical Publishing House.

Besant, Annie. (1932). *Principles Of Educaton.* Adyar: The Theosophical Publishing House.

Besant, Annie. (1939). *The Ancient Wisdom.* Adyar: The Theosophical Publishing House.

Besant, Annie. & Das, Bhagavan. (1939). *Sanatana Dharma– An Elementary Textbook Of Hindu Religion And Ethics.* Adyar: The Theosophical Publishing House.

Besant, Annie. (1942). *Builder Of New India.* Adyar: The Theosophical Publishing House.

Besant, Annie. (1942). *The Besant Spirit Series.* Adyar: The Theosophical Publishing House.

Besant, Annie. (1952). *Theosophy And The Theosophical Society.* Adyar: The Theosophical Publishing House.

Besant, Annie. (1961). *The Riddle Of Life.* Adyar: The Theosophical Publishing House.

Besant, Annie. (1962). *The Universal Textbook Of Religion and Morals.* Part I. Adyar: The Theosophical Publishing House.

Besant, Annie. & Leadbeater, C.W. (1967). *Man: Whence, How and Whither.* Adyar: The Theosophical Publishing House.

Besant, Annie. (1976). *The Inner Government of The World.* Adyar: The Theosophical Publishing House.

Besant, Annie. (1984). *The Theosophic Life.* Adyar: The Theosophical Publishing House.

Besant, Annie. (1992). *The Universal Law Of Life.* Adyar: The Theosophical Publishing House.

Besant, Annie. (1993). *The Brotherhood Of Religions.* (comp.) Surendra Narayan. Adyar: The Theosophical Publishing House.

Besant, Annie. (1995). *An Autobiography.* Adyar: The Theosophical Publishing House.

Besant, Annie. (1995). *Right Citizenship.* (comp.) Idarmis Rodriguez. Adyar: The Theosophical Publishing House.

Besant, Annie. (1999). *A Study In Consciousness.* Adyar: The Theosophical Publishing House.

Besant, Annie. (2000). *Seven Great Religions.* Adyar: The Theosophical Publishing House

Best, John W. & Kahn, James. V. (1996). *Research In Education.* New Delhi: Prentice Hall of India, Pvt. Ltd.

Bhatia & Bhatia (1995). *Theory And Principles Of Education.* Delhi: Doaba House.

Bhatia, K.K. & Narang, C.L. (1979). *Principles Of Education.* Ludhiana: Prakash Brothers.

Brubacher, S. John. (1947). *A History Of The Problems Of Education.* New York: Mc Graw-Hill Book Company, Inc.

Brubacher, S. John. (1950). *Modern Philosophies Of Education.* New York: Mc Graw- Hill Book Company, Inc.

Buch, M.B. (Ed.). (1974). *A Survey Of Research In Education.* Baroda: CASE, M.S. University.

Buch, M.B. (Ed.). (1979). Second *Survey Of Research In Education.* Baroda: CASE, M.S. University.

Buch, M.B. (Ed.). (1987). *Third Survey Of Research In Education.* New Delhi: National Council Of Educational Research And Training.

Buch, M.B. (Ed.). (1991). *Fourth Survey Of Research In Education.* New Delhi: National Council Of Educational Research And Training.

Buch, M.B. (Ed.). (1997). *Fifth Survey Of Research In Education.* New Delhi: National Council Of Educational Research And Training.

Chandmal, Asit. (1985). *One Thousand Moons: Krishnamurti At Eighty Five.* New York: Abrams.

Dhopeshwarkar, A.D. (1956). *Krishnamurti And The Experience Of The Silent Mind.* Bombay: Chetana.

Dhopeshwarkar, A.D. (1971). *Krishnamurti And The Mind In Revolution.* Bombay: Chetana.

Dhopeshwarkar, A.D. (1973). *Krishnamurti And The Texture Of Reality.* Bombay: Chetana.

Encyclopaedia Britannica. Inc. (1974). Vol 18. (15th ed.).

Encyclopaedia Of Mystical And Paranormal Experience. (1991). London: Grange Books Ltd.

Fourere, Rene. (1981). *Krishnamurti: The Man And His Teaching.* Bombay: Chetana.

Good, Carter. V. (1959). *Dictionary of Education.* New York: Mc Graw-Hill Book Company, Inc.

Grover, V.& Arora, R. *Great Women Of Modern India, Their Contribution To Political, Economic And Social Development–Annie Besant.* Vol I. New Delhi: Deep & Deep Publications.

Hirst, P.H. & Peters, R.S. (1970). *The Logic Of Education.* London: Routledge & Kegan Paul Ltd.

Holroyd, Stuart. (1991). *Krishnamurti: The Man, The Mystery And The Message.* Dorset: Element.

Husain, Dr. Zakir. (1959). *Educational Reconstruction In India.* Faridabad: Publications Division.

Illich, Ivan D. (1971). *Deschooling Society.* Harmondsworth: Penguin Books.

Bibliography

Jayakar, Pupul. (1986). *Krishnamurti: A Biography.* New York: Harper & Row Inc.

Jinarajadasa, C. (1932). *A Short Biography Of Dr. Annie Besant.* Adyar: The Theosophical Publishing House.

Koul, Lokesh. (1984). *Methodology Of Educational Research.* New Delhi: Vikas Publishing House Pvt. Ltd.

Krishnamurti, J. (1953). *Education And The Significance Of Life.* New York: Harper & Brothers.

Krishnamurti, J. (1954). *The First And Last Freedom.* London: Gollancz.

Krishnamurti, J. (1956, 1959, 1961). *Commentaries On Living.* (ed.) D. Rajagopal. Vol I, II, III. London: Gollancz.

Krishnamurti, J. (1963). *Life Ahead.* London: Gollancz.

Krishnamurti, J. (1964). *This Matter Of Culture.* (ed.). D. Rajagopal. London: Gollancz.

Krishnamurti, J. (1969). *Freedom From The Known.* (ed.) Mary Lutyens. London: Gollancz.

Krishnamurti, J. (1970). *The Only Revolution.* (ed.) Mary Lutyens. London: Gollancz.

Krishnamurti, J. (1971). *The Flight Of The Eagle.* New York: Harper & Row.

Krishnamurti, J. (1971). *The Urgency Of Change* (ed.) Mary Lutyens. London: Gollancz.

Krishnamurti, J. (1972). *The Penguin Krishnamurti Reader.* (ed.). Mary Lutyens. England: Penguin Books.

Krishnamurti, J. (1972). *Tradition And Revolution.* (ed.). Pupul Jayakar and Sunanda Patwardhan. New Delhi: Orient Longman.

Krishnamurti, J. (1972). *You Are The World.* New York: Harper & Row.

Krishnamurti, J. (1973). *The Awakening Of Intelligence.* London: Gollancz.

Krishnamurti, J. (1973). *The Second Krishnamurti Reader.* (ed.). Mary Lutyens. England: Penguin Books.

Krishnamurti, J. (1977). *Truth And Actuality.* London: Gollancz.

Krishnamurti, J. (1978). *Beginnings Of Learning.* England: Penguin Books.

Krishnamurti, J. (1978). *The Impossible Question.* England: Penguin Books.

Krishnamurti, J. (1978). *The Wholeness Of Life.* London: Gollancz.

Krishnamurti, J. (1979). *Meditations.* Madras: Krishnamurti Foundation India.

Krishnamurti, J. (1981, 1985). *Letters To The Schools.* Vol I & II. Madras: Krishnamurti Foundation India.

Krishnamurti, J. (1982). *Explorations Into Insight.* Madras: Krishnamurti Foundation India.

Krishnamurti, J. (1982). *On, Within The Mind.* Madras: Krishnamurti Foundation India.

Krishnamurti, J. (1982). *The Flame Of Attention.* Madras: Krishnamurti, Foundation India.

Krishnamurti, J. (1982). *The Network Of Thought.* London: Krishnamurti Foundation Trust Ltd.

Krishnamurti, J. & Bohm, D. (1985). *The Ending Of Time.* London: Gollancz.

Krishnamurti, J. (1987). *Krishnamurti On Education.* Madras: Krishnamurti Foundation India.

Krishnamurti, J. (1991). *A Wholly Different Way Of Living.* Hampshire, England: Krishnamurti Foundation Trust Ltd.

Krishnamurti, J. (1992). *The Collected Works.* America: Krishnamurti Foundation.

Krishnamurti, J. (1994). *Krishnamurti's Notebook.* Madras: Krishnamurti Foundation India.

Krishnamurti, J. (1994). *On Learning And Knowledge.* New York: Harper Collins Publishers.

Krishnamurti, J. (1995). *An Introduction To The Life And Work Of (1895-1986).–Unconditionally Free.* America: Krishnamurti Foundation.

Krishnamurti, J. (1996). *Questioning*. Brockwood Park: Krishnamurti Foundation Trust Ltd.

Krishnamurti, J. (1999). *The Little Book On Living*. (ed.). R.E. Mark Lee. England: Penguin Books.

Krishnamurti, J. (2001). *Sutras On Life*. Bangalore: Krishnamurti Foundation India.

Krishnamurti, J. (Alcyone). (1910). *At The Feet Of The Master*. Madras: Theosophist Office.

Lal, Basant Kumar. (1973). *Contemporary Indian Philosophy*. Delhi: Motilal Banarsidass Publishers Pvt. Ltd.

Lutyens, Mary. (1975). *Krishnamurti: The Years Of Awakening*. London: John Murray.

Lutyens, Mary. (1979). *Krishnamurti: The Years Of Fulfilment*. London: John Murray.

Lutyens, Mary. (1988). *The Open Door*. London: John Murray.

Mehta, Rohit. (1979). *J. Krishnamurti And The Nameless Experience*. Delhi: Motilal Banarsidass.

Michel, Peter. (1996). *Krishnamurti- Love And Freedom*. Delhi: Motilal Banarsidass.

Motwani, Kewal. (1951). *Three Great Sages: Sri Aurobindo, Dr. Annie Besant, J. Krishnamurti*. Madras: Ganesh.

Niel, Andre. (1957). *Krishnamurti-The Man In Revolt*. Bombay: Chetana Pvt. Ltd.

Pandey, R.S. (1993). *An Introduction To Major Philosophies Of Education*. Agra: Vinod Pustak Mandir.

Pandey, R.S. (1993). *Philosophsing Education*. Delhi: Kanishka Publishing House.

Patwardhan, Sunanda. (1999). *A Vision Of The Sacred*. Penguin Books.

Ransom, Josephine. (1938). *A Short History Of The Theosophical Society: 1875 to 1938*. Adyar: The Theosophical Publishing House.

Sanat, Aryel. (1999). *The Inner Life Of Krishnamurti: Private Passion And Perenial Wisdom*. Varanasi: Pilgrims Publishing.

Shringy, R.K. (1976). *Philosophy Of J. Krishnamurti: A Systematic Study.* New Delhi: Munshiram Manoharlal Publishers.

Singh, Jaspal. (2001). *Methodology And Techniques of Social Research.* New Delhi: Kanishka Publishers.

Stead, W.T. (1946). *Annie Besant: A Character Sketch.* Adyar: The Theosophical Publishing House.

Suares, Carlo. (1950). *Krishnamurti And The Unity Of Man.* Bombay: Chetana.

Thakar, Vimala. (1989). *On An Eternal Voyage.* Gujarat: Vimala Prakashan Trust.

Thapan, Meenakshi. (1991). *Life At School–An Ethnographic Study.* Delhi: Oxford University Press.

Trilokekar, C.S. (1956). *Of Pattern Of Things To Come: Annie Besant's Vision of The Future of India.* Adyar: The Theosophical Publishing House.

Vyas, Savitri. (1989). *A Critical Study Of J. Krishnamurti's Educational Thoughts.* Ahmedabad: Savitri Vyas Publishers.

Weeraperuma, Susunaga. (1974). *A Bibliography of The Life And Teachings Of Jiddu Krishnamurti.* Netherlands: E.J. Brill Leiden.

Weeraperuma, Susunaga. (1978). *Living And Dying From Moment To Moment.* Bombay: Chetana.

Weeraperuma, Susunaga. (1983). *That Pathless Land.* Bombay: Chetana.

Weeraperuma, Susunaga. (1984). *Bliss Of Reality.* Delhi: Motilal Banarsidass Publishers Pvt. Ltd.

Winch, Christopher & Gingell, John. (1999). *Key Concepts In The Philosophy Of Education.* U.S.A. : Routledge.

Reports And Periodicals

An Experiment In New Education For Students And Teachers. (1984). Vol I & II. Bombay: Paragon Publications Trust.

Ajeet, G.K. (1997-98). *Introduction To Theosophical Society.* U.P. Federation Theosophical Society.

Ajeet, G.K. (1993). *Prakash Punj: Annie Besant*. Allahabad: Anand Lodge Theosophical Society.

Anand Lodge: Theosophical Society (12th Aug, 1994). Allahabad: Anand Lodge Theosophical Society.

Concerning Education: Fundamental Questions (1995). Report Of The Krishnamurti Birth Centenary Educational Conference held at Rishi Valley School, Nov 27-30, 1995. Madras: Krishnamurti Foundation India.

Education and National Development. (1966). Report of the Education Commission 1964-66. New Delhi: National Council of Educational Research and Training.

In Honour of Dr. Annie Besant. (1990). (Lectures by eminent persons 1952-88). Kamachha, Varanasi: The Indian Section Of The Theosophical Society.

Journal of The Inter-University Centre For Humanities And Social Sciences, Education and Values. (2000). Vol 7, No. 2 Shimla: Indian Institute of Advanced Study.

Journal Of The Krishnamurti Schools. July 1998 (No. 2.), March 1999 (No. 3), May 2000 (No. 4), May 2001 (No. 5). Krishnamurti Foundation India.

Krishnamurti Birth Centenary Souvenir. (1995). Madras: Krishnamurti Foundation India.

Learning: The Treasure Within. (1996). Report to UNESCO of the International Commission on Education for the Twenty-first Century. France: UNESCO Publishing.

National Curriculum Framework For School Education. (2000). New Delhi: National Council of Educational Research and Training.

National Policy On Education, 1986 (with modifications undertaken in 1992). New Delhi: University Grants Commission.

Rajghat Besant School – Prospectus. KFI Rajghat, Varanasi.

Report of The Secondary Education Commission (October 1952- June 1953). Ministry of Education, Government of India.

Sarva Bhavantu Sukhina – Theosophical Order Of Service. (1999). U.P. Federation Theosophical Society.

Theosophy and World Problems. (1922). (Being the four convention lectures delivered in Benares at the forty-sixth anniversary of the Theosophical Society, December 1921). London: Theosophical Publishing House.

The Theosophist. (January 2000 – January 2002). Adyar, Chennai: The Theosophical Society.

The Link (1998, No. 15) (1999, No. 16) (2000, No. 18.). Switzerland: Krishnamurti Link International.

Vision And Activities. Chennai : Krishnamurti Foundation India.

Wake Up India. (January 2000–December 2001). Adyar, Chennai: The Theosophical Society.

Unpublished Material From The Krishnamurti Archives:

Krishnamurti, J. *On Life.* (reproduced from the original in the Henry E. Huntington Library and Art Gallery, California, U.S.A.).

Krishnamurti, J. *On Study Centres.* (from verbatim transcripts of the report of the International Trustees' Meetings in Ojai, 1977).

Rao, Sanjiva B. *The Story Of A Project For New Education.* (typed from the Original in the Krishnamurti Archives by H.F. May 1958).

Audio Cassettes

Education And Life's Challenges. (3 Cassettes). (talk to the children of Rishi Valley School (1970); talk to the students of Bombay University (1969); talks at the Rishi Valley Educational Conference (1979). Chennai: Krishnamurti Foundation India.

Index

Agnostic and Atheist 13
Agricultural Labourers' Union 11
Alcyone 34
All India Home Rule League 22
All India Women's Association 25
Ancient Wisdom 27
Annie Besant 3, 8
Annie Besant Shishu Vihar 194
Arts Faculty 195
Asha 209
Ashram Ideal 116, 140, 213
Atheism and Redical Politics 14
Atma 65-66, 81
Autobiography 27
Awakening of Intelligence 54, 91, 97
Axiology 101

Banaras Hindu University 20, 196, 207
Beauty 112
Beloved 47
Beyond Violence 54
Bhagavad Gita 27, 32, 212-213
Bhagirath Valley 51
Bhikshus 223
Biginning of Learning 87
Brahma 61-62, 103, 223
Brahmacharya 136, 138, 213, 220
Brahma is Truth 73
Brahma Vidya 16, 103
Brahmavidyashrama 21, 216
British Museum 12

Brotherhood of Humanity 18
Budhi 65-66
Builder of New india 27

Carter V Good *et al* (1953) 6
CBSE Board 200, 203-04
Central Hindu College 19, 113-14, 129, 139
Changing World 107
Chit and Ananda 62
Choiceless Awareness 95, 98, 100, 190
C Jinarajadasa 8
Commentaries of Leaving 42
Commonwealth of Humanity 112, 212
Commonwealth of India Bill 120
Communion 117
Concept of Universal Truth 16
Content of Consciousness 82

Delors Commission Report 157, 227-28, 230-31, 235
Dense Physical Body 64
Deschooling 159-60
Describing Words 201
Diologue 177, 187
Diologue as Inquiry 178

East India Company 109
Education as the Basis of National Life 109
Education and the Significance of Life 53

Education of Indian Girls 141
Ending of Time 46
Environment 110
Essentials of an Indian Education 27
Eternity 198
Etheric Double 64-65

Famous Central Hindu College in 1898, 19
Feeling of Being at Home 177
First and Last Freedom 53, 89
Freedom of Education from Government Control 117
Freethinker 211
Freebel 130

Great Bereavement 38
Grey and Agnostics 11
Gurukul System 129, 131, 138
Gurukul and Monastaries 3

Haridvanam 22
Hidden Curriculum 159
High School and Subsequent Level Stage 124-25
Hinduism and Theosophy 61, 212
Home Rule 22

Ideals in Education 27
Indian Culture 195
Indian National Congress 22
Indian National University Scheme 20, 113
Indian Scouting Movement 20, 113
Inspiration of the Bible 11
Integral Yoga 224

Jivatma 104
J. Krishnamurti 3-4
Just on Organisation 183

Kamachha 194
Kama Rupa 65
Kavi Sammelan 196
Kothari Commission (1964-66) 2
Krishnamurti Notebook 54
Kshatriya 140

Law of Karma and Reincarnation 111
Learning Webs 160
Life and Times of J. Krishnamurti 178
Lower Secondary School Stages 123

Mahabhata 212
Manas 65
Mass Education 228
Meditations 94-96
Messiah or Saviour 32
Monessori Method 9
Mudaliar Commission (1952) 2

Nation Education 119
Nations 115
National Household 22
National Policy on Education (1986) 2
National Secular Society 12-13
National Reformer 15
National Social Service (NSS) 196

O Coward 12
Ojai Valley 36-37, 40-42
Olcott Pancham School at Adyar 18
Open Door 46-47
Openness and Sensitivity 185
Order of the Rishing Sun 34
Other 85

Pariah 172
Path 37
Path and Its Qualification 27
Physical Space 88
Pragmatist 218
Prana 65
Prefact System 113
Primary School Stage 122
Pyjamakurta 48

Quaternary 64

Rajghat Education Centre 49-50, 183
Ramayana 212

Index

Rector 206
Reincarnation and Karma 68
Researches 194-196, 203, 207-209
Revisit 1
Rhetoric 202
Riddle of Life 27
Rishi Valley Education Centre 49-50, 183

Sacred 104, 179
Sacred Motheriarel 18
Sahyadri Krishnamurti School 52
Sanotana Dharma 212
Sanskrit Shivir 196
Satyagraha 24
Satyanasti Parodharmah 16
Secret Doctrine 15
Shanti Kunj 18, 196
Shudras 24, 140
Sibsey Church 11
Sinyavsky 232
Skill Exchange 160
Small Village 145
Sons and Daughters of India 19
Spirit 108
Star 34, 39

Theosophia 16
Theosophical Education Trust in 1913 20, 120, 194
Theosophical Library 196
Theosophical Society (1975) 14-17, 26, 31, 39-40, 45, 47, 111, 210
Theistic 11
Thinking Together 199

Truth 101, 103, 211
Turmoils 211

United Nations Educational Scientific and Cultural Organisation (UNESCO) 2, 157
United Nations Organisation (UNO) 2
Universal Law of Life 27
Upanayana 136
Upanishadic 223, 225
Urgency of Change 54
Utter Kashi Education Centre 51

Vague and Dreamy 31
Vairogya 70
Vaishya 140
Vanaprastha 136
Varna 140
Vasant Kanya Mahavidyalay 194, 196-97
Vedanta 90, 223
Vedas and Shastras 139
Vedic 141
Vehicle 113
Vernacular 143

What is, 210-11, 215, 225-26
Wholeness of Life 77, 87
Wisdom of the Upanishads 27
Wisdom Religion 16
Women's Education 228
World Teachers 7, 40, 113

Years of Fulfitment 47
Young Men's Indian Association in 1914, 19

115 13/6/08
modern book house